Following Christ
in a
Consumer Society

John F. Kavanaugh

Following Christ
in a
Consumer Society

The Spirituality of
Cultural Resistance

25th ANNIVERSARY EDITION

ORBIS BOOKS

Maryknoll, New York 10545

Founded in 1970, Orbis Books endeavors to publish works that enlighten the mind, nourish the spirit, and challenge the conscience. The publishing arm of the Maryknoll Fathers and Brothers, Orbis seeks to explore the global dimensions of the Christian faith and mission, to invite dialogue with diverse cultures and religious traditions, and to serve the cause of reconciliation and peace. The books published reflect the views of their authors and do not represent the official position of the Maryknoll Society. To learn more about Maryknoll and Orbis Books, please visit our website at www.maryknoll.org.

Library of Congress Cataloging-in-Publication Data

Kavanaugh, John F.
   Following Christ in a consumer society : the spirituality of cultural resistance / John Kavanaugh. — [Updated], 25th anniversary ed.
      p. cm.
   Includes bibliographical references and index.
   ISBN-13: 978-157075-666-5 (pbk.)
   1. Christian sociology—United States. 2. Christian life—Catholic authors. I. Title.
   BT738.K37 2006
   261—dc22
                                                             2006009460

To the Communities, the brotherhood, the families; and especially to those who in word and act helped bring this together: Patrick and Jeanne, Michael and Mary Beth, John and Julie; to Mahon, Tom, Jay, Catherine, Virginia and Ann.

When it comes to the Catholic church, I go to the right as far as I can go. But when it comes to labor, pacifism and civil rights, then I go as far as I can to the left.

—*Dorothy Day to Stanley Vishnewski*

Contents

THE SEARCH FOR A
PARADOXICAL READERSHIP

I write for two quite disparate groups, who share, if little else, the wholeheartedness of their diverse commitments to either social justice or the life of faith. I am especially writing for those who, while committed to faith or justice, have acknowledged and admitted a need for something to either embody their faith or sustain their passion for equity. In the past few years, I have been privileged by friendships with both kinds of persons. I have seen many priests and nuns committed to work in city ghettos, having lost their sense of faith or prayer, soon lose their passion for the poor. I have talked with married couples clinging to their faith, struggling to ward off a loss of passion for each other and for life. And I continue to dream of bringing together radicalized Christians who seek the support of a profound faith with intensely orthodox believers who seek to give their faith a concrete historical impact. Fideists and activists need each other to be whole. They need each other even to be who they are.

People who have taken social justice seriously are, quite simply, those still working at it. You may be a humanist with unshakable faith that men and women are not expendable. You may be a parish priest who wonders if there is any chance to reveal the ugly truth about racism and inequity to your people in a way that makes sense to you and challenges them to action.

You may be a young single or married person laboring with the poor or disenfranchised, working in political organizations or in our schools, and wondering if you can possibly hold on to your commitment while the fire of hope threatens to flicker out. You may be someone who feels betrayed by your own church while you aspire to live the gospel values it taught you.

The first half of this book will make sense to you. But it is the second half that is written for you. Laboring for justice demands the support of a culture-transcending faith. And the faith to which you are invited is found in the revelation of Jesus Christ and embodied in the deepest traditions of the Christian Church. I hope that you may discover the truly revolutionary, political, and social implications of Christ's message, of prayer and sacrament, of permanent commitment, and of community life.

The first half of this book, on the other hand, is written for the person who takes faith, especially the Catholic faith, seriously. You may find the second half of the book encouraging or even exhilarating, but the strength of anything it has to say is intimately related to the chapters of the first half, which you may well find irritating or disturbing.

You may be a married couple painfully wondering whether you are all alone in living marital fidelity in this society. You possibly have children whose hearts you feel are being seduced by some alien gospel and empty belief system. You may love the sacraments but wonder what connection they have to life. You may have a desire to know Christ more deeply as the Master of your life, but not quite feel his presence in your lived struggles. You may question what your faith calls you to in a culture of institutional abortion, pornography, and the decline of family life. You may be seeking methods to resist the injustices of the world, but not know where to turn.

The suggestion that this books offers to you is this: authentic faith is constituted by justice, expressed and embodied in our social relations as well as in our personal lives. The issues which bother you are economic and political problems, as well as moral and religious. And problems which may not bother you—armament, capital punishment, racism, and the like—are religious and spiritual problems as well as political ones. Although justice is not all there is to faith, when you are truly living your faith you are doing justice. And when you are doing true justice you are living your faith.

The danger in having such a strangely dual audience is that both groups could be either missed or alienated. The message I hope to communicate, moreover, can be lost in the perplexing confusion about faith and justice issues that is presently haunting our culture.

The rise of the "new conservatism" is a case in point. As I see this movement, often associated with morality and a form of Christian faith, it is not a conserving of what is richest and deepest in human beings, but a preserving of ourselves from the facts. It is a conservatism not of principle, but of pragmatism. It hungers for the legitimations of power and prestige—especially economic, military and ideological. And it represses all suggestions that right order has yet to be achieved in our country. It is a conservatism of self-interest.

This new conservatism is the fruit of two complementary but dangerous tendencies: the tendency to separate faith from the work of justice (active love and service) and the tendency to equate faith with a particular form of social, political, or national power.

The danger of the first tendency is that it fails to recognize that society and culture are intimately interwoven with spirituality and faith. The power of religious aspiration is rendered innocuous and ineffective when it is separated from the concrete demands of justice and love for others. Both the established "secular" and "religious" worlds feed this debilitating separation—not of church from state, but of faith from lived social reality.

Newsy journals chide bishops for trying to legislate morality in their protesting of abortion. Women missionaries who were brutally killed in Central America are passed off by some right-wing pundits as do-gooders who had no business working for the poor and oppressed. Social commentators taunt people of faith who take stands concerning world hunger, prisons, and the inequitable distribution of wealth. Church leaders are subjected to State Department pressure when they resist propaganda on arms spending, on military aid to El Salvador, on cutbacks in federal assistance to the poor.

On the other hand, when some clerics, religious, or lay persons try to speak to their own church people about justice, racism, capital punishment, or militarism, they are frequently told, "Don't bring politics into the pulpit. Talk to us of religion." It is not unthinkable that Mary, the mother of Jesus, would be unable to speak her Magnificat from our church sanctuaries, smacking as it does of poverty-talk, justice, and casting the mighty down from their thrones. And so the "people of God" join forces with *Time* and *Newsweek* in their prying apart of politics and spirituality, in their sundering of faith from justice.

It is a most dangerous separation. For it is precisely this splitting of faith from social reality that seduces the religious impulse into a stance of mere accommodation to political and economic power. Hence, the second dangerous tendency: the identification of faith with cultural standards, even cultural idols.

Recent events provide compelling examples of the ways that Christians are more committed in lived faith to the gospels of nation and culture than to the gospel of Jesus. When Pope John Paul II came to the United States, Roman Catholic commentators of the right and left went to great pains to explain to television audiences that the pope did not fully understand the "facts" of American Life—whether economic, military, or sexual. The actual problem is, however, that North Americans are not sufficiently critical of their own patterns of life—especially with respect to sex, war, and money. The pope was calling for an evangelical generosity in all areas—based upon the radical dignity of the human person revealed in the gospel of Christ. The pope also saw the intrinsic relatedness among all these areas, in the light of faith, and how they are influenced by cultural ideology rather than human sensibility. This relatedness, however, was ignored or repressed. For to confront it would mean to change our own attitudes and behaviors toward nationalism, poverty, and justice.

A second phenomenon is the fact that many of those who do claim to see the relationship between Jesus and politics have reduced Christ to Americanism and capitalism. Some of them, assuming the terminology of "morality" and "majority," continually associate Christianity with military ascendency, financial success, and vindictiveness against criminals or marginal people. They come close to extinguishing the fire and compassion of Jesus' own message and life. On many Sunday morning media presentations of Christianity, we hear much of money and success, often of psychological stability and social popularity, frequently of the glories of capitalism and the dangers of socialism, but rarely of the poor, the suffering, the rejected, and disenfranchised; rarely of the Christ who was crucified, unsuccessful, imprisoned, and abandoned. Such is the impoverishment of a faith intimidated and consumed by cultural imperatives.

The impoverishment and domestication of the Christian faith, consequently, is not only the central problem of my search for a paradoxical readership; it is also the central problem addressed by this book. I intend to show the intrinsic and necessary relationship between a living faith and an activist love. At the same time I will suggest how it is that men and women of faith can so easily be led into a position of submission before national, economic, and cultural idols.

I propose to activists that they become more profoundly rooted in faith: in the life and action of Jesus and in the life of a believing people.

I propose to people who profess a serious belief in Jesus that they become more deeply activist in their loving service and more fully critical of the ways their faith has become acculturated.

In answer to the problem of a faith ineffectually isolated from justice, this book offers neither more interiority nor more activism, but precisely an integration of both: an activism that is truly revolutionary and a faith that is fully holy: saintly revolution.

In answer to the problem of faith being co-opted by culture, this book suggests how the life of Jesus, how his saving action, how his people and its traditions, all offer a most stunning contrast to cultural idols. We must be willing to disengage our commitment in Christ from the illusions of nationalistic myth, military might, and economic supremacy. We must be courageous enough to undertake a life of resistance.

The problem of finding people who might respond to the whole of this book, consequently, is very much like the difficulty we face in confronting both Christ and culture in an integral manner. It is a risk, but it is worth it. And there are hopeful signs in the churches that the convergence of justice and spirituality is upon us. If persons of traditional Catholic faith are repelled by the social critique of America or the mention of Marx, at least they might be invited more deeply into the faith which calls them to justice and compassion for the poor, if they take that faith seriously. If social activists, disillusioned with the broken promises and inconsistencies of a sinful church, will not take seriously the talk of sacraments and prayer, perhaps at least they will be led into a deeper recognition of the imposing reality which confronts them. It may be hoped that they will see how high the stakes are, how great the need is for some sustaining hope or faith or person to live and die for.

Part One is a critique of American society under the controlling concept of the "Commodity Form." When we perceive ourselves and others as things, when we live and behave under the "form" or in the image of the commodity, we invariably produce lives of violence, fear, manipulation, and alienation. This critique is framed by a discussion of some insights which Karl Marx could offer for a Christian critique of society and a schematic presentation of a Christian anthropology. The purpose of Part One is to reveal the spiritual crisis at the heart of social and political and economic evils. Our problem is idolatry. Its presence is systemic.

Part Two is a presentation of the "Personal Form" of perceiving, valuing, and living as revealed in the person of Christ.

Its purpose is to reveal the societal and political implications of believing in Jesus Christ, and to suggest the ways of sustaining a Christian-activist life through sacramentality, prayer, commitment, family, and community. The way of Christ is the way of freedom. It, too, is systemic. His claim upon our lives is total; and it is in collision with our culture.

The entire book is largely interpretative—an attempt to see behind the veil of appearances in our culture and penetrate to the meaning of a religion so often supposedly fought for but rarely lived. Although I offer an annotated bibliography as appendix, I do not attempt in the text to document facts or observations. Rather, I ask you to direct your energy and attention to the lines of interpretation. Since, moreover, this is not a book of fundamental or philosophical ethics, no specific arguments are given to support my own positions against war, abortion, armament, sexual hedonism, or unrestrained capitalism. My purpose is not so much to establish the foundations of particular moral positions as it is to unveil the connections between them. I would rather reveal the relationship between death row and abortion factories than prove the inhumanity of either. I would rather suggest the collaboration of hedonism with the dissolution of marriage and with the free market than insist upon or demonstrate the evil of each.

Just as my ethical convictions are not established here but are offered as personal rational choices, so also my appeal to Jesus Christ is not "justified" by any apologetic or dogmatic argument. It is, as it stands, quite simply an appeal and belief that I invite others to share in commitment. I write as a social and political communitarian, an evangelical Roman Catholic, whose final trust rests on the love of God made manifest to humanity in Jesus Christ.

RISING HOPES, LOST OPPORTUNITIES

It might seem, at first sight, that the passing of ten years would seriously challenge any interpretation of cultural life. These last ten years, in particular, have brought changes in American culture and the world that were not only unexpected, but improbable. Indeed, some events have taken place that most people, only a few years ago, insisted were impossibilities.

The Berlin Wall has come down; it is now marketed as fragmentary memorabilia. Germany's reunification has been won, and not by force of arms. Political freedom has been achieved in countries where it was never supposed to happen —only to be once again threatened by the political and economic instability of Russia.

Chinese students erected a "statue of liberty" in Tiananmen Square and were brutally crushed for doing so. Free elections, despite terrific military and financial tampering by the United States, were held in Nicaragua, and a Marxist-led government turned over the reins. In South Africa, apartheid is dissolved and Nelson Mandela is free, although the circle of violence is not yet broken. Lebanon was brought to its knees and brutally violated while few in the West seemed to care. Ferdinand Marcos was cast down from a mighty throne once deemed impregnable. The victors exercised only "people power." His successor, however, is now under siege, assaulted both by the cries of the poor and the machinations of the wealthy and the rebellious.

The last decade has seen the assassination of Egypt's Anwar Sadat and India's Indira Gandhi. It has also witnessed a succession of "demons"—as many Americans have considered them.

The Ayatollah Khomeini, hostage-taking nemesis of President Jimmy Carter, has died. Moammar al-Qaddafi's residence was bombed by American jets. The country of Panama was invaded and maimed for the purpose of capturing a demon drug lord who had spent much of the decade in the employment of the invaders. The damage to humans and property is yet unacknowledged while the country continues to languish.

The most astounding events in the last few years, however, were the developments in Europe, especially in the Union of Soviet Socialist Republics.

In the spring of 1985 Mikhail Gorbachev was installed as the General Secretary of the Communist Party. In six years' time, he would win the Nobel Peace Prize and be named *Time* magazine's "Man of the Decade." One need not know his eventual fate or his political destiny to be assured that the most momentous of changes have taken place under his leadership. No matter the social or economic forces at work in his decisions, no matter the possibility that he might turn back to the ideology and violence of Leninism, irreversible events have taken place. In the spring of 1986, Russia, for the first time in seventy years, acknowledged a disaster in its own lands, the Chernobyl nuclear catastrophe. By the end of that year, political dissidents, including Andrei Sakharov, were being released from prison or exile. By the following summer, massive economic reforms were announced. In late 1987, Gorbachev indicted Stalin, whose guilt he characterized as "enormous and unforgivable." By the next summer, a nuclear arms cut-back was agreed upon with then-President Reagan, and the Soviet army was pulling out of Afghanistan. Early 1988 brought proposals of reforms in the military, the Communist Party, the farming system, and the Central Committee. Boris Yeltsin, in open opposition to the policies of Gorbachev, won a free election.

In late 1989 and throughout 1990 a tidal wave of change swept through Eastern Europe. A Catholic member of Solidarity was made premier of Poland. Lech Walesa achieved the elected presidency, having been in jail only a few years previously. An East German exodus to the West went unchallenged. The Berlin Wall would crumble on November 9. Free parliamentary elections were scheduled for Hungary, as a martyr of the 1956 Hungarian Revolution was reburied with honor. In Czechoslovakia, Alexander Dubcek, of the 1968 "Prague Spring," would hail the ascendancy of Vaclav Havel to Czech leadership. And the criminals of Romania would tumble in the space of ten hours.

The beginnings of this last decade of the twentieth century were rife with unparalleled opportunity. A great new Marshall Plan for the 1990s might have been unveiled. Disarmament, and the consequent reallocation of resources, might have been undertaken. The Third World, which had until this time been largely victimized by the conflicts of the First and Second World, might finally be addressed with cooperation and compassion.

The opportunities, sadly, may be lost.

The USSR is on the verge of falling apart or regressing into a military state. In the absence of massive technical and managerial assistance, and under pressure for liberation from its various republics, Russia faces disastrous economic failure and political sundering. This, to be sure, is primarily due to the internal failure of communism, its production system, its dispiriting bureaucracy, its often heartless ideology, and its extravagant military waste.

The opportunity lost may also be laid at the hands of the West, especially the United States, because of two lethal factors. First, the failure of communism has been interpreted as the unquestioned success of capitalism (not, as one might have thought, the triumph of the human spirit even in the midst of totalitarianism and material want). Second, the United States lurched into a war in the Persian Gulf.

The economic failure of communism is manifest. The International Monetary Fund and the World Bank have revealed that one in five families in the Soviet Union must wait five years for an apartment, that in some regions people are exposed to environmental hazards up to 100 times greater than that acceptable in the West, that fifteen million Russians still wait for telephone services, that per capita income is equal to that in Mexico—about one-tenth of per capita income in industrialized democracies—and that the Soviet Union habitually loses a fifth of its grain crop and its cows produce only half as much as those in the West.

On the other hand, few remain who would question the economic success of capitalism in terms of productivity, diversity of goods, and the range of human services. Although we ourselves may yet have to face serious crises in our own economy, it is uncontested that the United States and its economy have provided a dazzling array of products, product choices, career opportunities, health and education options, and technological advances. The previous decade occasioned the arrival of highspeed facsimile technology, the cellular telephone, home video games, videocassette recorders, compact discs, and personal computers available to millions of Americans, while many parts of the Second and Third World—even in the halls of universities—can barely find paper to write on. This dazzling array of consumer items has been one of the major arguments offered by the proponents of "Democratic Capitalism" over the last decade.

But when the first edition of this book was written ten years ago, it was not the achievement of capitalism's productivity that was called into question. Nor was it the economic or spiritual achievement of Marxism which was proposed for our consideration. Rather, it was the cost which capitalist achievements exacted from our personal existence that was questioned: not only the financial costs paid predominantly by the poor of our country or of "third-world" nations, but costs to human personhood paid by all of us—psychologically, spiritually, and culturally. And of Marxism, what was appealed to is what remains, even in the shambles of Eastern Europe: a critique of economic and political ideologies which alienate us from our personal and social worlds. In many ways, it was this very critique—offered by Marxist-humanists and Christian socialists of Eastern Europe—which contributed to the collapse of Marxist-Leninist ideology and totalitarianism.

Thus, as the communist world is forced to face the inadequacies and the destructiveness of its way of life, it is important for us to face the inadequacies and destructiveness of our own. This is the meaning of Pope John Paul II's warning in Mexico when he cautioned the First World not to neglect its own self-examination, especially of its abundance, while Eastern Europe reels in economic and political turmoil. Throughout the previous decade, the pope had admonished the wealthy capitalist nations that they were equally called to a critical evaluation of their own priorities and policies. In *On Human Labor* of 1981, he insisted upon the primacy of labor over capital and pointed out that "materialism" held sway as much in the West as it did in the Eastern Bloc. Similarly, in 1987, his encyclical *On Social Concern* was considered a daunting challenge to the capitalist world. Challenges such as these have often brought angry responses, usually from wealthy Americans, that there is no "moral equivalence" between communism and capitalism. There were also complaints that the pope was too backward as a Pole, too socialist in his impulses, and too sympathetic to the Third World, to understand the United States and its capitalist way of life. As was the case with some Catholic American reactions to the U.S. Bishops' letters on peace and the economy, these papal confrontations with capitalist or nationalist ideology were for the most part stifled or ignored in the conviction that the American consumerist way of life was morally unassailable.

But the inescapable reality within the United States over the last ten years was that the ideology of the consumer society had reached its apex. It might best be symbolized in a mid-1980s cover story of *M Magazine,* "For the Civilized Man." "I want, therefore I am," the article began approvingly. It noted that even though greed had always been the dominant motive force of capitalism, it had reached, in the Reagan years, a quality of unmitigated purity, without any moral or social limits. Congress would raise the minimum wage one dollar an hour, up from $3.25, but they would double their own 1980 salaries of $60,000 because, despite all the congressional perks, they found it too little to live on. Executives complained that they could not manage on $300,000 a year. Religion-marketing itself became a big-time success story of opulence and extravagant television shows. All this, while the number of homeless people tripled to three million. (The government claimed it was only 350,000.) Elections were won with outright appeals to the nation's greed: "Are you better off now than you were four years ago?"

A president who entered the White House with the promise of balancing the budget left office eight years later with hitherto unimagined debt: it had tripled, from $909 billion in 1980 to $2.9 trillion in 1991. Ronald Reagan was succeeded by a president whose major campaign promise was "no new taxes," especially for the very wealthy, even though the ratio of the average CEO salary to a blue collar worker was 91:1. In 1980 it had been 25:1. It was called the decade of wretched excess, of unbridled hedonism, a time when the "politics of the rich" suffocated the poor.

An estimated $1 trillion disappeared into thin air through the Savings and Loan debacle, a scam underwritten by the legislative and executive branches of government, exploited by financiers living in opulence, and ultimately paid for by the middle class at the rate of at least $3,000 per taxpayer over the next ten years. Even the so-called "bail-out" provided "sweetheart" deals for new robber barons awarded billions in subsidies, profit guarantees, and tax breaks.

The Stock Market crash of 1987, the scandals of the Environmental Protection Agency, the influence peddling of White House aides, the marketing of arms to Iran for the sake of overthrowing an unpopular government in Central America, all signaled an unraveling of the fabric in our economic and political life. Paul Kennedy, author of *The Rise and Fall of the Great Powers*, would note in *The Wall Street Journal* as the '90s began that our national indebtedness, our decreasing productivity, our mediocre educational system, our decaying social sensibilities were being ignored at the very time we were devoting massive amounts of money, material, and human resources to win esteem on the battlefield. Ominous signs of possible collapse in the banking and insurance industry suggest that the next decade will be exhausted in paying for the greed of the '80s.

The heroes were Reagan, Donald Trump, Michael Milken. Reagan had cut federal appropriations for low-income housing by 82 percent. There were three million more poor Americans at the end of the decade than at the start. While corruption marked Reagan's Department of Housing and Urban Development, the percentage of families owning homes declined for the first time since the '40s. Trump, notwithstanding a governmental bail-out for his casino and real-estate empire, embodied the strange paradox of a man in debt who still could manage to live in suffocating extravagance. Michael Milken, the junk bond king of Drexel Burnham Lambert, would earn $550 million in 1987 only to be indicted on 98 counts of fraud and other misdeeds. His mentor, Ivan Boesky, proclaimed to the graduates of the University of California School of Business Administration in 1985, "Greed is all right. Greed is healthy. You can be greedy and still feel good about yourself." And two months before declaring bankruptcy, Drexel Burnham Lambert lavished $260 million in bonuses upon its own. Some executives would receive as much as $10 million. In the end, the company "bonused" itself with twice the amount of money it could have used to avoid defaulting on its debts.

Between 1980 and 1990, the United States moved from being the world's leading creditor to being the world's largest debtor. The $700 billion national debt was complemented by our nation's personal savings dropping by one half. Over the decade, we consumed $1 trillion more than we produced in goods and services. As a nation, much of this spending was for munitions. While we could launch a $2.2 trillion military spending spree, our bridges, highways, public housing, schools, and environment suffered benign neglect. We were creating a huge, unattended "underclass," many of them born as "crack babies," subject to terror and neglect in an inferior education system, living unrooted in a culture where family bonds were loosening to the point of unraveling. In New York State, for example, the number of black men in correctional facilities was 24,000; the number of black men in New York state colleges or universities was 23,000.

Not only were the poor of our own culture further marginalized in almost nightmarish fashion. During the decade of greed, expenditures to help the poor nations of the world lessened as well. Foreign aid—except for military purposes and strategic influence—declined.

John Paul II, in Edmonton, Ontario, indicted the wealthiest countries for their inverted priorities:

> Yes, the South—becoming always poorer—and the North—becoming always richer . . . Richer, too, in the resources of weapons with which the superpowers and blocs can mutually threaten each other. In the light of Christ's words (Mt. 25), this poor South will judge the rich North. And the poor people and poor nations— poor in different ways, not only lacking food, but also deprived of freedom and other human rights—will judge those people who take these goods away from them, amassing to themselves the imperialist monopoly and political supremacy at the expense of others.

Thus, politicians of the consumer society would insist that we build armaments and even undertake a devastating war for "the sake of innocent lives," while they ignored the poor of our own society as well as the entire earth. Forty thousand people die of diarrhea, malnutrition, and other preventable causes each day in the developing world. Fifty million of them could be saved during the next decade if the world military establishment would devote one day's expenditure to them. It does not occur. A one percent cut in annual U.S. military expenditures would unlock more than enough to save the lives of those fifty million children. It does not occur. A one percent cut could similarly fund the entire ABC childcare bill, double the budget for AIDS research and treatment, and triple the federal budget for the homeless. It does not occur. One in four children in the U.S. under the age of 6 lives in poverty, but we seem not able to muster the resources to help them. Whenever any foreign aid or poverty relief bill is introduced to Congress, the refrain is, "but where will the money come from?" But to wage a war in the Persian Gulf at the cost of billions? The money appears. To pay for the trillion lost in the S&L failure? The money is there.

Personal and national priorities reveal the continued ascendancy of the Commodity Form of Life. The living of persons and personal living have dwindled with the decade of greed. And, fatefully, the graced opportunity to examine our own need for cultural reform may well have been suffocated by our own cultural triumphalism, its neglect of personal existence, and the willingness to go to war to "insure our way of life."

The war in the Persian Gulf is particularly instructive in that it brings together the devaluation of human persons, the expenditure of huge human resources in hightech warfare, and the propensity to violence that marks much of the commodity way of life.

This is the second side of our own lost opportunity. Not only have we remained uncritical of our own need for personal and national reform; we have also succeeded once again in externalizing our enemy. We have put at risk a decade of peace which was finally feasible due to the changes in Russia, and we have endangered our own livelihood. A threat to the wellbeing of future generations smoldered in the cultural chaos we were fashioning through the neglect of our young, the erosion of personal values, the fascination for entertainment, and the reckless waste of American wealth and ingenuity. But rather than face this bitter truth, we projected Saddam Hussein as the pseudo-threat to civilization and Western life.

A war that might so easily have been avoided through negotiations, through flexibility in accepting deadlines, through a willingness to hear the complaints of the Arab world, through agreement to a United Nations conference on the Palestinian question, was entered into with chilling premeditation. The greatest bombing campaign in history was launched with the hope that a man whom our leaders had portrayed as an insane second Hitler would come to his senses. It brought about the response that might have been expected from a ruthless leader, fiercely pan-Arab, relentlessly nationalistic, and endowed with a cleverness to match his military resources: the greatest environmental damage in history due to oil pollution, the bombing of civilian populations in Israel and Saudi Arabia, the possibility of chemical warfare, and the crushing of a nation's financial, communication, and military structure.

Even though this war was "won" and it can be blamed upon the invasion of Kuwait by the forces of Saddam Hussein, we will yet have to face the consequences of our own actions. The people of Iraq have faced incalculable suffering with the destruction of their health, communication, water, and power systems. Not only were a hundred thousand of their soldiers killed—for the most part while they were trying to leave Kuwait—but unnamed tens of thousands of Iraqi civilians became casualties. In addition, over three million refugees were added to the ranks of the world's homeless. Our celebrations of victory will not enable us to avoid the problems we have helped create. The Palestinian question will haunt the Middle East. The alienation and outrage of Arab populations will intensify. The clamoring for new weaponry, especially of the "star wars" variety, will drown out the cry of the poor. And the presence of the United States may be required for generations in the Persian Gulf. One may only pray that this was not our plan.

It was Vaclav Havel, in his address to the Congress of the United States, who reminded us of the dramatic changes of the last ten years and the portentous choices of the decade to come. A man from the Second World was speaking to leaders of the First World and suggesting to them that there was more to be done than declare victory over communism. We must, he said, learn to put morality ahead of politics, science, and economics and realize that our responsibility is to "something higher than my family, my country, my firm, my success."

Having lived through the convulsions which occurred in Europe as it was facing its "great lie," Havel had offered his own warning to the affluent West, if it were willing to face its deceptions. In the mid-1980s the warning appeared in his work, *The Power of the Powerless*. Now, in the last decade of the twentieth century, we have yet to attend to his words.

The profound crisis of human identity brought on by living within a lie, a crisis which in turn makes such a life possible, certainly possesses a moral dimension as well; it appears, among other things, as a *deep moral crisis in society*. A person who has been seduced by the consumer value system, whose identity is dissolved in an amalgam of the accouterments of mass civilization, and who has no roots in the order of being, no sense of responsibility for anything higher than his or her own personal survival, is a *demoralized* person. The system depends on this demoralization, deepens it, is in fact a projection of it into society.

It would appear that the traditional parliamentary democracies can offer no fundamental opposition to the automatism of technological civilization and the industrial-consumer society, for they too are being dragged helplessly along by it. People are manipulated in ways that are infinitely more subtle and refined than the brutal methods used in the post-totalitarian societies. But this static complex of rigid, conceptually sloppy and politically pragmatic mass political parties run by professional apparatuses and releasing the citizen from all forms of concrete and personal responsibility; and those complex foci of capital accumulation engaged in secret manipulations and expansion; the omnipresent dictatorship of consumption, production, advertising, commerce, consumer culture and all that flood of information; all of it, so often analyzed and described, can only with great difficulty be imagined as the source of humanity's rediscovery of itself . . . In a democracy, human beings may enjoy many personal freedoms and securities that are unknown to us, but in the end they do them no good, for they too are ultimately victims of the same automatism, and are incapable of defending their concerns about their own identity or preventing their superficialization.

I have ended with the words of Czechoslovakia's president because they so powerfully confirm the thesis of this book and the introductory remarks of this second edition. They also indicate that the critique of the consumer culture which is offered here is not just the screed of a disenchanted American ungrateful for all the goods of capitalism which people of Eastern Europe envy. We have our own problems to face. And just as the newly liberated peoples of Europe might turn to us for assistance with our skills at productivity, entrepreneurship, or management, so also we might learn from them the spiritual insight which would help us admit the deficits of our own culture and economic system.

Some readers of the first edition have written me with the suggestion that the strong critical tone might be lessened. Indeed, while I have tried to note throughout the book that the United States is profoundly graced and that human technical productivity is an endowment meriting the highest of gratitude, the book was—and now remains—largely critical of our way of life. This is not due to a lack of love for the people and institutions of the "consumer society," or a blindness to the merits of capitalism in democratic societies. It is due rather to a belief that the best values and hopes of those peoples and institutions are in danger of extinction. The threat remains: not things and material possessions, but the idolatry of them; not technology, but the submission to it; not even capitalism, but its enthronement as a "way of life," as a Commodity Form of human existence which suffocates persons and personal values.

If this is the case, some negativity may indeed still be in order. Critique, albeit with faith, hope, and love, is imperative.

Over the past ten years I have found out that my hope to reach two quite diverse readerships was in many ways fulfilled. Men and women of profound faith and spirituality have realized that if their faith is to be real and effective in their lives, it must have political, social, and economic expression. For some of them, this book has been a helpful encouragement in their lives, whether they were confronting the consumer society and apartheid in South Africa, whether they were speaking on behalf of the homeless and the poor in England and Ireland, or whether they were defending aboriginal rights in Canada or Australia. Others, who had come to a reading of this book already with a conviction that there was something dreadfully wrong with American society and that a commitment to justice was central to their lives, have found the linkage to personal solitude, integrity in relations, and a community of faith challenging and enriching to their social consciousness.

I have found the greatest resistance and challenge to my ideas from people who might be located at either far end of the spectrum. Some of them seem to have so strongly identified faith with Americanism that they reject any critique of the United States as being communistic or even anti-Catholic. Others, it seems to me, have become so identified with American secular liberalism that they see any appeal to a radical Catholic or Christian faith as mere pietism. I continue to be challenged by both groups. I hope that, within both groups, there will remain some who might yet entertain the challenge of this book.

The most recent example of our unwillingness to be challenged is found in the reaction of some American Catholics to the encyclical letter *Centesimus Annus* written by Pope John Paul II to commemorate the centenary of Pope Leo XIII's encyclical, *Rerum Novarum*. A conservative newspaper ran the front-page headline, "'Free Economy' Must Replace Dead Socialism And Welfare State." Similarly, the *Wall Street Journal* enlisted another conservative Catholic source for an opinion column entitled "The Pope Affirms the 'New Capitalism.'" It sports a sidebar with the statement: "Capitalism is the economic corollary of the Christian understanding of man's nature and destiny."

It is astounding that in articles such as these, the undying attachment to our present way of life blinds commentators from recognizing that the entire fourth chapter of the encyclical is a systematic warning to the West and its capitalist countries about the dangers of the "business economy." These include: the inequitable distribution of the earth's goods, the militarizing of the world at the cost of the poor, the "domination of things over people," the marginalization of the least powerful, the "senseless destruction of the natural environment," the fragmentation of the family, the seduction of "consumerism, when people are ensnared in a web of false and superficial gratifications," the alienation of work, and the overpowering of cultural and moral life by a radical capitalist ideology.

Indeed, the pope equally focuses on the situation of the world today in light of the collapse of communist governments and Marxist-socialist economies. His analysis of the failure continues his long-standing indictment of a dehumanizing system grounded in an atheism incompatible with Christianity because it affirmed class warfare and state dictatorship while denying human spirituality and freedom. What is more, he commends the values of a free economy, of working for profit, and of economic freedom as long as they are ordered to the proper end of service to God and neighbor. In this regard, he goes to great lengths to insist that these are inadequate and even dangerous values if they are not grounded ultimately in a love for others, especially the poor, and a commitment to justice.

It is a brilliant, even-handed, and challenging document; but its message will be lost if we in the consumer society presume that it presents capitalism as the economic expression of human nature and destiny in the wake of communism's collapse. "The Western countries, in turn, run the risk of seeing this collapse as a one-sided victory of their own economic system, and thereby failing to make necessary corrections in that system."

Those "necessary corrections" involve nothing other than the reinstitution of a personal form of life in faith, economy, and culture.

Changes in this edition involve an updating of some statistics and cultural references throughout the chapters and significant additions to the annotated bibliography. In addition to this new introduction, the first chapter offers a different approach to a critique of our culture through "reading the life of the Consumer Society." Its sections parallel, to some extent, the "reading of the life of Christ" in Chapter Eight.

The material of the old Chapter One, "The Christian Marxist Matrix," is integrated into other sections of the book. Many people suggested that such a change would make *Following Christ in a Consumer Society* a more accessible book. The old chapter was so highly theoretical that some readers were discouraged from continuing. Also, the discussion of Marx's theories and use of his concepts made it impossible for some to be sympathetic to the goals of the book. I hope these changes will be of some value in making the reading less abstract and the willingness to criticize our social, political, and economic world more concrete.

There are also some short expansions of Chapters Three and Eleven in the treatment of our personal response and resistance to the "Commodity Way of Life." Some shortened and schematic forms of these new materials and observations have appeared in the Canadian Jesuit journal, *Compass;* the English journal of spirituality, *The Way; Commonweal;* and various lectures in Europe and Australia.

Finally, I wish to express my gratitude to the staff at the Center for Health Policy and Ethics at Creighton University for their generous time and instruction in matters not only of medical ethics but of the computer. Robert Ellsberg, the editor-in-chief of Orbis Books, has helped me as much with his hard work as with his encouragement. And if dedications would be proper for revised editions, this most assuredly would read: "To Patrick Murray and Jeanne Schuler and their two sons, a family which lives with such grace and fidelity what this book hopes to be about."

TURMOIL AND TRUST

The pontificate of Pope John Paul II roughly parallels the life span and themes of this little book. From 1978 to 2005 John Paul II offered an integrated vision of Christian faith and practice, a vision too often repressed or ignored by both the liberal and conservative wings of the Catholic Church. His indictment of untrammeled consumerism was perhaps most forcefully formulated in a statement for the World Day of Peace late in his pontificate.

The history of our time has shown in a tragic way the danger which results from forgetting the truth about the human person. Before our eyes we have the results of ideologies such as Marxism, Nazism and Fascism, and also of myths like racial superiority, nationalism and ethnic exclusivism. No less pernicious, though not always as obvious, are the effects of materialistic consumerism, in which the exaltation of the individual and the selfish satisfaction of personal aspirations become the ultimate goal of life. In this outlook, the negative effects on others are considered completely irrelevant. Instead it must be said again that no affront to human dignity can be ignored, whatever its source, whatever actual form it takes and wherever it occurs.

Such were his words for the last year of the twentieth century.

As the new century dawned, Thomas Friedman's bestseller *The Lexus and the Olive Tree* had an introduction titled "The World Is Ten Years Old." Although the motif was concocted in an advertisement, it was in many ways true. So much had happened since the fall of the Communist empire. It is easy to forget things. Consider this: United Press International reported in 2002 that the latest opinion poll in Britain found that the death of Princess Diana was the most momentous event in British history—more important than the Reformation, two world wars, the breakup of the empire, and even the Beatles. Such is the affliction of shortness of memory.

The Friedman quote alluded to the events of 1990, the year when the second edition of this book was being written. The preface to that edition, as you can read herein, was marked by hopes for a new Africa and a new Russia and by worries that we would enter a new era of warfare and capitalist expansion, heedless of the moral vision of Pope John Paul II. Sadly, Africa is in turmoil, Russia is in dissolution, we are at war with a new "evil empire," and capitalism has conquered even China. If the face of the world can change so dramatically over a decade, to look back over two and a half decades is to look at a different world indeed.

THE COLONIZING OF A NATION

CNN, EWTN, and C-SPAN call-in programs were launched twenty-five years ago, our news and spiritual teaching having been found until that time in newspapers and churches. Most people still went to libraries to find information about religion and politics, not to a computer. Amazon is only ten years old (remember how strange the ads sounded at first?). Google was a "project" in 1996, a humble enterprise with a staff of three in 1998. Now it is a giant, delivering 2.5 billion searches a month. The term "blogging," having surfaced in 1999, represented by 2006 an astounding 23 million personal publishers. These, to be sure, are great achievements of entrepreneurship and capitalism. The power of communication, moreover, may well have been the principal factor in bringing about the fall of the USSR. Chinese Communists realized this fact and blocked communication as fast as they could. For Africa, it may be mass communication, not religion or politics, which eventually alters its plight.

The media explosion may be the most strategic force of the last twenty-five years. Worldwide all-day news networks brought a startling immediacy to events. The Oklahoma City bombing and the trial of Timothy McVeigh, the destruction of the Branch Davidians in Waco, the Los Angeles rioting after the video of Rodney King's beating, the Challenger and Columbia catastrophes, the slaughter at Columbine High School, the awesome drama at Tiananmen Square, the thrill of seeing the Berlin Wall come down could be witnessed by almost everyone.

We became familiar with the crimes in Bosnia and Rwanda, experts on "smart bombs" in the first Gulf War, "embeds" in the second one. Politics became more personal as we witnessed the charisma of Reagan and a Polish pope, the turbulence of the Clintons, the shaming of the professoriate and judiciary in the Anita Hill–Clarence Thomas strife.

We attended liturgies of grief and celebration for a pontiff buried and a pontiff elected. The death of a holy woman from Calcutta was overshadowed by that "most important event in British history," the obsequies of Princess Di. We learned of "hanging chads" and kept vigil for 36 days to find out if we had a president. We became courtroom experts with the assistance of William Kennedy Smith and O.J. Simpson.

An indelible trauma was felt by Americans on September 11, 2001, when our two most prominent symbols of wealth and military power were struck by terrorists for whom personal life seemed utterly insignificant. This was a definitive assault on any illusions of human invulnerability. Equally numbing, however, in the span of one year we would witness, with horrific immediacy, the fragility of human life before the might of nature. Hundreds of thousands would die in the Indian Ocean's tsunami. Millions would be displaced by earthquake in Pakistan. A great American city seemed to disappear before our eyes.

A time traveler from 1980 or 1990 would likely be shocked by the content of television. Ads warning of four-hour Viagra-induced erections seem ubiquitous. Sex lives of presidents, rock stars, and athletes are clinically described. "Reality Shows"—the most inappropriately named genre in the history of the media—celebrate the egocentrism of anyone from a bride to a businessperson. And the rawness in the presentation of easy sex and unrestrained violence, made possible by cable television, moved to the major networks that still do not allow four-letter words. The paradox is that some of the most praised and talked about programs, such as "Sex in the City," "The Sopranos," "24" and "Nip and Tuck" also serve as devastating critiques of American culture.

There was much that was preposterous. Money, fame, and media crystallized on Monday, June 13, 2005, at 4 p.m. central time. Every major network, all cable news channels awaited the Michael Jackson child-molestation verdict. Fans of the King of Pop gathered around the courthouse. The crowds stopped in Times Square. The verdict: "Not guilty."

Daniel Henninger in the *Wall Street Journal* had observed a week before: "There is more of him [Jackson] in us than we might want to know . . . We live in a freaky culture. It is a culture confused about many things—about personal behavior, about identity, about norms of any sort."

He might also have added, "We all plead, 'Not guilty.' "

What could be more un-American than being guilty, than repentance and the admission of sin? Guilt-denial may be a human problem haunting each conscience and every culture, but we seem to have made a science of it.

We learn denial from our earliest years. Some toddlers invent a little friend or evil twin to blame mistakes on. Others, like four-year-olds I've seen off and on over the decades, just accuse the nearest bystander. "See what you made me do???" Accepting and acknowledging sinfulness may well be the last things we learn, if we ever do. And yet, perhaps this is what we Americans most need to do.

Denial and projection of guilt are tactics not only employed by individuals. They are also the ploys of nations, classes, genders and religions that demonize the enemy while protesting their innocence. Imagine you live in Iran or have a cousin in al-Qaeda: Whose sins do you seriously ponder? Who are the "evil ones"? And then come back to America and think about the sins we see and do not see in the world. Who are our "evil ones"? To ask such a question is not to propose moral "equivalence." It is merely to point out the omnipresence of sin-denial and to suggest how much is lost by it.

Rather than admit sin, the best we seem able to do is admit that we "made a mistake." Better yet, "A mistake was made." The passive voice is always more palatable. "Something bad happened while I was in the vicinity." And even admitting that is like pulling teeth. The most common confession we hear these days is this: "If anyone was offended, I'm sorry you have to feel that way." As Fred Barnes said one Friday on Fox News—"Fair and Balanced as Always"—"A president never makes mistakes." And Barnes was approving the president's unwillingness to admit that he had any regrets about anything, other than saying, "Bring it on." The flight from moral responsibility is nothing other than the flight from our personhood.

If we are faithful to our personhood, however, responsibility must be owned and admissions, indeed, should be made. That is the only way to repentance and recovery. As Alcoholics Anonymous wisely recommends, a ruthless inventory of our lives is a prerequisite for a sober life.

1. Stewardship of the Earth and Human Solidarity. Our patterns of consumption will not allow a sustainable planet. If China alone fulfills its aspiration to consume as we do (we are five percent of the world and we consume twenty percent of its resources), there would be no natural resources left. Deng Xiaoping was frighteningly prophetic: "To get rich is glorious." We who are gloriously rich, however, must show as

much human ingenuity and generosity in conservation as we
do in waging war. Moreover, in face of the growing problem
of starvation in the underdeveloped world, we must turn our
armaments into plowshares.

2. *The Wages of War and American Moral Exceptionalism.* This nation is at a precipitous moment in the execution
of its military policies. If we move beyond the boundaries of
the Just War theory, as is now being proposed by advocates
who are willing either to distort its principles or actually to
cast them off as outdated, we may reap a terrible harvest of
global violence. The true ugliness that marks the terrorists we
decry is their willingness to cast off all reason, all limits and
all distinctions in achieving their goals. With our own talk of
pre-emptive, even nuclear, strikes, of justified torture and of
"being willing to do anything" to stop terrorism, it is terrorism itself that will seduce our consciences.

3. *The Lessons of 9/11.* Amid the countless calls for
vengeance that could never heal the terrible trauma, the endless chattering about loss of liberties and the mindless conspiracy theories of right wing and left, we refuse to address
the hardest question raised by the destruction of New York's
Twin Towers. Whither our relationship to Islam? If only one
in a hundred Muslims is a radical extremist, this means there
are fifteen million of them. It is an illusion to think they can
be beaten into submission, not to Allah, but to the U.S. vision
of the future. The proponents of "The New American Century" who seem to have orchestrated the second invasion of
Iraq may ridicule the option of dialogue, but fair discourse—
much of which must be done within Islam itself—is the only
way to peace. If the U.S. pushes Muslim nations and peoples
further into the ranks of resentment, there will never be peace.
And the Twenty-First Century will be a century of war.

4. *The Mirror of Money.* If we do not believe that greed is a
fatal problem in the United States, we must be sleepwalking.
Covetousness, as Dorothy Sayers reminded us, is still a deadly
sin, even though it is considered bad form to remind us of the
fact. The super rich and their apologists have been so successful

at eliminating greed from the catalogue of sins that it is considered envious to even raise the point. Greed, as it always has, threatens the American economy. Greed has pushed the middle and lower-middle classes—so many laid off or relegated to service jobs— into free fall. Greed got us a tax boondoggle for the wealthiest of our country and a monumental debt for our children. The poor and middle class, by and large, are enlisted to fight a $400 billion war of choice. One wonders whether any political leader will ever appeal to the generosity of the American people.

5. The Margins of Human Life. While universities now hire well-paid specialists in animal rights, an increasing number of human beings are being excluded from the privileged class of rights-bearing persons. Pre-implantation genetic diagnosis allows us to eliminate unwanted imperfect embryos. Rather than just destroy them, however, we are learning to harvest any desirable cells they may have. For those embryos lucky to enter the fetus stage, there is absolutely no protection for them under the law. Be not surprised if it is soon proposed that, rather than destroy second-trimester fetuses in abortion, they, too, should be harvested for cells and organs at the service of high-tech cannibalism. Some ethicists, realizing that a newborn is much more like a fetus than a teenager, have announced that infanticide is not only defensible but is often desirable. As for the margin at the end of human life, again when persons are defenseless, dependent and often unwanted, the deadly utilitarian calculus has already suggested that it would be better to terminate such burdens than care for them. Will we make the best of it by harvesting them as well? Why would that not be desirable in a nation that maximizes profit and celebrates choice? We may ask the same question of the Christian churches.

THE CHASTISEMENT OF THE CHURCH

The task of the Catholic and other Christian communities in the reform of the nation is the reform of the Church. This should be an inescapable truth in the light of its own failure in fidelity.

As painful as the clergy sexual-abuse scandals have been for victims, perpetrators, and all believers, it is a matter of justice and an occasion of grace that evil has been revealed and named. That is all for the good. But special pleading continues. Responses to the scandal are a litmus test for ideology. It is interesting that two of the dominant voices on this matter over the recent years came from the Catholic right (George Weigel) and the Catholic left (Garry Wills). What is uninteresting and expected is that they disagree. Weigel, thinking that all could be resolved if we were all more conservative, seems to believe that clericalism, authoritarianism, and secrecy have little to do with the crisis. Wills, thinking that all could be resolved if we were more liberal, seems to think the culprits are celibacy and chastity—the very two principles that were obviously violated. What is known for sure is that there was an appalling violation of vows and persons, a legitimization of it, an enabling of it, and a covering up of it.

The damage that the clergy-abuse scandal has brought to the Catholic Church will be felt for years, if not decades. The financial loss, it will someday become clear, is insignificant when compared with the weakening of the Church's teaching and witness. It has been rare indeed that a bishop or priest actually admitted guilt, sorrow, and repentance. In a Church that has traditionally seen some of the most severe moral judgments passed upon the sexual sins of its laypeople, this is discouraging, to say the least. Have there been any parishes visited by a priest found guilty, not of sin alone, but of crime, speaking honestly of his sins, the ways of temptation, the seductions of deception, and the possibilities of healing grace? Have there been bishops to speak of the outrage, unafraid of legal repercussions? We all lose at this game of denial. The only winners are the lawyers and their courts, where, if things are not "settled" in secrecy, people plead no contest or not guilty; and we never face the reality of the wounds we have inflicted on our people and their trust.

There may be a saving grace to our chastisement as a Church. The honest acknowledgment of profound infidelity to the Gospels in sexual matters may lead to an admission that the call of Christ to forgive, to heal, to make peace and to attend to the poor has equally been ignored. It is not just pleasure that seduces the heart and mind. Power and property do as well.

In a time of closing parishes and dwindling attendances, of a youth seemingly not drawn to priestly life, religious life, ministry or service, perhaps we might ask ourselves whether we have been offering them a way of life that is a mere variation on a capitalist, depersonalized and de-Christianized world. The failure to grasp the whole Christian message, to fully accept Christ as truly the Way, the Truth, and the Life, is the core of the problem. We may say we believe in Jesus Christ. We act as if we do not.

This is why the legacy of John Paul II is so important. He drew people, young and old, not because he was a "media master," but because he fully believed what he preached and lived what he believed. And it was an integral faith. Discipleship meant following Christ in matters of sexuality, property, power. Thus he spoke and lived against a world of sexual exploitation, constructing a robust phenomenology of the personal body and a thickly reasoned defense of spousal love. He spoke endlessly about the dignity of personal life, especially at its most vulnerable beginning and ending stages.

His views on sexuality, abortion, and euthanasia were well known. But unfortunately, things stopped there. Many people, duped into thinking that sex is the most important thing in life, did one of two things. A) Hating what he said about sex, they rejected everything else he said. Or B) Loving his positive and sacred view of sex, they didn't take seriously what he said about anything else. "Politicians know best about war." "Capitalists know best about money." "I know best about my bedroom and my body." The result was that the message of John Paul II, much like the gospel itself, was mutilated by the very Christians who proposed to follow it.

When the last edition of this book appeared in 1991, Pope John Paul II released *Centesimus Annus*, his encyclical commemorating *Rerum Novarum*, the social encyclical written a hundred years earlier by Pope Leo XIII. Celebrating the fall of Communism's "Real Socialism" and acknowledging the value of the free market and private property when they are put at the service of the common good and the help of others, John Paul II cautioned the capitalist countries of the First World. "The Western countries, in turn, run the risk of seeing this collapse as a one-sided victory of their own economic system, and thereby failing to make necessary corrections in that system. Meanwhile, the countries of the Third World are experiencing more than ever the tragedy of underdevelopment, which is becoming more serious with each passing day." He saw clearly the looming "tragic crisis" of the coming years if internationally coordinated efforts are not taken. He saw, moreover, that the plight of the poor is not limited to the Third World. "In the countries of the West, different forms of poverty are being experienced by groups which live on the margins of society, by the elderly and the sick, by the victims of consumerism, and even more immediately by so many refugees and migrants."

The second great warning of the encyclical concerned the issue of war. Noting that the fall of the USSR was accomplished, not by the presumed inevitable war, but by "the non-violent commitment of people who, while always refusing to yield to the force of power, succeeded time after time in finding effective ways of bearing witness to the truth." The truth of non-violence was contrasted with the way of violence that "always needs to justify itself through deceit." He specifically mentions the false justification of pre-emptive war by "defending a right or responding to a threat posed by others"(23).

His warning against a deceptive claim to be "responding to a threat" was like a prediction for the tactics used to start the Second Gulf War, a war he strongly opposed despite the efforts of some American Catholics to enlist his support (and their later rejection of his moral position in favor of their government's leaders). His rejection of the second war should have come as no surprise. In *Centesimus Annus*, written fifteen years ago, he reminded us of his rejection of the *first* Gulf war:

> I myself, on the occasion of the recent tragic war in the Persian Gulf, repeated the cry: "War—never again!" No, never again war, which destroys the lives of innocent people, teaches how to kill, throws into upheaval even the lives of those who do the killing and leaves behind a trail of resentment and hatred, thus making it all the more difficult to find a just solution of the very problems which provoked the war. Just as the time has finally come when in individual states a system of private vendetta and reprisal has given way to the rule of law, so too a similar step forward is now urgently needed in the international community. Furthermore, it must not be forgotten that at the root of war there are usually real and serious grievances: injustices suffered, legitimate aspirations frustrated, poverty, and the exploitation of multitudes of desperate people who see no real possibility of improving their lot by peaceful means. (52)

To act in loving resistance as Christians against a Christian country that makes pre-emptive war its highest priority and assistance to the poor its lowest priority requires generosity, fortitude, and sacrifice. They are the same counter-cultural virtues of evangelism that personal lives of sexual and familial integrity require from us.

This is the legacy of an integrated faith in Christ that Pope John Paul II bestowed upon us. It is a vision shared, moreover, by a growing number of believers in the Evangelical tradition. In a 2005 article that appeared in *Books and Culture*, Ron Sider's "Scandal of the Evangelical Conscience" asks, "Why don't Christians live what they preach? Scandalous behavior is rapidly destroying American Christianity. By their daily activity, most 'Christians' regularly commit treason. With their mouths they claim that Jesus is Lord, but with their actions they demonstrate allegiance to money, sex, and self-fulfillment." The same year, an uncommon manifesto, written by Bill McKibben for *Harper's*, appeared with the title "The Christian Paradox: How a Faithful Nation gets Jesus Wrong." Lamenting that the Christian Coalition of America, founded to defend Judeo-Christian values, made its top legislative priority "making permanent President Bush's 2001 federal tax cuts," he unmasks the violence, excessive wealth, and self-indulgence of a people wearing the garb of Christianity, but not having the heart of Christ. "Having been told to turn the other cheek, we're the only Western democracy left that executes its citizens, mostly in those states where Christianity is theoretically strongest."

THE CONSOLATION OF A PERSON

During the year of this book's first revision, Wendell Berry in "Peaceableness Toward Enemies" advised us that if we want to be at peace we will have to waste less, spend less, use less, want less, need less. The most alarming sign of the state of our society now is that our leaders have the courage to sacrifice the lives of young people in war but have not the courage to tell us that we must be "less greedy and less wasteful." Since that time fifteen years ago, I have seen a stirring of the Holy Spirit in the lives of many lay people and the university students I teach. There is an open professing of faith. There is a commitment to service and the help of the poor. There is deepening dissatisfaction with America's leadership in the world, a disquiet about the massive inequities of wealth. There is a hunger for transcendence. Despite living in a consumer society, they desire to follow Christ.

As the world has changed, so have I. Despite the urgency of this 2006 preface, I have somehow gotten more patient with the world and more forgiving of our culture. Admission of the many ways my own life has been colonized by capitalism has helped me see the nature of the ongoing compromises I embrace in following the Lord: compromises that perhaps even his disciples faced. Whether it be in acknowledging the comforts, denied to most of humanity, of my own life or the weakness of a human will unable to give up smoking for any serious period of time over fifty years, I realize that grace has yet grown in my life and full redemption awaits. Whether reflecting on one's self, thinking of or worried about loved ones, pondering the crises of the Church or the wounds of the world, one ultimately can only hand it over to the Father revealed in Jesus.

Like the second edition, this edition involves some minor and major changes. In the early chapters I have tried to update statistics and cultural references that have changed over the last fifteen years. In this respect, Chapter One has been considerably rewritten. The last chapter of the annotated bibliography is changed in both style and matter. Well over half of the material is new, with even some suggestions about the internet. Many of the older recommendations, out of print or (more importantly) no longer pertinent, have been dropped. The bibliography, like other additions, has been enhanced, I believe, by my growing contact with radical evangelical writers who are not in the Catholic tradition. (I am grateful to Professor Eleonore Stump, whose gift subscription to *Books and Culture* has helped me find many new companions on the journey.) The last six pages of what was Chapter Eleven have been expanded into a full chapter. This was done at the request of many people who were looking for a deeper explanation of the "disciplines" of personal living in the context of the Gospel. Finally, various passages of the new edition, usually in different form, appeared in *America* magazine, a publication of the Jesuits of the United States.

My gratitude to Robert Ellsberg, Editor-in-Chief of Orbis Books, remains undiminished. It is extended as well to Philip Fischer, S.J., whose copyediting and corrective encouragement helped me complete this edition. Fifteen years ago, my dedication was to Patrick, Jeanne, and their sons, now graced by their sister, Savita. If a new dedication were allowed for a twenty-fifth anniversary edition, it would surely be for my nieces and nephews and their children, but especially for Julie (a constant witness of faith to me), her husband, and three girls.

PART ONE

THE COMMODITY FORM

CHAPTER ONE

READING THE LIFE
OF THE CONSUMER SOCIETY

Repeat. Do you read? Do you read? Are you in trouble? If you are in trouble, have you sought help? If you did, did help come? If it did, did you accept it? Are you out of trouble? What is the character of your consciousness? Are you conscious? Do you have a self? Do you know who you are? Do you know what you are doing? Do you love? Do you know how to love? Are you loved? Do you hate? Do you read me? Come back. Repeat. Come back. Come back. Come back.

Walker Percy, *Lost in the Cosmos*

The late Walker Percy, in his brilliant satire on American culture, aptly subtitled "The Last Self-Help Book," concluded with this fantasy appeal from an extraterrestrial voice. It is addressed to a culture whose people have lost all sense of their interior lives. They are incapable of communicating with each other, even though they expend endless energy trying to communicate with other planets and chimpanzees. They are earnestly romantic about their entertainment and about material objects, but deadly suspicious and cynical about persons. They are assiduously productive and yet on the edge of self-destruction.

3

Percy's words are a call for a "return" to our human personhood, to relationship, to the admission of inadequacy, to love and transcendence. But the words of renewal and reform demand from our society the very attitudes that we most promptly suppress: the acknowledgment that something is wrong and the willingness to change. We are after all "a city shining on the mountain," a "thousand points of light," and a "beacon" to all the backward nations of the world. We have been told, from the beginning of the new century, that our enemies are "evil ones" who hate us not for what we do but for what we are and for how we live. How can there be any need for us to examine ourselves, to "come back," or to repent?

What is more, the "lostness" of our selves, of our personhood, is reinforced systematically throughout our cultural consciousness. No matter where we turn—to ourselves, to others or to society at large—we find personal reality overshadowed by the omnipresent immensity of objects, whether it is in producing them, buying them, amassing them, or relating to them.

The Consumer Society is a formation system: it forms us and our behavior. It is also an information system: it informs us as to our identity and as to the status of our world. Its influence is felt in every dimension of our lives, and each dimension echoes and mirrors the others. The individual's "lost self" is paralleled in the dissolution of mutuality and relationship. The personal and interpersonal breakdown is reflected in the social and economic worlds through a general socialized degradation of persons, through a flight from human vulnerability, especially found in marginal people, and through a channeling of human desire into the amassing of possessions.

If we turn to the texts of our cultural life, our books, our media, our magazines, our newspapers, our heroes and heroines, a troubling interpretation suggests itself: the "end of man" and the deconstructed personal self which has been trumpeted by postmodern thinkers is the philosophical world's expression of the consumerist way of life, wherein personhood disappears.

THE EMPTY INTERIOR

One man who knows Trump well does see a rhyme and reason. Trump is a brilliant dealmaker with almost no sense of his own emotions or his own identity, this man says. He is a kind of black hole in space, which cannot be filled no matter what Trump does. Looking toward the future, this associate foresees Trump building bigger and bigger projects in his attempts to fill the hole but finally ending, like Howard Hughes, a multi-billionaire living all alone in one room.

Time, January 16, 1989

In other words, we are what we eat, what we build, what we buy.

Advertisement for *Time,*
Advertising Age, July 22, 1985

Insofar as people have adopted the "American dream" of stuffing their pockets, they seem to that extent to be emptier of self and soul . . .

Our consumer culture persistently teaches that we can counter insecurity by buying our way to self-esteem and loveworthiness. The pervasive message, passed on in popular media, advertising and celebrity-modeling, is that we will feel better about ourselves if we are surrounded by symbols of worth.

Richard Ryan, foreword to Tim Kasser's
The High Price of Materialism (2002)

Create a More Beautiful You. Tummy Tuck, Eyelid Lift, Breast Augmentation, Collagen Face Lift, Facial Resurfacing, Forehead Lift, Breast Lift, Nasal Surgery, Liposuction, Vein Treatment, Microdermabrasion, Botox

Plastic Surgery Advertisement,
Texas Monthly, January 2002

Donald Trump may be only the most prominent example of our quandary: the more we try to ground our identities in external possessions or triumphs, the more we plaster our names on everything we can accumulate, the more we cling to surface and style, the less we find underneath. We undergo what a *New York Times* Business Section article termed "The Strange Agony of Success." Many of our most accomplished achievers and acquirers "tell their therapists that they have lost all sense of themselves, that they consider themselves frauds in their very success and that money has become the main symbol of their human worth." As for Trump, although he slid into a $900 million debt in the 1990s, by the turn of the century he was again "worth" more than a billion dollars. By 2004, he was the star of a "reality" show called *The Apprentice*, wherein aspiring executives compete to win his approval.

The consuming self, unmasked, reveals a terrible absence. There is no substance to our being, nothing there but the appearances, the "outside," the "looking good," which has become, as the ad says, "everything." There is a hole underneath it all. It is a discovery frighteningly made in those moments of true solitude when we are no longer producing, consuming, marketing, or buying. The demise of the self takes place long before any death suffered by one's own hand. It occurs when first the myth that we are nothing but "what we eat, what we build, what we buy" is lodged in our mind.

The fear of our human frailty, of our unguardedness, of our creaturely existence takes manifold expression in the consumer society. Underneath the differing examples is a hidden rejection of our very selves, our personal limits, our deficits of mind and body. It can be found in the depressed self-rejection that the young, especially women, experience. A Princeton study of the late 1980s found that one in four young teenage girls reported herself as being "extremely depressed." Oddly, the more time they spend on shopping, hairstyling, and applying makeup, the more depressed they get.

Self-rejection inhabits and covertly motivates the addictive patterns of our lives: "He's drinking himself to death."

Or, with the rates now estimated at 400,000 deaths a year, "She's smoking herself to death." Television medicates our feelings, dulling our sensitivities, numbing our interior lives. Our average children will have 19,000 hours of TV by the end of high school, more time than they will spend in classrooms. The more depressed of the children tend to watch television in greater quantities. As the "rebelmothers" website reported, psychologists Allen Kanner and Tim Kasser in 1999 warned of advertisements that induce a sense of inadequacy in children unless they buy products, a dynamic that contributes to "the formation of a shallow 'consumer identity' obsessed with instant gratification and material wealth."

The flight from the solitary personal self haunts our compulsion to work, our urgency to produce. We often seem incapable of living in the present moment while paradoxically we feel robbed of time. Professor Geoff Godbey of Pennsylvania State University observes that we have devised marvelous stratagems to save, borrow, manage, lose, beat, and kill time, but we avoid personally living in it. "In America, there's a great need to define ourselves by what we do. We don't see ourselves as born with a fixed identity, so what we do becomes a sign advertising who we are."

The diversity of techniques for avoiding our interior feelings, the saturation of our consciousness with images, impulses, and noise, the avidity with which we feel we must produce, and the seriousness with which we invest our identity in money-making are all symptoms of a dispossessed and forgotten interior world.

THE BROKEN RELATIONSHIP

The '80s were about acquiring—acquiring wealth, power, prestige. I know. I acquired more wealth, power and prestige than most. But you can acquire all you want and still feel empty. What power wouldn't I pay for a little more time with my family! What price wouldn't I pay for an evening with friends! It took a

deadly illness to put me eye to eye with that truth, but it
is a truth that the country, caught up in its ruthless am-
bitions and moral decay, can learn on my dime. I don't
know who will lead us through the '90s, but they must
be made to speak to this spiritual vacuum at the heart
of American society, this tumor of the soul.

"Lee Atwater's Last Campaign," *Life*,
February 1991

Do your own thing. Seek your own bliss. Challenge
authority. If it feels good, do it. Shun conformity.
Don't force your values on others. Assert your personal rights (to own guns, sell pornography, do business free of regulations). Protect your privacy. Cut
taxes and raise executive pay (personal income takes
priority over the common good) . . . Such sentiments
define the heart of economic and social individualism,
which finds its peak expression in modern America.

David Myers, *The American Paradox*, 2000

There have been a lot of jokes made about the number
of marriages that go on the rocks because people would
rather sit in front of a computer terminal than spend
time with their spouses, but it's no joke, says professor
of psychology at the U.S. International University in San
Diego, Michael Yapko. "People are having substitute
relationships with their cars, computers, VCRs and
bank accounts."

"High Technology and the
Decline of Human Caring,"
Saint Louis Post-Dispatch, July 9, 1986

I got knocked up by half a cubic centimeter of defrosted
sperm that had been FedExed in a nitrogen tank from
an East Coast donor facility to my doctor in Los Angeles. Now, if all goes well, my dream will become a reality: I'll be a single mom . . . Without the emotional con-

text, finding a donor seemed less like the intimate act of choosing my child's father and more like buying a car. I could select a basic model (tall, good-looking, healthy) and then accessorize with options . . . Ordering the father of my child on a Web site was especially difficult for me, because I'm not a good online shopper.

Lori Gottlieb, "The XY Files,"
Atlantic Monthly, September 2005

Unable to engage our interior lives, we are incapable of engaging the interior lives of other people. Not knowing ourselves, we are unable to reveal who we are before the face of another person. And we are unable to receive them in their personhood since we are out of touch with our own.

The commodity-hucksters reassure us that their products will comfort us more than persons could, anyway. "I'm looking for a meaningful relationship, and I found it at Saks Fifth Avenue." "Toyota, I love what you do for me." "Fall in love without paying the price." "Loves having a trust fund, hates feeling guilty about it; hates, loves, hates, loves; wants a better relationship with money." Thus advertisements evangelize us.

As C.S. Lewis wrote in *The Four Loves*, if we want to avoid the pains and vulnerability of love, we had better not even love a cat. We should wrap our hearts in tinsel and trinkets, and they will never be broken; they will become unbreakable. Dead. Like the objects we cling to. And so human passion, which can only be fulfilled by encountering persons, is channeled into possessions. We are warned of the betrayals and vulnerabilities often discovered in relationships. We might be "found out" as we really are. We might be rejected and certainly wounded. This cautionary theme is the gist of a run-of-the-mill *Cosmopolitan* article of the 1980s. "As we've heard a boring number of times, a child is only lent. If you clutch a loved one too closely, that person might disappear . . . But there's no need to hold back when you're dealing with possessions. Clasp a sensuously soft cashmere as tightly as you like (assuming your fingernails are well cared for). It will never walk out on you."

The Consumer formation system trains us for a life of fragmented relatedness. According to Source Priority Management Systems, Inc., eighty-five percent of the business people in the U.S. work more than 45 hours a week. Eighty-one percent experience stress, forty-eight percent every day. Eighty-nine percent take work home with them. Sixty-five percent work more than one weekend a month. Forty-two percent don't read to their children. Fifty-three percent spend less than two hours a week looking after their children. As one man said to his wife, who was painfully wondering why they never spent time together or with the children, "Honey, it's not you. It's just that I don't know how not to work."

Relationships are also assaulted by the media culture—not only by the content of the media, which so often demeans committed intimacy, but by its almost imperial hold on us. When we are not producing and consuming, we watch. By 2004, 60 percent of children aged 8 to 16 had a TV in their bedroom. Half of American households have three or more televisions. We sit, passive again, like objects, lulled into the world of "it" which dominates our conscious action and labor. We look at images of images and fancy them real. Our life project seems to have become, in the words of Neil Postman, "Amusing Ourselves to Death." More of our conscious life is spent witnessing commercials than communicating with our spouses, children, community. Taking a cue from Orwell's *1984*, Mark Crispin Miller has written, "Big Brother is You, watching." The Consumer formation system, through its media, speaks to our souls and utters its pronouncement: "We shall squeeze you empty, and then we shall fill you with ourselves."

Kevin Roberts, CEO of Saatchi & Saatchi, has discovered the secret of the empty soul, bereft of relationship. It is *Lovemarks,* the title of his book and the message of "marketing" speeches he gives throughout the world. He has five insights into our commitments to favorite brand names: "Lovemarks capture emotion . . . Lovemarks are irreplaceable and irresistible . . . Lovemarks earn both love and respect . . . Lovemarks touch mystery, sensuality and intimacy . . . Best of all, we can *measure* Lovemarks." The deepest desires of humanity can be measured because they are found, not in relationship with others, but in relationship to products.

The upshot of it all is this: the culture of lost interiority is paradoxically a culture of lost intimacy. Alone with our passive aloneness, but not in true solitude, we find that our ability to relate to other persons has atrophied. We know not how to give ourselves to the other since it is an empty fortress we call the self. And we know not how to receive the other's love, since one cannot love what one does not know. The fragmentation of relatedness and intimacy is the hidden termite eating at the foundations of commitment to others. It is manifested in the breakdown of family life, in the increasing rate of divorce, in the abandonment of our children to the streets and the airwaves, in the decline of civic and neighborly community, in the growing popularity of "prenuptial" contracts made fashionable by the rich and famous, in the new malady called "time famine."

In my own discussions with parents and their children concerning the problem of family stress and fragmentation, I know of no other force so pervasive, so strong, and so seductive as the consumer ideology of capitalism and its fascination for endless accumulation, extended working hours, the drumming up of novel need fulfillments, the theologizing of the mall, the touting of economic comparison, the craving for legitimacy through money and possessions, and unrelieved competition at every level of life.

Having expended our lives in the husbandry of commodities, we feel robbed of any time we might give each other. And we starve in the midst of plenty.

Thus the words of Lee Atwater, the campaign manager for the first President Bush, were prophetic. In his forties, dying of a brain tumor, painfully bloated from chemical medication, he speaks out from the pages of *Life* magazine to the people of the hard-driven consumer society. It is a "tumor of the soul."

THE CRAVING FOR THINGS

The money society has expanded to fill the vacuum left after the institutions that embodied and nourished those values—community, religion, school, university, and especially family—sagged or collapsed or sometimes even self-destructed. Now we live in a world where all values are relative, equal, and therefore without authority, truly matters of style. Says Dee Hock, former chief of the Visa bank card operation: "It's not that people value money more but that they value everything else so much less—not that they are more greedy, but that they have no other values to keep greed in check." Or as University of Pennsylvania sociologist E.D. Baltzell puts it: "When there are no values, money counts."

Myron Magnet, "The Money Society,"
Fortune, July 6, 1987

Now we may have reached the apogee of consumerism. Many of us can no longer afford what our fathers could—a house, an education for our children—but an enormous percentage of us can afford practically anything else, and we buy it. What is more, we have made the very act of pursuing it almost an end in itself. We have built pleasure domes of commerce dedicated to the search, great agglomerations of shops under one roof, climate controlled, adorned by trees and fountains that never see the sun, places where some people spend entire days, unashamed. In California the bumper stickers say, "I Shop, Therefore I Am." Nowadays, this is only half a joke.

"The Gimme Generation," 1980s supplement
to *Wall Street Journal*

The essential conservatism of Mr. Bush's approach is all the clearer if you compare it with the big-government liberalism of the 1960s . . . Mr. Bush is not using government to redistribute wealth (unless you own an oil company), to reward sloth or to coddle the poor. And government in America remains a shriveled thing by European standards. Some 40 years ago after the Great Society, America still has no national health insurance; it asks students to pay as much as $40,000 for a university education; it gives mothers only a few weeks of maternity leave.

John Micklethwait and Adrian Wooldridge,
"Cheer Up, Conservatives,
You're Still Winning,"
Wall Street Journal, June 21, 2005

Bereft of any interior life and starved for relationship, it is only logical that we feel driven to fill the emptiness that is within us and the absence that is between us.

A July 1987 cover story for *Fortune* magazine, entitled "The Money Society," provided an extensive examination of the existential yearning at the heart of the consumer society. It begins with a religious allusion: "Money, Money, Money is the incantation of today. Bewitched by an epidemic of money enchantment, Americans in the Eighties wriggle in a St. Vitus's dance of materialism . . . Under the blazing sun of money, all other values shine palely." The liturgical and ritual context is apt. As the *Journal of Consumer Research* pointed out in June 1989, there is a confluence of "The Sacred and the Profane in Consumer Behavior." While religion has become secularized, buying and consuming have become vehicles for experiencing the sacred. The infinite longing of the human heart has been introjected into products—the newest, the best, the costliest, the always interminably improved. Our malls are "cathedrals of consumption." Eternity is found in Calvin Klein bottles. Infiniti in a Japanese automobile. One's heart, no longer a throne wherein the transcendent personal God might dwell, no longer engaged by a knowing and loving trinitarian encounter of other persons, is restless until it rests—now anchored or even chained by the promise of possessions.

Thus, accumulation is king. The *Fortune* article notes that we clamor for $175 tennis shoes, $40,000 fur coats, and a $4,000 toy Mercedes. We are told that, while in 1967 forty percent of U.S. college freshmen thought "being well off" was important to them as opposed to eighty percent who thought "developing a meaningful philosophy of life" was important, by the late 1980s the numbers had reversed. It was not so much that money and possessions were seen as being a value in one's life; they were becoming the only value. And having more of them was becoming the only goal.

Many were succeeding. By 1990, millionaires numbered over 1.3 million people, six times as many as there were in 1970. The richest 1% of Americans, who owned 31.8% of the national wealth in 1963, had upped their share to an even heftier 34.4% of it two decades later. As Kevin Phillips revealed in *The Politics of the Rich and the Poor: Wealth and the American Electorate in the Reagan Aftermath,* the amassing of wealth in the United States was only beginning, and it was being redistributed away from the middle class and poor and into the hands of the super-rich. By the year 2005, the *Wall Street Journal* reported that the number of millionaire households had risen to 7.5 million. *Forbes* listed almost 700 billionaires. It is noteworthy that even as the new century dawned, the top one percent of the population was getting a bigger share of after-tax income than the bottom 40 percent. The 2.8 million wealthiest Americans were earning more than the 110 million poorest. President Bush's response was to push through tax cuts. An extended analysis in the Sunday, June 5, 2005 issue of the *New York Times* showed that these tax cuts benefited the very wealthiest (about 150,000 taxpayers) the most.

The craving for "more," wedded with a powerful sense of isolated individualism, erodes our sense of solidarity. The doctrine of capitalist "freedom" is an appeal to supposedly "self-made" individuals who make and spend money in a society of unfettered celebration of private choice. The costs to the democratic civil community, however, are great. Former Treasury Secretary Robert Rubin has estimated that if the tax cuts of 2001 and 2003 for earners over $200,000 were repealed and the reformed inheritance tax were continued rather than repealed in favor of the super-rich, any Social Security shortfall would be covered for 75 years. But our leadership has appealed to the dogma, "we know best how to spend our own money." The problem, however, is this: is there any "we"?

Thus, conservatives are told to "cheer up" in a *Wall Street Journal* opinion piece. "You're still winning." Sloth is not rewarded in America. Poor people are no longer coddled. Government is shriveled. America has no national health service. Universities cost $40,000 a year for students to attend. Mothers have only a few weeks of maternity leave.

If this is "compassionate conservatism," what on earth might "a culture of life" mean?

THE INJUSTICE OF DEPERSONALIZATION

American children watch an average of three to fours hours of television daily. Television can be a powerful influence in developing value systems and shaping behavior. Unfortunately, much of today's television programming is violent. Hundreds of studies of the effects of TV violence on children and teenagers have found that children may: become "immune" to the horror of violence, gradually accept violence as a way to solve problems, imitate the violence they observe on television, and identify with certain characters, victims and/or victimizers.

*American Academy of Child and
Adolescent Psychiatry*, April 1999

"Threaten the Men in Your Office in a Whole New Way"

Advertisement for the Hummer, 2005

We should invade their countries, kill their leaders and convert them to Christianity. We weren't punctilious about locating and punishing only Hitler and his top officers. We carpet-bombed German cities; we killed civilians. That's war. And this is war.

Ann Coulter, syndicated column on the
9/11 terrorists, September 13, 2001

Where can you get the idea that sexual violence against women is fun? From a music store, through Walkman earphones, from boom boxes blaring forth the rap lyrics of 2 Live Crew.
"To have her walkin funny we try to abuse it
A big stinking p——-y can't do it all
So we try real hard just to bust the walls."
That is, bust the walls of women's vaginas. 2 Live Crew's lyrics exult in busting women—almost always called bitches—in various ways, forcing anal sex, forcing women to lick feces. "He'll tear the p——-y open 'cause it's satisfaction.' Suck my d——k, bitch, it makes you puke." That's entertainment.

George Will, "America's Slide into the Sewer,"
Newsweek, July 30, 1990

The lost interior person, whose consuming and producing has become self-destructive, is capable only of injurious relationships. People are reduced to functions of their identity and gratification as consumers and possessors. Inevitably, this personal and interpersonal reality is "writ large," Plato might say, in the republic, in society. The form it takes is systemic injustice—which is nothing other than reducing a human being to the status of a thing. Depersonalization in the individual and relational spheres is universalized in the social and political world.

Violence and violation haunt our media. Stylized mayhem ranging from Quentin Tarantino's *Kill Bill* to Saturday morning cartoons, the World Wrestling Entertainment and gangsta rap videos are complemented by saturation cable news coverage of murdered children, celebrity murders, molestations, spousal homicide. In regular television programming, 61 percent of programs contain violent acts, with 44 percent of the incidents involving attractive perpetrators having no immediate punishment or long-range condemnation.

Sexual violence, so graphic and brutal that it cannot be described in the newspapers which defend it in the name of free speech, is commonplace in our cultural life. Over the last twenty years we were treated to the sadomasochistic videos and public appearances of Madonna and the male sexual modeling of Aerosmith's Steve Tyler, his pants falling off, his cheeks and lips seemingly swollen with silicone, his concession to change lyrics from "he raped," to "he popped." Robert Mapplethorpe's photographic exhibits were lionized as daring and challenging, even though he displayed men with whips in their rectums and sexual acts which were the primary occasion for the spread of AIDS. By the new century, mainstream sadomasochism was celebrated by a *Vogue* magazine article titled "Beyond Good and Evil." A curator of a museum of photography marvels at the influence of Helmut Newton: "Who could have predicted that the culture would follow his vision as if it were some sort of game plan for the future? That everybody would be wearing chains and stiletto heels as part of their daily dress and embrace S&M as a fashion statement?"

The denial of the human person's dignity and grace is evident as well in our geopolitics. A conservative columnist once recommended that we retaliate against Arab terrorists by striking Shiite villages and over-killing them at the ratio of 500 to 1. There was no outrage at such a proposal. He was not excommunicated from his church or laughed off the political scene. That is because his logic, for the most part, is accepted in our social world. An international policy which suggests that Arabs are expendable is echoed in the call-in talk shows where callers recommend that we "make an ash tray of all those Arab countries." Since the abomination of the destruction of the World Trade Center, forms of violence once considered unthinkable as American policy are now in effect (pre-emptive war) or under consideration (torture).

Under threat from the "evil ones," some commentators revealed a new ferocity in their opinion. *Time* magazine ran a Lance Morrow piece, "Case for Rage and Retribution." It was more than a rejection of any peaceful solution. It was a cause for a holy war of our own, filled with loathing not only for the terrorists, but also for those who cheered them on and had given them support. "America needs to relearn a lost discipline, self-confident relentlessness—and to learn why human nature has equipped us all with a weapon (abhorred in decent peacetime societies) called hatred." Andrea Peyser in a *New York Post* column demanded that the United Nations "get the hell out of town" and characterized Christiane Amanpour as a "war slut."

When a young Arab-looking man, having run from London police in the early days after the terror bombings in the summer of 2005, was killed instantly by five shots to the head, John Gibson in his July 22 Fox News segment "My Word" commented: "Five in the noggin is just fine. Don't complain, 'that's barbaric.' We are fighting barbarians." The fact that the young man turned out to be a confused immigrant from South America is not the most troubling aspect of Gibson's commentary. What is most distressing is that he continues the dehumanizing rhetoric that first surfaced after September 11, 2001, when he suggested that America imitate the methods of Syria's Hafez Hassad, who obliterated a Syrian town that harbored his enemies: "He shelled the town until everybody was either dead or gone and literally paved over it. It was cruel. It was heartless. It was merciless. It was unfair. But he didn't have political problems with his opponents again. Works for them. So why is it so bad for us?"

Institutionally legitimated violence, whether it be reckless retaliation against enemies, capital punishment, racism, the astounding abortion rates or the growing euthanasia movement, can only occur when a culture has lost any sense of intrinsic personal dignity. Some "cause," some heartfelt goal, some desirable result justifies wiping out persons. Yet it seems impossible for us to ask ourselves: if "national interest," personal happiness, or freedom justifies any action, do those same goals justify the action of "the enemy"? We do not have to go so far as apply the logic to Islamic extremists. Timothy McVeigh, an extremist for what he thought was the cause of American freedom and patriotism, chose to kill hundreds because he needed a "body count" to make his stand against *tyranny.* Wearing his favorite T-shirt, *sic semper tyrannis,* on the day of his Oklahoma City bombing, he would never regret the act. "In any kind of military action, you try to keep collateral damage to a minimum. But a certain amount of collateral damage is inevitable."

Consumer culture, of course, is not the cause of violence and depersonalization. One need only reflect on Maoism, Pol Pot, Rwanda and Saddam Hussein's Iraq. The challenge for people living in a consumer society like our own is to question the unique ways that capitalism generates its own forms of injustice and violence against persons.

When consumerism becomes a full-blown philosophy and way of life, all social depersonalization, whether in violence or degradation, carries a common theme. Women and men are reduced to the status of means and instruments, whether it be for profit, for "enlightened" self or national interest, or for pleasure. Though almost half a million people die from diseases related to smoking, we continue to subsidize the tobacco industry. Though we are witnessing a frightening creation of an unrooted and uncared-for "underclass," we spend our money on arms and refuse further taxes. Though we say that "nothing is ever solved by violence," we embark upon a war, the consequences of which are horrific, in the name of preserving "our way of life."

THE FLIGHT FROM THE WOUNDED

My real undoing came a few weeks later. The subject was *binding moral duties.* We find such duties compelling; they significantly affect the way we act, I claimed. For instance, "I would like to go to a movie, but *ought* to visit a friend in the hospital . . ." These statements show the tension between what we find pleasurable and what we experience as a moral commitment. It *feels different* to enjoy a movie than to do what is right, even—or especially—when the hospital is far away, the visit is tedious and being there reminds us of our own vulnerability. Most students didn't accept this line of reasoning . . .

I clearly had not found a way to help classes full of MBAs see that there is more to life than money, power, fame and self-interest.

Amitai Etzioni, "Money, Power and Fame,"
Newsweek, September 18, 1989

Since Sept. 11, 2001, the U.S. has launched a war on global terrorism, but it has neglected the deeper causes of global instability. The nearly $500 billion that the U.S. will spend this year on the military will never buy lasting peace if the U.S. continues to spend only one-thirtieth of that, around $16 billion, to address the plight of the poorest of the poor . . . just 15 cents on every $100 of our national income. The share devoted to helping the poor has declined for decades and is a tiny fraction of what the U.S. has repeatedly promised, and failed, to give.

Jeff Sachs, "The End of Poverty,"
Time, March 14, 2005

Needless to say, the real market here is not the pets themselves but their owners, who spent more than $34 billion last year on [them] . . . according to the American Pet Products Manufacturers Association. (The 2005 "trend report" on the trade group's Web site notes a surge of companies getting involved in "pet attire" and claims that faux mink coats and monogrammed sweaters are among the offerings.) Perhaps pet lovers can be accused of treating their animals as mere props to be decorated as broad extensions of their owners.

Rob Walker, "Dog Chic,"
New York Times Magazine, August 7, 2005

Things are not woundable. They do not bleed or suffer or die. And the culture that enthrones things, products, objects as its most cherished realities is ultimately a culture in flight from the vulnerability of the human person. It is the unguardedness of personal existence which is fled when we escape from interiority, or evade committed intimacy, or harden our hearts to the unjust degradation of people.

Amitai Etzioni, while serving as visiting professor at Harvard Business School, was puzzled by his students, whose prime conviction was "consumer sovereignty." The poor do not exist for them, and even if the poor should be present in the form of a friend sick in a hospital, there is no imagined response of duty or compassion. They responded to his case of visiting a friend rather than going to a movie with the claims that he would be just trying to get rewarded by the friend, that he was trying to impress his other friends, that he wanted to make himself feel good. They were "boiling down whatever is noble in human behavior to base motives (self interest, the quest for reputation, or simply whatever is fun), denying the existence of morality, and, in the process, undercutting its significance."

Such a response is actually a further withdrawal from the personal dimension of life, from responsiveness and responsibility, from compassion and empathy, from a recognition of human fragility. Robert Reich, a political economist from Harvard, characterized it as the "Secession of the Successful" in his early 1991 article for the *New York Times Magazine*. Successful Americans are holding themselves off in psychological and economic enclaves where they do not have to confront the wounds of humanity or the world.

The distractions, entertainments, and "stuff" of our lives allow us to live not only apart from wounded humanity but also in a world of illusion. Many Americans, thinking we are the most generous people in the world, believe that we already give too much to the poor nations; and yet we spend on our pets more than double the amount we give to the six billion poor persons in the world, 20,000 of whom die, each day, from the effects of extreme poverty. Facts such as these prompt skepticism from the rest of the world when U.S. government officials cite "humanitarian" reasons for invading Iraq when millions were killed in Rwanda and starved in Niger.

As for "private" giving, the *Chronicle of Philanthropy* reports that Americans making over $70,000 give 3.3 percent of earnings to charity. (The percentage of gifts goes up as income goes down: those making between 30 and 50 thousand dollars contribute close to 9 percent.) The Urban-Brookings Tax Policy Center, moreover, estimates that the estate tax rollback will cost charities $10 billion a year.

Our flight from the wounds of the world's poor is mirrored in our private difficulties in accepting our own vulnerability as embodied persons. There is a mounting ideological delusion that humans at the margins of life surely do not count as persons like the rest of us. We are productive. We manage our lives. We take care of ourselves. We are independent, free, and in control. Thus we are led to question whether we have any personal community with humans in their most unmanageable, vulnerable, and dependent stages of life. Surely mute fetuses, dependent infants, and diapered or dysfunctional old people are not "full persons" like the rest of us. This observation may be shocking to some readers but not to those who use terms like "blobs of protoplasm," "vegetables," and "heartbeating cadavers."

Our antidote, again, is what we most fear: the shedding of the armor (which has become our cage); the opening of our eyes to the wounded (whose existence we deny); the touching of our hearts by those for whom the consumer dream is at best a false promise, at worst a proven nightmare.

The marginal. The sick. The dying. The poor. The old. They might teach us. But we deny our need for learning.

One of the stories of the Buddha might best express the paradox. He was young and wealthy and depressed. His parents gave him everything and shielded him from anything which might distress him. They even had the inside windows of his carriage painted with lovely pictures so that he might not see the pain of the world around him.

Then, one day, being carried through his kingdom, he opened the windows and saw the "Four Sights," though at first he was not even able to name what he saw. He saw people: looking for food, mourning a loss, caring for the ill, facing their old age. His driver told him the names of the sights.

And Buddha left his kingdom. His journey led him to the Bo Tree where he experienced his enlightenment. He would become a Buddha for others.

And wherever you go in the Far East or around the world, you find the statue of the Buddha. And he is smiling. Enlightened by human vulnerability, he is no longer depressed.

Could we take the story of the Buddha as our own? Might it be that the people of the "joyless economy" will be best enlightened when they open their hearts—experientially—to the marginal of their society?

It is our refusal to hear the cry of the poor and wounded which is the final component of our systemic alienation from personal existence. Walker Percy's voice from the wilderness that we "return" to ourselves and "come back" to our human personhood will demand not only a rediscovered interior life, a renewal of interpersonal relationships, a reawakening to the joys of simplicity, and a rediscovery of our passion for justice. It will also require a reopening of our hearts to the marginal people of our world.

The problems that we face are interwoven, since the consumer society and its values are the fabric of our lives. Connecting all of the parts of our experience with a hollow texture of meaning and purpose, consumerism becomes a thing of huge significance, a religion, in effect, supported by its own philosophy and leading to its own theory of behavior. This insight will help us understand the deformation of personal life that has taken place, even in our ways of knowing, willing, and acting. What is more, it will help us see that, once having encountered the life of Christ and his redemption of people, every one of which has a unique personal existence, any response we might make must be a total one, informing not only our private and interpersonal lives, but our social, political, and economic worlds.

CHAPTER TWO

BEHIND BELIEF AND
THE CULTURAL GOSPEL

GOSPEL AS "FORM" OF LIFE AND PERCEPTION

A "gospel" is a book of revelation, an ultimate source or reference wherein we find ourselves revealed. A gospel is a response to the questions of who we are, what we may hope for, how we may aspire to act, what endures, what is important, what is of true value. A gospel, then, is an expression of who or what is our functional god.

No longer are people so much concerned with the issue of atheism. We used to hear questions like, "Do you believe in God?" But today it is no longer a significant question (if it ever was one). The question more crucially before us is, "What god do you believe in?" The myth of the "value-free" science, much less any other human enterprise, is dead. Everyone, any scientist, any philosopher, any politician, economist, or blue collar worker, has a functional god or some ultimate basis of value. It is not a question of *whether* to believe, *whether* to value, but *what* to believe and value. In other words, once our pretenses of neutrality are given up, where do we really find ourselves and our destinies revealed? What is our book of revelation? What is our gospel?

25

We will inevitably be confronted with at least two competing gospels or books of revelation in American society. These
gospels differ as radically as light and darkness, life and death,
freedom and slavery, fidelity and unfaithfulness. They serve as
ultimate and competing "forms" of perception, through which
we filter all of our experience. Each form, moreover, provides
a controlling image for our consciousness in apprehending
our selves and our world. These competing life-forms can be
expressed as the "gospels" of Personhood and Commodity:
the Personal Form and the Commodity Form; the Person-god
and the Thing-god. Each has its own "church," you might say,
its own cults and liturgical rites, its own special language, and
its own concept of the heretical.

One form of life, one gospel, reveals men and women as
replaceable and marketable commodities; another gospel, inalterably opposed to the first, reveals persons as irreplaceable
and uniquely free beings. Some people having formal mem-
bership in a Christian church may in reality follow the gospel
of the culture, and belong to the secular church of "the thing."
Others, not formally belonging to a Christian church or to a
synagogue, may actually be giving their life-commitments to
the message and truth revealed in the covenantal Lord of the
Jewish Bible or in Jesus Christ as true God and true human
person.

CULTURE AS HUMAN:
AMERICAN CULTURE AS GRACED

Setting up such an opposition has, of course, its dangers,
oversimplification not being the least of them. A culture is a
human creation, with human possibilities for pathology as
well as for grace and health. A culture, presumably, is as re-
deemable as a person. At least we might accept such a possibility as an open question. But I wish to focus upon our own
culture as the embodiment of immanently reinforced and legitimated values which permeate our institutions, sustain the
accepted "wisdom" of the day, and underwrite our notions of

"what really counts," of "what talks." It is in this sense that I will speak of the American culture as a pathological phenomenon which assumes for us an objective reality of its own, and against which we judge ourselves, evaluate our worth, seek our fulfillment, and find our meaning and purpose.

I will be emphasizing the negative aspects of our cultural values, well aware that we have no corner on the market of unfreedom, repression, and injustice. Our culture is not the first nor is it the worst to have discovered evil. But it is the only one we live in, the one we are most in need of subjecting to critique.

It is true that our American society is graced in countless ways. We nurture a promise of what millions see and experience as a good and free life. We have a marvelously fertile land and an accomplished technology. Our people have often overcome massive internal opposition in attempting to deal equitably with racism, poverty, the needs of other nations, and institutionalized dishonesty at the highest levels of government. We sustain perduring democratic impulses toward equality, fairness, and the checking of our darker impulses. We are privileged with a press which is for the most part free, despite corporate controls and its dependency upon advertising. Americans by their labor and legislation have achieved almost full literacy, health, food and retirement programs and a force of productive workers invested with self-respect, political power, and considerable security.

But these same "graced" accomplishments, these gifts themselves, are in danger of extinction. American society (and religious faith, including Christianity, to the extent that it has identified with this culture) is in great peril. Human commitment, true personal productivity which serves the human interest, our institutions of family community and citizenship, our sense of justice and respect for freedom, the valuing of life and affection, are all under massive attack. It is for this reason that it is so important for us to be willing to acknowledge our own need for reform, our own need to repent, our own need to change—as painful as that may seem to be.

The admission of our own moral and social failure is not a rejection of our culture's grace and goodness: it is really an effort to preserve and be faithful to it.

As it is in the love for a person, so also it is in the love for a people or one's nation. There can be no grounds for love other than the truth. Otherwise our love is merely for an illusion, not for the truth of who and what we really are.

CULTURE AS INHUMAN:
AMERICAN CULTURE AS DISGRACED

Our severity in judging our value system should not be mitigated by pointing to the failures of other eras or countries in the hope of softening our self-critique. It is none other than ourselves whom we must reflect upon and, if necessary, seek to have changed. We do no service to the truth, much less to the country we profess to love, if we insist that the frequent appearance of evil in other countries and ages somehow absolves us of the evils strangling us. The failures of postrevolutionary France, of Leninist Russia, or of contemporary dictatorships should serve only to warn us rather than to justify their reduplication in our own lives. The fact that I may love my family and even prefer it to all others does not mean that I shouldn't challenge or change it, especially if it is in danger.

It is only at great cost to ourselves and our integrity that we ignore the one million dead in Southeast Asia who purportedly brought us "peace with honor." The dead do not experience it that way, nor do the one hundred million killed since 1900 in the name of an always "final" but disappearing peace.

It is morally fatal for us to repress the truth of our actions and their consequences. It does no service to our country to cover up the thousands in El Salvador and Nicaragua who have died because of our meddling, to pretend that our previous interventions in Iran or South American countries are unrelated to the hostility their elected leaders have for us, or to allow a sitting vice president to deny that he was misleading the country into a war by declaring in the summer of 2002: "Simply stated, there is no doubt that Saddam Hussein now has weapons of mass destruction. There is no doubt he is amassing them to use against our friends, against our allies, and against us." The repression of truth only leads to the deadening of conscience.

It can only be foolishness, not patriotism, to ignore the realities of the present. We *already* live in a country in which the old of our society are victims of what Claire Townsend calls the "last segregation." We already know that some New York insurance companies will pay willingly for the termination of pregnancies but not for deliveries. It is already the case that women from Bedford Stuyvesant, illiterate but hoping to give birth, are directed to abortion-referral lines when they are seeking prenatal counseling.

We already live in a country represented by people who seem to think that the food problem of the world can be solved solely by contraceptives rather than by a more equitable distribution of wealth. We inhabit a country in which euthanasia laws have been introduced into state legislatures, in which the highest court of the land has institutionalized abortion by reducing the issue of fetal human life to a matter of property and privacy. State executions, nuclear escalations, pregnancy terminations, and disposal of the brain-damaged are arbitrated in terms of cost-benefit analysis.

We already live in a country which feeds its dogs a better diet than a fourth of the world's humans are fed—a phenomenon made painfully clear in our latest marketing discovery of diet-food products for our hapless overweight dogs. We consume more products to take off weight than some countries spend to put it on. We have doubled our meat consumption in the last few decades and increased the death-related health hazards caused by dietary superfluity. Meanwhile, there is much earnest talk of "lifeboat ethics" and the abandonment of the world's poor because there is "not enough to go around"; and at the same time we continue to suffocate in our pollution-generating abundance. We already live in a country which has prosecuted illegal wars in secrecy, which has seen fit to execute the greatest saturation terror-bombing in history, which has lionized leaders who have shown little more than contempt for people of the Third World, and which has manipulated, controlled, and ended entire governments of other countries.

Although the illusion of a "kinder, gentler" nation marked by "compassionate conservatism" is the stuff of political rhetoric, the reality is more often a social and political meanness. The degrading and dehumanizing pictures from Abu Ghraib prison and the reports of secret detentions in Eastern European and Middle-East "black sites" for the purposes of torture have been termed "rare exceptions" and un-American. This would seem to be confirmed by Senator John McCain's successfully convincing ninety senators to ban "cruel, inhuman and degrading" treatment of any prisoner. And yet, as a December 2005 Harris poll reported, most Americans disagree with the Senate. A slim majority believes that "rendition" to secret prison camps where torture is used, as well as torture itself, is sometimes or often justified. An even larger majority of 80 percent (apparently not believing the president's claim that the United States does not torture) think that we actually do.

The famous civil liberties and defense attorney Alan Dershowitz in *Why Terrorism Works* argues for a legalization of torture in the face of an imminent attack threatening thousands. Charles Krauthammer, a member of the second President Bush's Commission on Bioethics, in an extended article for *The Weekly Standard* proposed that torture is not only permissible, but "a moral duty." Even though a "monstrous evil . . . as degrading and morally corrupting to those who practice it as any conceivable human activity," he insists we must do anything to prevent mass murder.

The stated goal of some strategic "think tanks" is that the United States allow no country or group of countries to reach the status of a military threat. The president of a country that has produced more "weapons of mass destruction" (and actually used them twice against civilian populations) than any country in history warns that countries must never aspire to having such weapons. Such a policy of exceptionalism for American "toughness" is echoed in call-in shows that ring with voices of vengeance, recommending that we "kick butt" by nuking Iran and "turning those Arab countries into a big ash tray." Our toughness in military matters, moreover, is mirrored in our toughness on crime with our astounding percentage of civilians behind bars and our singularity as the only democracy to execute criminals.

Our toughness in military or penal matters complements our toughness with the poor. Each year delivers more burdens to them in decaying cities, lack of health insurance, poor education and decreased buying power. Despite astounding expenditures for our Pentagon, and unprecedented expansion of wealth for financial elites, we are told that it is the poor—those on social security and fixed incomes, those on minimum wage, those not making a living family wage—who must tighten their belts. As we entered the twenty-first century, the wealthiest 20 percent of taxpayers earned 50 percent of the nation's total income and paid almost 60 percent of the taxes. This struck some people as being unfair to the rich and a disincentive to growth, although the wealthiest profit most from our infrastructure and the 1990s witnessed massive economic expansion. When the first edition of this book was published, Chief Executive Officers in the United States were paid 42 times more than the average worker. Now, twenty-five years later, those executives are paid 419 times the rate of workers. And yet, although no one was calling for it, and the country was facing a massive debt, the President pushed through a tax cut, 78% of which went to our top earners. The *Wall Street Journal* could shamelessly proclaim, "It's payback time for the business community."

The media world enables the repression of reality and construction of illusion. In the entire year of 2004 ABC News supplied a total of 18 minutes on the horrendous Darfur genocide in Sudan (NBC offered 5 minutes, CBS 3 minutes).

As Nicholas Kristof reported in *The New York Times*, Martha Stewart received 130 minutes of coverage by the three networks. In one month, all major news sources collectively ran 55 times more stories on Michael Jackson than they did about the Darfur atrocities. This happens, of course, because Jackson and Stewart are a boon, Darfur a bust, for advertising.

We have the luxury of spending almost $260 billion a year on an industry that is in countless ways a nationally institutionalized deceit—a drumming up of false needs and the hucstering of false promises. Our world of advertising, the "life-blood" of our economy, tells us from our earliest years that we are despicable and inadequate because of our lack of products. "Datsun saves, sets you free." "Buick is Something to believe in." "I'm looking for a meaningful relationship and I found it at Saks Fifth Avenue." "Coke is the Real Thing." "Love is Musk." In a country that is already suffocating in the commodities it produces, advertisers admit that they are no longer selling products, since we really don't need any more products; they are selling us the values introjected into them. "Boss." "Hero." "Knowing." "Opium." "True." "Triumphs." "Slims."

This is the culture that is already with us, that we breathe and inhabit, often without even knowing it. It is the unquestioned "real world," which we are told we must accept and adapt to. It is the world that is appealed to when friends or students or associates say, "After all, money talks, power talks." It is the world of our cultural gospel, a world which must be challenged by critique.

THE HIDDEN UNITY BEHIND THE APPEARANCES

In speaking of the Consumer Society as a form of life, the Commodity Form of life, I have likened it to a gospel because the buying and consuming of material things has taken on religious, even theological significance. It serves as a "way of life," a truth about "the real world," a method of achieving meaning and fulfillment in our existence. Behind all of the buzzing phantasmagoria of dehumanizing problems and de-personalizing experiences, there is an overarching unity which "forms" or gives shape to our experience.

Even though we might not at first see the relationship between seemingly diverse issues, there is a connection. There is a connection between "clean" and precise surgical bombings and our antiseptic delivery rooms, both of which administer a so-called sanitized death. There is a web of meaning which attaches street violence to the degradation of women in the media and the heartless neglect of our children. There is a relationship between the attitude that millions in the Third World might be better off dead and our new technologies of euthanasia and assisted suicide for those who have "no meaning" or no "quality" of life. There is a logical thread between "getting over the Vietnam syndrome"—supposedly fighting with "one hand tied behind our back," even though a million Vietnamese were killed and the only bombs we neglected to rain upon them were atomic—and the pretense that the first Iraq War was won with few casualties, even though there were over a hundred thousand Arabs killed and three million refugees created.

The unified theme is that persons do not count, unless they are certain kinds of persons. If they are not endowed with value by power, affluence, productivity, or national interest, they may be sacrificed at the altar of "our way of life." What is "ours," what we possess, what we own and consume has become the ultimate criterion against which we measure all other values. As an ultimate, this criterion has become our functional god.

The notion that an economic way of life might serve as a religious surrogate was first suggested to me when I read Karl Marx over thirty years ago while writing a doctoral dissertation. I found his famous work, *Das Kapital*, intriguing, not so much for its endless economic statistics and analyses, as for its comparisons of economic and cultural life with religious belief. The term he coined to express how we have perversely related to material objects was "fetishism of commodities," wherein men and women increasingly worship the products of their own hands. We not only relate to things as if they were substitute persons; we relate to them as if they were our gods, giving us meaning, purpose, and a reason for living. And, what is more, as this is done, we increasingly relate to each other as if we were mere things, bereft of our humanity.

A "fetish" is something that is fabricated, the product of human work; but it is also something that we relate to in worshipful devotion. Even though it is something that we ourselves have made, we invest it with power over us and we re-fashion ourselves in its image.

In some ways I suspected that Marx had been influenced by his uncle and grandfather, both prominent rabbis, since his notion of fetishism seemed so similar to that of the Psalmist in Psalm 115:

> Their idols are silver and gold,
>   the products of human hands.
> They have mouths that cannot speak,
>   and eyes that cannot see;
> they have ears that cannot hear,
>   nostrils, and cannot smell;
> with their hands they cannot feel,
>   with their feet they cannot walk,
>   and no sound comes from their throats.
> Their makers grow to be like them,
>   and so do all who trust in them . . .

The commodity "fetish" was actually a way of life, a form of existence in which men and women became "formed" in the image and likeness of marketable objects. Living only to labor and to consume the products of our labor, we become re-created, not in the image of a living personal God, but in the image of dead things which can neither see nor feel nor listen nor speak. Entrusting our identity to dead objects, we take on their characteristics and imagine ourselves to be mere things without capacity for listening, feeling, or truly communicating. Thus we become estranged from our very selves, from each other, and even from the living and true God. Human relationships, activities, qualities become thing-like relations, actions, and qualities.

We become transformed *into* the idols we *trust*. In worshiping those products, in living for them, in measuring ourselves by their qualities, we have created a false god which exacts from us our freedom and personhood. Idolatry in all of its forms displaces proper human relationships and turns upside down the ordered human world. Idolatry victimizes the person whose life and purpose becomes reduced to serving a state, or material possessions, or technology, or any religious or political ideology.

It is this connection between religious and socio-economic sensibilities which motivates much of the writing of Pope John Paul II. Many Americans, especially, find it difficult to understand his frequent indictments of consumerism and liberal capitalism. They seem puzzled that he is not more appreciative of the great successes in the West. What he is warning us of, however, is the danger that in achieving high economic freedom and productivity, we might fall into a more profound form of unfreedom: a slavery to consumerism itself. Thus, in his first encyclical, *Redeemer of Humankind*, for the most part a letter on Christology and spirituality, he focuses his central passages on the ways that men and women can be enslaved by a process of political, economic, and media manipulation—so much so that we lose our very selves. "Humans cannot relinquish themselves or the place in the visible world that belongs to them; they cannot become slaves of things, the slaves of economic systems, the slaves of production, the slaves of their own products."

The Polish Pope—and his opinions are sometimes passed off as the benighted misunderstandings of an Eastern European—knows that the peoples of the Eastern Bloc have been quite cognizant of their oppression. He is not quite so sure, however, that people in capitalist societies are as aware of their own condition of oppression. Thus, even in his visit to

Mexico in 1990, in the full wake of communism's turbulent retreat, he warned the champions of liberal capitalism against superficially assuming its triumph. This observation to the business leaders in Durango was reinforced a day later in his homily to workers in Monterey. "Without denying the good results achieved by the joint efforts of the public and private sectors in countries where freedom lives, we cannot, however, be silent about the defects of an economic system which has money and consumption as its main power source, which subordinates the person to capital in a way which, without taking personal dignity into account, considers him or her to be only a gear in production's mammoth machine where one's work is treated as a simple commodity at the mercy of supply and demand."

It is my belief that we have such difficulty accepting these challenges and warnings because our national and personal identities have become intractably grounded in the consumerist "way of life." It has become almost impossible to imagine any other approach to life because it has become life itself for us. The Commodity Form has become gospel.

But that does not mean it has become good news.

CHAPTER THREE

THE COMMODITY FORM: CONSUMING AND MARKETING

In an early autobiographical section of his book *The True and Only Heaven*, Christopher Lasch reflects upon the cultural chaos of North American society. To see this world from a parent's point of view, he says, is to see it in "the worst possible light."

This perspective unmistakably reveals the unwholesomeness, not to put it more strongly, of our way of life: our obsession with sex, violence and the pornography of "making it"; our addictive dependence on drugs, "entertainment," and the evening news; our impatience with anything that limits our sovereign freedom of choice, especially with the constraints of marital and familial ties; our preference for "nonbinding commitments"; our third-rate educational system; our third-rate morality; our refusal to draw a distinction between right and wrong, lest we "impose" our morality on others and thus invite others to "impose" their morality on us; our reluctance to judge or be judged; our indifference to the needs of future generations, as evidenced by our willingness to

saddle them with a huge national debt, an overgrown
arsenal of destruction, and a deteriorating environment; our inhospitable attitude to the newcomers
born into our midst; our unstated assumption, which
underlies so much of the propaganda for unlimited
abortion, that only those children born for success
might be allowed to be born at all.

Lasch's complaint is a catalogue of personal and social
dysfunction; and by even mentioning the range of symptoms
in the same sentence, he troubles liberals and conservatives
alike. He believes that these problems fit together in a society
cast under the spell of progress. His book is thus a historical
and cultural interpretation of that mystification.

I believe, however, that there is a theological and philosophical interpretation that is both complementary to Lasch
and may be even more suggestive. It is this: With consumerism
functioning as a system of reality (a philosophy of what is
most real and valuable) and a religion (a belief in what
saves us and gives us ultimate meaning) it has occupied every
piece of territory in our personal and social lives. Consumerism and its Commodity Form of life must be understood as an integrated unity that lives in and through, lives
off of, our various experiences. One must comprehend it as a
total worldview, if one is to understand how it dwells in all
the assorted parts of our lives. It does not just affect the
way we shop. It affects the way we think and feel, the way
we love and pray, the way we evaluate our enemies, the way
we relate to our spouses and children. It is "systemic." It is
"dialectical."

In the same way, the Gospel of Jesus will have to be addressed as an integrative unity which penetrates and unites the
seemingly separate dimensions of our life-world. It is not just
for prayer time or Sundays; it is for all our time. Believing in
Christ, if it is indeed real, does not merely change the way we
worship; it changes the way we labor and play, the way we
buy and sell, the way we make love or make war.

Could it be that there are *economic* conditions that *foster* the breaking of the Ten Commandments? Does a given economic or social system inhibit personal commitment, prayer, or the sharing of our goods? Is there a cultural bias against the living of lifelong vows? Does chastity have a political impact? Is it bad news for business? Is simplicity? Is the Prince of Peace bad news for nationalism? Is marital fidelity and steadfastness in bonding with children a force for social justice?

In answering such questions, we must more fully realize that there is nothing in the realm of the social, the political, or the economic which does not influence or is not influenced by the realm of Spirit. And there is nothing in the realm of Spirit which does not influence or is not influenced by history.

The present situation in the United States is one in which the producing, purchasing, and consuming of objects provides the ultimate horizon of meaning for persons. Its "lived" gospel, its "real world" is the Commodity Form.

The pre-eminent values of the Commodity Form are producing, marketing, and consuming. These values are the ethical lenses through which we are conditioned to perceive our worth and importance. They have profoundly affected not only our self-understanding but also our modeling of human behavior (into manipulation and aggression), human knowledge (into quantification, observation, and measurement), and human affectivity (into noncommittalness and mechanized sexuality).

A number of years ago the Associated Press ran a story about a Dr. Darold Treffert of the Winnebago Mental Health Institute in Wisconsin and his theory that teenagers were being victimized by what he called "The American Fairy Tale." The story read in part:

Amy, 15, had always gotten straight A's in school, and her parents were extremely upset when she got a B on her report card. "If I fail in what I do," Amy told her parents, "I fail in what I am." The message was part of Amy's suicide note.

"The American Fairy Tale," Treffert claimed, "begins with two themes: that more possessions mean more happiness, that a person who does or produces more is more important."

These themes are also the foundational motifs of the Commodity Form. In the family where love must be earned, competed for, won, or proved; in education where value is exclusively rated in terms of production, quantified grades, and competitive standings; in religion with communion counts and Madison Avenue vocation promotions; in the job sweepstakes or in retirement of the expendable: in all these areas, marketability is king. "Will it play in Peoria?" is not only the standard of the marketed dishonesty found in the Watergate travesty and its daily declared "inoperative truths"; it has become the criterion of selfhood. Will *I* sell? Will they buy *me*? Diplomas, skills, talents, and roles are mustered from our earliest ages as guarantees against the planned obsolescence characteristic of our products and our persons. If you are unproductive you are useless, worthless. You are unwanted, whether you be one of the economically poor, a starving Bengali, a death-row criminal, or a bothersome five-month fetus. The crises that children face in their terror at being replaced is the first premonition of that demeaned life to which so many of our elder retired succumb in their feelings of being worthless and discarded once their producing days are over.

What this means in effect is that there is no intrinsic human uniqueness or irreplaceable value. The person is only insofar as he or she is marketable or productive. Human products, which should be valued only insofar as they enhance and express human worth, become the very standards against which human worth itself is measured. If our life's meaning is dictated by mercantilism and production, then our purpose and value are defined essentially in relation to what we can buy, what we can sell, or—at the very least—what we can hold on to. The uniqueness of an individual's way of being, of the unrepeatable personal qualities in knowing and loving, of relating to life in such a way that can never be duplicated by another person, much less by a thing—these human qualities inevitably disappear in a universe whose ultimates are productivity and marketing.

The form of the commodity which legitimates personal devaluation is also the hidden but functioning criterion at the bottom of less crucial but nonetheless significant complaints. Highly specified markets gave rise to the professional magazines and the variations of *Playboy*. It was also the marketing factor which has made it difficult for family television programming, the public broadcasting network, and programs which appeal to senior citizens. Sign-carrying protesters against pornography are protesting nothing other than marketability, even though they do not know it and might refuse to acknowledge the fact. It is not the communist conspiracy which is behind the marketing of pornography—any businessperson will tell you that. And it is far from clear that it was the demonstrations of pacifists that ended the war in Vietnam; quite likely it was merely the cost-benefit analysis of staying in or getting out. A powerful American Secretary of State once threatened war in the Middle East—not in the name of Israel's autonomy, but for the sake of the American oil-based economy. Supposedly he would have had us continue buying huge oil-consuming automobiles and go to war rather than become self-sufficient in petroleum by producing autos which would consume at a rate equal to European or Japanese cars. His position was restated in a "born again" president's State of the Union address. And it became a multibillion-dollar military policy in the first war of the Persian Gulf—so crucial to us that we would pay Egypt to join our war effort and pay Israel to keep out of it. The dollar stands behind the expropriation of our spirit.

A veil of illusion deceives us because we are lulled into believing that principles motivate us rather than profit. Yet, if we were honest with ourselves corporately and individually, we could acknowledge that we actually live according to a commodity-ethics. We consume what is marketable and we are marketable according to our powers of consumption. "You are what you eat." "More is better." "What does your car say about you?" We consume ideas, junk foods, news, the latest unneeded plastic gadget, or other persons. Anything has the potential for being sold, once a need can be artificially created and then identified with a marketable commodity.

Friendship, intimacy, love, pride, happiness, and joy are actually the *objects* we buy and consume, much more so than the tubes, liquor bottles, Cadillacs, and Hummers that promise them and bear their names. And since none of these deepest human hopes can be fulfilled in any product, the mere consumption of them is never enough; "more" of the product, or a "new improved" product, is the only relief offered to our human longings. Thus the seller drives us to greater purchasing with even more extravagantly concocted promises: more commodities are the solution to anxiety stimulated by media manipulation. Consumption, consequently, is not just an economic factor. It emerges as a "way of life." It is an addiction.

Is it any wonder, then, that one-sixth of the world continues to struggle mightily to consume up to half of the world's energy and a third of its food, or that a nation could have more radios than people, more television sets than homes or families, and more cars per family than children? When the Commodity Form of valuation approaches full dominance, consumption inevitably becomes more important than life itself. And the sacred phrases about quality of life collapse into meaning little more than quantity of consumption.

Our "life boat" ethicists are willing to abandon drowning nations or toss unproductive peoples over the edges of humanity's lifeboat supposedly because we are all facing the "difficult questions" of there not being enough to go around. Yet the hidden reality behind their perversions of language is that we are actually on a luxury liner sinking from the sheer weight of our automobiles, televisions, empty foods, fertilizers for golf courses and cemeteries, and parakeet diapers. We are terrified at the prospect of people having children, but we inexplicably entrust ourselves to machinery which consumes most of the nonrenewable natural resources we supposedly fear depleting.

Paradoxical realities cloud and crowd our consciousness: we fear the mention of new life and whisper of population "explosions," yet even if the most horrible 1960 predictions of population expansion in the United States had held true until the year 2000, we still could have fit every American into the front seats of our automobiles. We have become biased against our very personhood. A person who challenges us to relate in mutuality and responsibility is more threatening, makes more claims on our being, than some "thing" we can call our own. We will clean up after our pets, groom them, and lovingly wash them and feed them, we will manicure our lawns and meticulously clean the grime from our cars—but we are repulsed at the thought of doing the same for our disabled old, who have given us our culture, our lives, and our substance.

The commodification of our desires, our values, and ultimately our selves is revealed, in its most intense form, by our relationship to the media. Although we do have more than five radios per home in the United States, the visual media are the most pervasive influences on our commodity consciousness. A Kaiser Family Foundation media study in 2005 found that children in the United States are exposed to 8 1/2 hours of TV, video games, computers and other media each day. Eight- to eighteen-year-olds responded to questions about television use: 63% said it is usually on during meals, 51% said that it is on most of the time. Just in terms of the amount of our lives spent in relationship to the media-object, rather than other persons, the figures are amazing. Estimates of the average American watching-time run from 29 hours a week to the equivalent of 13 straight continuous years of our average life span. Since up to 27 percent of prime time can be given to advertisement, we could possibly spend, on an average, the equivalent of three solid years of our lives watching solely commercials. And this is their relentless message which assaults the self-worth and perceptions of millions: your hair is too long, your hair is too short, your skin is too light or too

dark, your smells are noxious, you are too fat, too thin, too
blemished, you must have a training bra in fifth grade or you
will have no friends, your breasts are too large or frightfully
small, and you will be frigid or impotent if you do not use
Opium or Musk. Our narcissistic buying is motivated by an
anomalous self-loathing.

If we believe that this assault has no effect upon us, then
we should be especially attentive to the way children watch
television, the way they are channeled and manipulated in
their values, tastes, and demands, and the way they can be
convinced that they are miserable without the latest piece of
junk for Christmas. Two hundred sixty billion dollars a year
is not spent on advertising because it is ineffective. And in the
face of such expenditures (and the profound, obvious trust in
the power of advertising and behavior modification) the
claims that the violent or banal content of television programming have no effect upon the behavior of children have
a disconcerting hollowness, if not the ring of deceit.

Research by the University of Southern California has determined that elementary students experience a drop in all but
verbal creative abilities when they are exposed to intensive television watching. In other studies, children have been found to
be more aggressive in interpersonal relationships, more passive
in self-initiating behavior, more hyperactive in nervous action,
and more regressive in living and enjoying life as a result of television. From our earliest years, our ways of perceiving ourselves, our value, our self-acceptance, and our behavior are
molded into commodity-like forms. The average prekinder-
gartener spends 64 percent of his or her waking time watching
television game shows (the content is often a combination of
wild, heart-throbbing avarice in competition for money or
commodities), soap operas (the principal characters of which
are often identified by small children with their own parents),
cartooned violence sponsored by empty junk foods, and frus-
trating commercials devoted to convincing them that they are
despicable and desperate creatures who can achieve peace and
happiness only in possessing and consuming products.

With such consumerist propaganda and our consequent obsession for things, it is no surprise that if the rest of the world consumed and wasted at our rate all known world resources would be lost within one generation. It is no surprise that we see the population crisis as a question of survival: they must stop propagating, they are better off dead, else we cannot continue to survive as infinitely open consumers. The compulsion to consume has become for us as deep as the exigency to survive because the Commodity Form reveals our very being and purpose as calculable solely in terms of *what* we possess, measureable solely by what we have and take. We are only insofar as we possess. We are what we possess. We are, consequently, possessed by our possessions, produced by our products. Remade in the image and likeness of our own handiwork, we are revealed as commodities. Idolatry exacts its full price from us. We are robbed of our very humanity.

Our fifteen-year-old "Amys" whose lives are prematurely lost in one way or another have learned their commodity-gospel lessons well. And the American Fairy Tale of consumption, competition, and marketing one's personhood lives on—not only in our children's sense of loss, but also in the loss of our own selves.

CHAPTER FOUR

MISSING PERSONS

KNOWING AND BEING KNOWN AS A COMMODITY

Marketing and consuming infiltrate every aspect of our lives and behavior. They filter all experience we have of ourselves. They become the standard of our final worth. Marketing and consuming ultimately reveal us to ourselves as things; and if we find ourselves revealed as things it will follow that our diverse capacities for knowing are reduced to the truncated conditions of thing-like or commodity knowledge. I am not merely trying to point out here that knowledge itself has become a salable commodity, or that our universities have been compared to product-manufacturing industries. What I am speaking of is a more subtle collapsing of human knowing into models and patterns which are more appropriate to cognition of things or commodities.

A thing does not possess, nor is it known by self-reflection, internal consciousness, or any other method of interiority. Instrumental intelligence, technical knowledge, or quasi-mechanical cognition characterize our knowing of a thing. These qualities also characterize "knowing" *by* a thing, and it is on this level that some scientists have attributed "intelligence" to computers. Interiority or self-reflection is rarely being recognized as the distinctively radical foundation of human intellectual knowledge. The basic ways of knowing an object are external observation, external measurement, prediction, manipulation, and quantification—the most suitable cognitive tools for dealing with the producing, buying, and selling of commodities.

In the world of the Commodity Form, thing-like knowing has become the sole criterion for determining reliable knowledge about human persons and even one's knowledge of oneself. This is true of the behavioral sciences and their still increasing emphasis upon quantification in economics, social science, psychology, and the philosophy of the human sciences. It is true of the criteria we employ to evaluate the quality and promise of students. And it is also, and more significantly, true of the criteria we use to weigh the reliability of our personal experience.

The texture and nature of our immediate experiences (the condition of any scientific knowledge in the first place), our consciousness of freedom, our experiences of love, compassion, and hope, our longing for fidelity or equity, are all called into question because they cannot be verified by the methods of instrumental commodity-knowledge. The intense skepticism concerning our most intimately human thoughts and feelings is in considerable part caused by reducing human knowledge to technical intelligence. We take for granted that technical intelligence is some grand historic leap forward in humanity's ongoing rush to perfection. And we do not even suspect that such an imperialism of object-knowledge over our consciousness might be related to the rise of advanced industrial capitalism and the enthronement of the commodity as the center of our lives. We do not consider the possibility that the dominance of thing-knowledge goes hand in hand with an ideology that has substituted consumption and marketing for the development and realization of human persons.

Faith in a person as well as faith in an ideal, in a future possibility, or even in ourselves—the very forms of knowledge which yield newness or solicit commitment in life, work, and love—are banished from a constricted world of measurement, quantification, and external observation. These personal forms of knowledge are marked by an inescapable vulnerability and risk which cannot be scientifically apprehended or resolved. Risk and mystery, inherent to personal encounter, are precisely the aspects of living and knowing which must be minimized in thing-knowledge.

Consequently, if technical scientific knowledge or instrumental reason is the ultimate criterion of reliable knowledge, then human experience, and the forms of knowing, such as intuition, feeling, emotion, aesthetic judgment, sensuousness, wisdom, purposefulness and ethical judgment, can all be dogmatically passed off (as B. F. Skinner does in *Science and Human Behavior*) as "prescientific." Even more destructively, the most human dimensions of our knowing are subjected to a skeptical erosion of confidence. The personal experience of being loved or being believed in, the act of trusting or caring for another person, the knowledge of certain moral principles concerning human dignity and potentiality, all become inaccessible when only thing-type knowledge is acceptable. The "peak experiences" of our lives, experiences which Abraham Maslow pointed out as being founded upon a nonquantifiable, nontechnically controllable "being-cognition," are often described as scientifically immature or unreliable forms of knowing. Only the publicly verifiable and repeatable, only the measurable experience, is regarded as truly trustworthy. Thus, in thingified knowledge, what is most human in us becomes most alien to us, its possibility having been defined out of existence in a universe of discourse whose perimeters are established by the limits of thinghood.

The commodification of human knowledge has far-reaching implications, whether it be in the postured "value free" investigations of scientific experimentation or in a child's estimation of self-worth through quantity and competition measurement. The formative influence of capitalism and ever-expanding consumption upon our categories of thought and experience is not called into question; our humanity is. At the deepest reaches of our self-consciousness, thing-knowledge achieves its most stunning impact upon the ways we have become possessed by our commodities. Trusting most wholeheartedly in commodity-formed knowledge, we begin to understand and recreate ourselves in the image and likeness of the products of our hands. In our popular scientism, in our literature and art, we are most mystical about things. We are most mechanistic when we speak of persons.

VALUING AND WILLING
UNDER THE COMMODITY FORM

As we know, so we act. And human action, throughout a spectrum ranging from the geopolitical to the most intimate, is modeled after the things which possess us and the thing-knowledge in which we have immersed ourselves as the sole criterion of our self-understanding. In the behavioral area of ethics and morals the connection is most immediately evident. Skepticism and relativism in ethics are the necessary correlatives of personal skepticism in our self-understanding. Morality, once it is restricted by the categories of measurement, description, observation, and quantity, becomes reduced to a by-product of custom, utility, force, and the free market of preference. This is a consequence of the supremacy of the commodity-as-moral-reality, but it is also bolstered by the more extensive cognitive dimensions of the Commodity Form mentioned above.

Moral relativism is the ethical embodiment of *laissez faire* economics: non-interference from the centralized agency of our personhood or from our common, objectively shared humanity with its natural potentialities seeking to be realized. Moral relativism, like *laissez faire* economics, is non-communitarian, it is nonsharing, it is isolationist, and it is rampantly individualistic. "You do your thing and I do mine," a phrase of self-styled cultural liberation, is in no way a challenge to capitalism or the traditions of the Commodity Form. It is merely the moral linguistic currency of the mythical free market, regulated only by the marketing principles of preference and number, Gallup polls, social pressure, encrusted custom, or the ruling ideas of the ruling class.

What we are not aware of and do not question is what makes "my thing" mine. Is it most intimately and humanly mine, or is it my idiosyncratic and blind introjection of competition, hedonism, and marketability? When hidden by the veil of illusion, ethics are helplessly subjected to the laws of selling, to the dialectics of supply and demand, to the play of respectability's market. Thus, in our discussions of wiping out prisoners on death row, of eliminating unwanted children, of manipulating South American economies, of soiling the environment, neglecting the old, and escalating the arms race, morality is easily relativized according to the canons of expediency. The most shrill immediate need, the popularly accepted dogma, the institutionally supported prejudices, the pragmatic and the profitable, are the norms of commodity ethics.

Taking a moral stance has become an increasingly rare phenomenon. Unsure of the most primal laws of human personhood, trusting in number and production, our ethical commitments weaken as our moral sense of the irreplaceable person capable of self-understanding and judgment slowly erodes. No power of number or social acceptance could have established the interior grounds of resistance to racism in the United States in the 1940s or to the anti-Semitism of the Third Reich. It was precisely the marketability, the social acceptability, the feasible technical rationality, and the money value of racism and anti-Semitism which legitimated their very being and made so difficult an individual's stand against them.

Commodity ethics, the ethics of quantity, relativism, and cultural acceptance, is the legitimation of what *is*. This is why we suffer such a dearth of people willing to take a moral stand on social or personal forms of evil. What *is*, is accepted or affirmed. What *might* or *should* be, is beyond comprehension, victim of a failure in imagination as well as nerve. Thus, university students today are often at a loss for words or rational discourse when you ask them: "Would it be moral to exterminate 10 million people if it would end all of our troubles, if 80 percent of our people approved of it, if the law approved, and if they were a lethal threat to our security?"

Commitment demands human risk in an act of personal freedom; and it is the extinction of that act of freedom, ultimately, which results from the imperialism of the commodity.

The object, lacking interiority and subjectivity, is not free. But since men and women have patterned their knowledge after thing-knowledge, the inescapable conclusion is that they are not free within themselves, and *a fortiori* are incapable of free commitment to others. If self-understanding is not a legitimate form of knowledge, how can self-possession, much less self-donation in loving, be acceptable as a real possibility? In the absence of self-donation as the expression of human autonomy, commodity consciousness has displaced freedom with the myth of the free market. Just as our shriveled powers of affection are invested in soap operas and sweaters for poodles, so our lost freedom is mythologized into an "as if" reality called a "free" market. Our "freedom to choose" is between more products, between scenarios for success, between empty promises.

But we know that even this freedom is an illusion: it is merely a functional and culturally serviceable concept of freedom applied to a mercantile dynamic. It is a freedom controlled by oligopolies, a submissive servant of impersonal forces and conditioned-to-buy automatons. It is a "freedom" appropriate only to a passive object.

HUMAN INTERACTION COMMODIFIED: VIOLENCE

We do not give invitations to or make requests of objects. Our behavior towards things is use, demand, force, manipulation, and, if required, destruction. Within the Commodity Form of life, since self-worth and self-evaluation are measured in terms of quantitative production, consumption, and competition, we are conditioned to relate to each other as things—or, more frequently, as obstructions. If quantity is the goal, conflict is the method. Our value and dignity are rooted, not in the capacity to perform free human acts of knowing and loving, but in the dynamics of domination. The interaction of commodity with commodity is not one of the reciprocal mutuality or the collaboration of subjects. It is rather one of price competition (is it true that "every man has his price"?), quantitative supremacy, and the power forces of commercial uniformity, control, repetition, and material exchange.

In this context it is interesting to note that "power" has become the byword of so many of the recent years' political-social movements. The virtues of compassion or empathy have now become associated with "wimpishness." Elections have been won on the willingness of candidates to be tough enough to push the nuclear button or to execute the criminal or to extend the power of life and death over the unborn. Some clerics and politicians serve up the rhetoric of forgiveness and service to others, but they remain vigilant in protecting their own authority and power. Some black organizations make it quite plain that while they are surely concerned with equity and justice, they are more interested in having a bigger share in the very structures and values of submission and dominance which have oppressed them. Some women's groups, while rightfully contesting the inequity of wages and false division of labor, have focused relentlessly on control and power. Equality in violence, dominance, and machismo is often the underside of demands not for the revolution of a people's consciousness, but for the repetition and expansion of the patterns of injustice which have oppressed both men and women in the first place. The only change is a broader sharing of injustice.

This is nothing new. The "given order" has for a long time institutionalized power and domination in a geopolitical metaphysic of deterrence (the word means "out of fear"), balance of power, and first-strike capacities, as the ultimate means of human interaction and problem solving. "Mutually assured destruction" was the byword of the now defunct Cold

War. And yet it remains, now in the context of a "war on terror." As David Gutmann wrote in the September 2003 issue
of *The American Enterprise*, "Counter-terror and even torture are sometimes required to extract vital information before the next bomb goes off. In effect, the counter-terrorist
will only gain his enemy's respect if he shows a savagery that
is equal to the enemy's." Terror and violence, having become
our only final security, have become us.

It is important to note here that the Commodity Form of
life is not the only socio-culture structure that leads people into
treating others as mere objects or replaceable things. The Imperialist Form, the Statist Form, and even the Religio-Fascist
Form—all ways of life that reduce persons to the status of being
mere tools of ideology—invariably objectify people and make
them candidates for destruction. The Commodity Form is the
particular seduction of American Consumerism which so easily
enlists religion, business, arts and even education into its cause.

Fear, force, and threat are not prerogatives reserved to advanced industrial nations or gigantic corporations. These values form the fabric of the "rising expectations" of third-
world countries which must buy arms from the United States
and the Soviet Union, of underdeveloped nations seeking to
come of age through the rites of nuclear passage. These very
values were the ballast of many "counterculture" movements
which lionized alienation, violence, hedonism, relativism, and
manipulation—the reincarnate Commodity Form. Thinglike
values underlie the shrill rhetoric of Christian writers and omnipresent commentators who sabotage every effort of the
Christian churches to call capitalism, armament, capital punishment, and social inequity into question. And it is the worship of the Thing, with the violence it requires of us, which
motivates the Catholic nationalist to profess that our only
hope is in the bomb, or the Catholic leftist to think that the
surest hope of the poor is found in the barrel of a gun.

Thus the chains of violence and domination are not shed.
They are merely painted a different color. The commodity absolute can be painted in endlessly different hues. Within the

almost cosmic categories of the Commodity Form, most reforms come to fruition as nothing other than variations of the dialectic of dominance.

The aspirations of women, the demand for the recognition of human dignity irrespective of race, belief, age, or technological sophistication, the appeal for the recognition of the human fetus's claim to personhood, the resistance to armament and militarism, the reformation of our goals of infinite consumption, the appeal to the wealthy of the world on behalf of starving millions, are not the hodgepodge of vested interests and partialities that they might first appear to be. There is an underlying issue at the foundation of these demands: Do we perceive men and women as persons, or as commodities? Are people of irreplaceable dignity, or are they expendable before the altars of planned obsolescence, competition, ideology, and vested interest?

It is this foundational issue that is most difficult to apprehend, since we have in so many ways been subjected to the Commodity Forms of perception, value, and existence. Once a man or woman, be he or she oppressor or oppressed, whether dressed in silk or sprawled in a Calcutta slum, whether on a battlefield or in a delivery room, whether bourgeoisie or proletariat, whether criminal, president, or both, is perceived as a thing or in terms of the commodity, he or she is thereby rendered replaceable. The fetus is a "blob of protoplasm." The criminal is "scum and vermin." The brain-damaged are "vegetables." The poor are "like animals." The Iraqi is "the enemy." The wealthy or the police are "pigs." The "enemy" is an obstruction—quantifiable, repeatable, manipulable, expendable, the legitimate object of our hatred and violence. Only on this level of understanding can the questions of violence in the street or among nations, on death row or in hospitals, be adequately addressed as fragmented symptoms of a totality which itself so often escapes our attention and critique. Does a poor person kill a refusing grocer for the sake of property, for food and freedom, for security, for self-defense, for enlightened self-interest? Of course. So does a nation.

Critique and true change call for a massive personal resistance to the values of the Commodity Form which are en-
cased in our institutional structures as well as in the liberation
or revolutionary movements which would oppose them. The
common denominator of most segments of our society (even
segments opposed to each other) is the implicit belief in force,
coercion, and violence—which are "as American as cherry
pie," as a black revolutionary once phrased it.

He was not altogether wrong. The very president who was
warning black militants that "violence will get you nowhere,"
was conducting the greatest saturation bombing in human
memory—in a war that some Americans still insist was fought
"with one hand tied behind our backs." It was violence we
turned to when we felt threatened by Central Americans "in
our own back yard." It was violence we unleashed in Grenada
on the very weekend our marines were slaughtered in Beirut.
It was violence, of a most horrific kind, we embraced to challenge the brutality of Saddam Hussein.

Many of the structures of government and education, the
too frequently legitimizing churches, and the romantic rhetoric of their antagonists are freighted with the language and
methodology of fear, power, threat, aggrandizement, and self-
defense. One can always find, moreover, the power-ethic of
money and profit supporting legislated economic sanction for
birth control, abortion for the mercantile purposes of greater
affluence (not subsistence reasons), population scares, the
threat of a Middle-East war, and a justification of national
priorities by capitalist self-interest. Greater accumulation is
the omnipresent, a priori "given." And its language is that of
the absolutized commodity.

Once self-worth is defined in terms of appropriation, the
cultural myth will relentlessly be one of materialism, property,
consumption, buying-power, competition, and greater economic exploitation. It is this "gospel" with its valued "givens"
which prevents us from *seeing*, much less responding to, the
needs of the nation, the community, the neighbor, even the be-
seeching person next to us. We perceive objects to be used,

enemies to be overcome. We no longer see persons. We see *things*. And things, like idols, are dead.

THE BODY AS COMMODITY:
SEXUAL MECHANICS

If the worth of men and women is measured by the thingified values of the Commodity Form, if persons can be known only in terms of the mechanical, external, and instrumental, and if their interpersonal behavior is most adequately expressed in manipulation, force, and violence, then the world of personhood is replaced by the world of objectness. And if the human person is an object, the dominant form of body-consciousness in that world will be thing-consciousness. The body is a commodity. The body is a thing.

There is a strange paradox in our fixation on the objectness of personal bodies. On one hand, we magically separate our "minds" or "selves" from our embodied condition. On the other hand, we repress our personhood and collapse our identities into our sheer physicality. In the first case, the recent years have seen a growing insistance that our "personhood" is somehow disconnected from our bodies. Highly paid ethicists and professors propose that we are not the same kind of being as helpless diapered infants or hopeless diapered alzheimer patients. Somehow "we persons" are different than our bodies, their lowly origins and diminishments.

At the same time, we are witnessing a movement that suggests we are mere computers. Bill Joy, the founder of Sun Microsystems, wrote in an April 2000 issue of *Wired* magazine that the advancements in genetics, molecular technology and micro-robotics will make possible not only the refashioning of our bodies, but the rejection of them. He notes, in this alarmist essay, that some scientists would not hesitate to trade their bodies for silicon and thereby live 200 years. This seems to be a dream not only of popularizing "futurologists" but also of some philosophers who imagine that the entire content of our experience could be "downloaded" into a computer that would never suffer the shame of our bodied condition.

The strongest pop-culture phenomenon expressing this separation of our personhood from our bodies and then the reduction of our personal lives to mere physicality is found in commodified sexuality. We first divorce our personhood from sex. Then we lose our personhood in it.

In August of 1979, an article appeared in the *Archives of General Psychiatry* which expressed perfectly the relationship between violence, sexuality, and the marketing of the body. Dr. Robert Stoller in "Centerfold: An Essay on Excitement" reported that "a woman who poses for soft-core pornography reports that she has never belonged to her body, that she is and wants only to be an erotic product manufactured by a team of specialists for the use of a viewing audience." She has become schizophrenically separated from her own sexuality and gender, a true fetish, representing "fantasies of revenge in which the consumer imagines he is degrading—dehumanizing— women."

The report was a prophetic prognosis for a decade in which MTV would be born and flourish on Heavy Metal and "Rap" images of violated and degraded women, in which Guess Jeans would become the most successful clothing phenomenon through the hawking of sadistic and masochistic advertisements featuring hapless blonds. Madonna could launch her career as the "material girl" who was a "Boy Toy," and mature into the great businesswoman who had achieved the status of being "in control" of her own humiliating and vengeful fantasies. It was also a decade which would see the almost catastrophic social and medical results of a depersonalized sexuality which was marketed in the name of new freedom.

Commodified body-consciousness is expressed in a variety of forms. There is the obvious marketing of sexuality in advertisements, the sale of sex in a variety of prostitutions, the high incidence of sexual domination in the media's emphasis upon rape, sadomasochism, and bondage. At the same time we witness the continuing growth of what Rollo May has called the "new puritanism," an inversion in which love and sex are magically sundered so that falling into sex without falling into love is the commonest expectation.

There are three particular aspects of advanced industrial and capitalistic sexuality which are worthy of special mention. It is strikingly voyeuristic; it has a highly developed technological rendition of sexual relations; and it is marked by a severing of human sexuality from the totality of the human person, and *a fortiori* from personal commitment.

Observation and description are as characteristic of our acculturated sexuality as they are of our forms of knowledge. Sex, in fact, has become experimentalized and objectified by its reduction to measurement and observation. But this is only one aspect of the marriage of science and sex. Voyeurism, in a sense, is quite scientific, whether one is a voyeur of life or merely of sex. To be a voyeur is to be at a distance, to be outside of and yet somehow in control of the happenings (paying for or peeking in on the object). It demands no personal involvement, no commitment, no recognition of the personhood of the sexual object. It is "value-free."

Technical detachment and description (which are not unrelated to voyeurism itself) are hallmarks of the mechanization of sexuality, in which technique, performance, and how-to-do-it are controlling perimeters of investigating. In sex, as in our lost self-understanding and ideologized scientific knowledge, final causes (purpose, value, and meaning, related to the question "why?") have been subsumed under efficient causes emphasizing mechanics, description, valuelessness, and exclusive concentration on the answers to the question "how?" Even the supposedly liberated books of sex education like *The Sex Book* and *Show Me!* are composed and edited like some over-fleshed "Popular Mechanics." Meaning questions, value questions, personal commitment questions, are utterly absent.

Our cultural romance is with the mechanical and the manageable. We experience an incredible poverty of language which could reveal or suggest the world of personal passion, sustained feeling, suffering love, ecstasy, promise-keeping, or the gift of one's self. It is true that Rollo May, Abraham Maslow, and even Masters and Johnson have spoken of the inadequacy of sex without passion or the committed bond. But such observations are ineffectual without a more totalizing critique of culture. Cultural consciousness is saturated by mercantile media which for the most part reject any relationship between sexuality and human affection, and often identify sex with violence, domination, escape, consumption, exploitation, and thinghood.

Objectified sexuality is convincingly portrayed by the ideological propaganda of advertising. Specific relationships with husband, wife, children, and friends are supplanted by purchasable commodities. "I bought a wagon out of wedlock." "I bought it because it looked like it [a Gremlin] needed me." "This baby [auto] won't keep you up nights." "How to cradle your twelve-year-old [scotch]." "Think of her [an airline stewardess] as your mother." "A heart-to-heart talk with Climatrol Computer." The sexual relationship itself is reduced to cash value by image industries of capitalism. Cigarettes and alcohol are substitute intimacies. Women are portrayed in magazines as relating erotically to their products. Men find potency in Brut, Burley, Musk, and Viagra. There is a persistent suggestion of loathing for the natural body—especially the woman's—and for the natural, long-range heterosexual union of commitment.

Teenage girls are educated by *Seventeen* and *Mademoiselle*, the preponderant content of which is advertisement and editorial copy advising the packaging of the face, body, and personality: "How to wrap your package" (Warner's Bra). "If your hair isn't beautiful the rest hardly matters." "Ecusson territory." "A new belt for your motor." "The twelve-dollar neck." "Having a female body doesn't make you feminine" (F.D.S.). This objectification of the body is the theoretical underpinning for the body as product, for a systemic attack upon family life and intimacy, and for the high incidence of violence in high-fashion magazines. Violence is the ultimate objectification.

Rape is the thingifying of another person sexually, negating invitation and commitment. Sadism is sexual satisfaction in thingifying the other. Masochism is sexual delight in being thingified. All three themes appear in advertising. The connections between commodified sexuality, capitalism, infidelity, and violence is patent in Madison Avenueland.

As a new century dawned, themes of violent sexuality in advertising were attracting the attention of national news sources. The *New York Times*, although it had earlier featured an article on the sado-masochistic themes of Versace and other clothes designers, reported that a major fashion photographer's images "engage issues of power. The power to shock, provoke, seduce, titillate or arouse. The balance of power between those who desire and the objects of their fixation. And the commercial replication of this psychological dynamic in fine stores everywhere." Not much later the *Wall Street Journal*, in "Anything Goes," commented that "Fashion advertisements have indeed been pushing the envelope lately. You don't have to look too hard to find images that suggest rape and S&M—or just suggestive stuff you don't want to think about."

Rape, sadism and masochism are essentially related to treating the human body as an object. They are themes of high fashion advertising only because we have a culture where discourse about human sexuality is radically depersonalized. These are the tenets of the ideology:

1. We are objects. Our products are called "Me" and "Self." "I found myself in my McCall's catalogue." "It lets me be me." "The Easy-to-be-me Pantyhose." "What does my car say about me?" "You never forget your first Girl" (beer ad).

2. Our bodies are the packages of our object-identities. Sexuality is the coming-together of things that "perform," "make it," "do it," "turn on," "hook up," and "get it off." Our products are sexual substitutes for the intimacy we are taught to loathe or fear.

3. Since the body-person is a packaged object, sexuality can be portrayed as a matter of commerce, competition, planned obsolescence, selling oneself. More lethally, revealed to each other as sexual objects, we relate in objective patterns of domination and submission (Dior, Calvin Klein, Charles Jourdan, Guess Jeans).

4. In this process, the heterosexual covenant is discussed with ridicule in editorial content, while advertisements suggest: "If your husband doesn't like it, leave him." "My wife got the house, but I got the Sony." "We can marry you. We can separate you." And *Forbes*, the self-styled "capitalist tool," can run a cover story on the "big business of divorce." The disenfranchisement of human relationships, of the natural body, of intimacy, is good capitalism.

5. Finally, the disenfranchisement of activities and relationships unmediated by the market (solitude, intimacy, friendship, love of nature, family) intensifies the ache of languishing for the fulfillment promised in the new products: "You can Buy Happiness." "There is only one Joy." "Sharing, Caring." "Martin [paints] understands." "Serena [clothes] understands." "A Problem-free Relationship" with an AMC car. "Fall in Love Without Paying the Price" (Honda).

In 1945 Aldous Huxley described advertising as the organized effort to magnify and intensify our craving in such a way as to stimulate the principal causes of our suffering and wrong-doing: it is the highest barrier between our personhood and our fulfillment. Eighteen years later, Jules Henry condemned advertising as the brutalization of human desires and the degrading of our humanness. And now forty years after the first appearance of Henry's *Culture Against Man*, the worldview of advertising has become a national philosophy of life, supporting and supported by the Commodity Form.

Here, in its most evident and undeniable form of advertising and what it does to us, the commodity-fashioned universe dominates our understanding as well as our sexuality. Yet we fail to get in touch with its virulent hold on our consciousness: some conservative moralists are more upset at the sight of naked women in *Playboy* or internet pornography than they are at the economic system which objectifies women, which makes *Playboy* the successful advertising phenomenon it is, and which offers a view of life that is the full embodiment of capitalistic hedonism. On the other hand, persons concerned with women's liberation attack boldly the midgets of our society while they remain silent before the titans of Madison Avenue, who have become the greatest force for the objectification of women in our culture.

With human sexuality objectified, voyeurized, and technologized, there is little place for the full relationship of one human being to another. Sexuality as an expression of the self, as a *saying* of the self, as an embodiment of interiority, is lost because the self is lost in the dictatorship of commodity consciousness, in the world perceived through the filters of the Commodity Form. We have modeled our sexuality, our fertility, and our intimacy after the image of the automated products to which we have entrusted ourselves.

Our acceptance of our bodies is constantly frustrated by the onslaught of propaganda from the world of infinite consumption. One's own body, like that of one's partner, is continually portrayed as hopelessly, disgustingly inadequate, marred by lumps and acne, scarred with stretch marks and age spots. Our breath and natural odor are revolting to everyone around us to such an extent that even our best friends will not tell us of the horror. Seduced into a fretful dissatisfaction with our bodies and with our loved ones, we seek that so-called "problem-free relationship." The planned obsolescence of intimacy and marriage covenants is patterned after the career of our automobiles. The average American marriage lasts scarcely longer than the average car. Our families aspire to have more automobiles than children. Sexuality is automated and mechanized in more ways than we dare suspect. As *Forbes* magazine, the "capitalist tool," said of divorce in its advertisements, "The *business* keeps growing" (emphasis mine).

Finally, the misnamed "counter-cultural" view of sexuality—as we have already seen in the area of domination and violence—has failed to call into question the depth-values of our culture's view of sexuality: it has duplicated the problem but in a different set of clothes. With the de-emphasizing of commitment in human sexual relationships, with the intensification of hedonism in a new form of repression (Marcuse accurately characterized the new sexuality as a desublimation which has actually repressed personhood, historical commitment, and critical consciousness), the "counter-cultural" sexual lifestyles are not really counter-cultural at all. They are the intensification of the depersonalized universe of the commodity.

In their denial of commitment, the new styles have legitimated the assault upon freedom and upon the capacity of the human person to make and keep promises. In their assault upon chastity, they have perpetuated the dualism of self and body, and have sold out the possibilities of sexual integrity and life-love to the merchants of rock, rap, hip-hop and style. In the counter-culture's denial of marriage it has joined hands with the disco and jet set in weakening a powerful base which could provide children with the experiential data of trust, intimacy, covenant, and an integrity capable of suffering for love—the kinds of experience which might help form men and women strong and stable enough to resist the imperialism of the market.

A family which strives to embody the qualities of personhood can be the most primal and resilient support for resistance to dehumanization. Thus understood, the family is essentially counter-cultural and subversive. No wonder it is under such a relentless attack in our culture.

CHAPTER FIVE

IDOLATROUS APPEARANCES
OF THE COMMODITY FORM

The Commodity Form is in many ways a world "view." It is a view *of* the world, a way of viewing all the parts of that world, including ourselves, our bodies, other persons, our goals and fulfillments, our possibilities. We could compare it to tinted glasses, which filter all seen objects in a prejudiced way. But the "filter" in our case is not merely visual. The Commodity Form filters *all* of our experience, our attitudes and feelings, our emotions and drives, our perceptions, our behavior.

At the same time the Commodity Form has a specific content which it adds to our experience, and a specific result which it brings about through our experience. The content of the Commodity Form is marketing, producing, and consuming; and its result is a revelation of ourselves as replaceable objects whose goal and value are dependent upon how much we market, produce, and consume. With our worth and purpose dependent upon the commodity, we ourselves are reduced to the qualities of commodity: quantifiably measurable, non-unique, price-valued, replaceable objects.

The Commodity Form appears in every area of our lives, in all of our experiences and enterprises. It insinuates itself into the ways we understand our capacity to know—restricting our knowledge to thing-knowledge. Trust is produced and marketed, not discovered and adhered to. Quality is reduced to quantity. Knowledge is non-personal, noncommittal, "value-free"—objective, in the sense that our subjectivity is mistrusted. Interiority and self-awareness are held in suspicion. External observation, measurement, numbers, repeatability, are held in awe. We consume our knowledge; we are no longer enhanced by it.

We have also seen how the affective dimension of our lives—attitudes, emotions, feelings, willing, choosing, committing, and loving—are similarly filtered through the Commodity Form of experience. The paralysis of moral relativism inhibits personal commitment. We are taught to have the passivity of objects. Immediate gratification emerges as our only willed ideal. Scientific determinism explains our choices through the criteria of measurement, weight, observation, and blind satisfaction of need. Life commitments are deemed impossible by our media, by the arts and by the "received wisdom of our day." Intimacy, trust, and desire for covenanted love, the capacity to endure for a dearly held belief, are all repressed. Such is the patterning of "thing-willing."

Our understanding of ourselves in terms of thing-knowledge and thing-affect is the link to our discussions of "thing-behavior." We behave like things because we believe ourselves capable only of thing-like activities. Consequently, in three crucial arenas of human behavior—the arenas of power, of possession, and of pleasure—the great moral struggles of our time are in actuality spiritual struggles of men and women in the grips of the Commodity Form.

We become expert not in the power of relationship, or in life-giving love, but in the spurious power of force, violence, and self-defense. Terrified at the thought of the obsolescence to which we as things are condemned, we perceive our lives as conflict, as competition with other person-things or nation-things. We feel we must make ourselves invulnerable before the threat of the other, who might overcome or replace us. Manipulative control, domination, and technique become our trust and allies. People are produced. People are marketed. People are consumed.

Possessions which might otherwise serve as *expressions* of our humanity, and enhance us as persons, are transformed into ultimates. Our being is in having. Our happiness is said to be in possessing more. Our drive to consume, bolstered by an economics of infinite growth, becomes addictive: it moves from manipulated need to the promise of joy in things, to broken promises and frustrated expectation, to guilt and greater need for buying. Property is no longer instrumental to our lives; it is the final judge of our merit. So vast is its pre-eminence, it is worth killing for.

Finally, hedonism and escapism serve as opiates. Pleasure is no longer found in the integration of body and interiority, for there is no interiority in a thingified life. Immediate gratifications dominate consciousness. Our bodies, like ourselves, are objects, packages, tools, and instruments. Commodification splits sexuality from selfhood. And sexuality, no longer the embodied expression of our now repressed personhood, itself becomes a thing for exchange and price, a battleground for competition, a stage for aggression and self-infatuation. Voyeurism replaces intimacy. Technique replaces tenderness. Free commitment and life-covenants are stricken from the lexicons of love and sex.

Such, in summary, are the manifold ways in which the Commodity Form appears in and underwrites our cultural gospel, the idol of capitalism.

Many parts of this total worldview are not, in themselves, intrinsically damaging to our humanness. The best examples are perhaps scientific and technical intelligence, which, when placed at the service of human dignity, actually exalt and enhance the lives of men and women. The life and writings of Christy Nolan, with his lyrical appreciations of chemical therapy and IBM Selectric—both of which unlocked his tightly wound and uncontrollable body—are stirring testimony to the gift of human technology. It is when the ends-means relationship is inverted, when the scientific model of human knowing becomes imperial or ultimate or when it serves an end other than human dignity, that the transformation into idolatry takes place.

Moreover, when the whole spectrum of our experiences and expectations serves as a reinforcing system of ultimate thing-hood, when commodity values are legitimated and fostered by a powerful economic dogma with its media, its advertising network, and its value-formative industries like television, radio, music and arts, the commodification of the human person is relentless and omnipresent. We are actually educated and trained to behave and think like things and to relate to each other as things. Thing-knowledge and thing-behavior in turn support and legitimate violence and domination as the resolution to human problems of power and possession; and uncommitted, mechanized sexuality is offered as the resolution of the problem of human affectivity.

There are countless other dynamics whereby the Commodity Form meets and reinforces itself while oppressing human personhood. Thing-knowledge, as an ultimate, renders any act of *human faith* (whether in an ideal, another person, or a God) impossible. Faith disappears into the security of invulnerable facts and the capacity to control and manipulate the other. A thing need not, cannot, believe. At the same time, when appropriation, competition, and consumption are ultimates, *human hope* is rendered obsolete: if our hope lies only in the accumulation of what "is"—in greater quantity—true hope is extinguished. The very intelligibility of hope entails human risk and vulnerability—a reality qualitatively different from the observation or repetition of what is. Finally, *human love* is rendered impossible. The denial of commitment, the retention of the self, the escape from our capacity to give our selves away are nothing other than rejections of our capacity to affirm the other for his or her own sake. Love, by its very nature rife with risk, vulnerability and freedom, can exist only in a world of Persons.

Underlying the gospel of the Commodity Form in all its appearances mentioned above is a concerted and systematic rejection of *human freedom*. By freedom I mean the human potentiality for self-commitment or self-defining gift, based upon our limited capacity for self-understanding and self-reflection. When we confine human knowledge to description, manipulation, and control, we automatically eliminate freedom as a possibility. When we channel human behavior into fear, domination, violence, and mechanized sexuality, we inhibit the mutuality of personal freedoms. When we allow scientism to reduce human action to external blind causes, we methodologically repress any discussion of freedom. When we embrace escape and hedonism as cultural ideals, we exclude free commitment. And when we deny the possibility of hoping, believing, or loving, we are actually prohibiting the exercise of freedom which is the very condition of those human acts.

The Commodity Form, in effect, represses those qualities which are most intimately and most specifically human. Such is the meaning of Psalm 115 which was previously quoted in relation to Marx. Persons relate to things as if they were persons; they relate to persons—including themselves—as if they were things. Having patterned ourselves after the image of our commodities, we become disenfranchised of our very humanness. Reduced to commodities, we lose the intimacy of personal touch. We cannot truly see or listen as vibrant men and women. We do not speak, limited as we are to the repetition of computed input. We do not walk in freedom, since we are paralyzed by what is. Such is the result of idolatry. Those who make idols and put their trust in them become like them.

In summarizing the framework of the Commodity Form and its values, I want to focus once again on the crucial point. I am concerned with idolatry: the dispossession of our humanity in the name of our artifacts. I am speaking of ultimacy: thing-values which have no other limiting principle than themselves. Thus the following observations are important.

A. Productivity, marketability, consumption, technique, scientific method, are not evil themselves. They are beneficial to the well-being of humanity and as such are "graced" values. It is only when the relation of persons to production is reversed, when the instrumentalities become the measure of the persons, that the Commodity Form of life rules and ruins us.

B. The Commodity Form is primarily a frame of perceiving and valuing. It is not the only or total cause of human frustration so much as it is the foundation for a matrix of values which make human frustration quite likely. A case might be made, however, that the primary cause of human suffering, failure, and evil is the propensity of persons to turn away from the vulnerability of their very personhood and to entrust themselves instead to the false security of pretending to be self-enclosed things.

C. Capitalism is not the only cause of the Commodity Form, although it seems to be one of the most fertile environments for its flourishing. If capitalism is unchecked by any other universe of values but its own, however, it necessarily leads to the Commodity Form. It is, at the same time, extremely difficult to appeal to any other universe of moral values once the Commodity Form predominates in a capitalist society. Since the Commodity Form has reached such power and pervasiveness in our present situation, I have presented it as a dominating gospel or "belief system" in our culture. As a worldview and belief system, its dimensions have become socially authoritative, unquestioned, intimidating, and humanly depleting.

D. There are other instances of idolatry besides the Commodity Form. The collective state, the bureaucratic church, the institutionalization of the personality cult, are all equally powerful forms of human impoverishment under different conditions or in different social systems. The point of my exposition has been to show how the value-ultimates of capitalism in our culture reappear as a Commodity Form of consciousness. In effect, my aim has been to show why such disparate values as family, commitment, human life, pacifism, equity, justice, faith, hope, and love have become increasingly difficult to talk about, and more difficult to live, in a society that has systematized the worship of commodities.

Once having made these reservations, however, it is important to realize that the very nature of our economic system provides a faith challenge for those who wish to live the Christian life. In an economic world that is based upon continually expanding consumption, in a society that already has a superabundance of goods and services, in a society that makes consumption, marketing, and producing such absolute values, there are questions that must be raised. What kind of person is *most suitable* for such an economic system? What kind of person, what kind of behavior is *least desirable*?

When people, at least on a per capita basis, have most of their needs fulfilled, how are you going to get them to continually want and buy more? Is it possible that it would be more financially rewarding if people were conditioned to be dissatisfied cravers rather than appreciators of the goods of the earth? Does one buy *more* if one appreciates and relishes things, or if one is continually dissatisfied and distressed and craving? Is it profitable that dissatisfaction be induced into the life-consciousness of a people? Will the stimulation of anxiety and tension (closely associated with the experience of need) be economically desirable? Will persons buy and consume more if they have been taught to be unhappy, to be distressed, to be unsure about personal identity, sexuality, and relationships?

Another way of putting this problem of the commodity formation of self-consciousness is to suggest what kinds of behavior are not "good news for business." Let us suppose that you are a married person with children. If you are relatively happy with your life, if you enjoy spending time with your children, playing with them and talking with them; if you like nature, if you enjoy sitting in your yard or on your front steps, if your sexual life is relatively happy, if you have a peaceful sense of who you are and are stabilized in your relationships, if you like to pray in solitude, if you just like talking to people, visiting them, spending time in conversation with them, if you enjoy living simply, if you sense no need to compete with your friends or neighbors—*what good are you economically in terms of our system?* You haven't spent a nickel yet.

However, if you are unhappy and distressed, if you are living in anxiety and confusion, if you are unsure of yourself and your relationships, if you find no happiness in your family or sex life, if you can't bear being alone or living simply—you will crave much. You will want more. You will have the behaviors most suitable to a social system that is based upon continual economic growth.

The Commodity Form, as we have seen, affects us at every level of our existence. Our fear of solitude, which is one with the fragmentation of individual identity, our valuing of ourselves solely in terms of external criteria, is beneficial to the commodified way of life. Our lack of intimacy, community, personally enduring relationships, our sense of competition and lack of solidarity nudge us into possessing and accumulating things in order to fill up the lack we experience by missing persons in our lives. Our sense of powerlessness in changing the social system and its disordered priorities only serves to confirm and support our economic way of life. Our inability to live simply, to enjoy life without a continual sense of craving and dissatisfaction, is good news for economic growth. Our ignorance of the poor and the disenfranchised, our *fear* of encountering them in truth, intensifies our flight from our own vulnerability and the truth of our own creaturehood.

This is what is meant when we say that the Commodity Form of life touches us systematically. It cuts across every human activity. For there is an economics of intimacy and happiness: covenanted love is not very profitable. There is an economics of the vows: poverty, chastity, and obedience are not very helpful to economic growth. There is an economics to prayer and solitude: they are financially worthless. These are the very activities which are held up to derision in our media propaganda. We are taught to believe that what is most human and most personal in us is impossible. And with our continually increasing expenditure of time in relating to the media, we actually decrease our uniquely human and interpersonal activities. Thus the content and the form of the media reinforce the economics of the Commodity Form of life.

We might ask: can it be that when Pope John Paul II speaks in *Redeemer of Humankind* of being slaves to production, to economic systems, to the possessions produced by our own hands, he is not only warning those who may live in a totalitarian state? Can we in the United States be similarly held in thrall by a totalitarian state of mind?

Such has been the thesis of the first part of this book. We have not offered a critique of capitalism so that we might find a utopia or discover a perfect model of life in another culture or nation. It is this land, this culture which we have been gifted with and burdened by; and it is this society which we must challenge for its economic idolatry and our enslavement to it. We have also tried to suggest that a total "way of life" or gospel such as the Commodity Form, which infiltrates every aspect of our experience, must be equally confronted at all levels by an alternative "way of life" claiming our allegiance.

We are not only called to resist the programming of the consumer society; we are also called to affirm the following of Christ. For it is he who reveals us as we truly are: not expendable objects defined by the dead idols we have crafted, but irreplaceable persons, created in the image of a communitarian God who has empowered us to take part in the Godly life: the Personal Form of human existence realized in Jesus Christ.

PART TWO

THE PERSONAL FORM

CHAPTER SIX

TOWARD A CHRISTIAN PHILOSOPHICAL ANTHROPOLOGY

PERSONS

When I speak of the "Personal Form," I am referring to a mode of perceiving and valuing men and women as irreplaceable persons whose fundamental identities are fulfilled in covenantal relationships. A covenantal relationship is a mutual commitment of self-donation between free beings capable of self-conscious reflection and self-possession. Covenant as the free gift of self, the promising of oneself, is a characteristic unique to such free beings.

Various philosophers as well as religious thinkers have emphasized this "form" of human consciousness; but ultimately I will turn to the fullest revelation of the Personal Form in Jesus Christ as I have encountered him in history, tradition, Scripture, the communal endeavor of believers, and personal experience. I turn to him in an act of faith—a free human act which is neither logically nor historically necessitated and which, while founded upon the certitude of encountering another person, is accompanied by both insecurity and risk. I believe in him just as I might say I believe in any other person or in that person's love for me, but the content of my belief is that he is the fullness of revelation of what it means to be true God and true human person. Jesus Christ must be approached as a totality—not as some combination of isolated personal experiences, not as embodied in dogma alone, not as the mere summation of moralistic texts, not merely as a historical reality living in a believing community, and not apart from his own history as a Jew and mine as a Christian. All of these aspects have to be considered if I am to be able to encounter Jesus as a total personal reality.

It is also important to point out that the "Personal Form" is not the prerogative of the Catholic church, the Christian churches, or even revealed religion. The Personal Form is revealed and manifest, at least in some way, whenever and wherever human beings are faithful to their personhood. At the same time it is equally true that church people or Christians are not necessarily the fullest embodiment of Christ's revelation. Christians have at times been notoriously out of touch with their personhood, as well as with their Lord Christ. Moreover, any believer lodged in history and society is as subject to the pathologies of history and society as non-believers are. Quite simply, what I appeal to here is the revelation-as-a-totality that is found in the full dimensions of Jesus Christ. And that reality always includes in some way, when it is closest in integrity to its calling, the church.

At least part of my encounter with the revelation of the Personal Form in Jesus Christ is made in the context of my categories, my self-understanding, and my general worldview. Revelation is not made or received in a vacuum; rather it is mediated through history, both in the context of nation, church, and culture, and in the context of my own human career.

It will be helpful to clarify how I understand the nature of the "human person." For to speak of "culture," "society," and even "Christianity," is necessarily to imply in some way a previous understanding of personhood. This principle also applies to action and purpose, not to say alienation or human devaluation. All of our reflections depend to a great extent upon a philosophical anthropology, or general view of self-consciousness, human potentialities, human drives and needs, human realization. This is not to say that I must define human nature in some static, wholly invariant manner which can once and for all be definitely categorized; rather, it simply means I contend that humans have species-wide, commonly shared characteristics, exigencies, and inherent demands—all of which, if violated (whether in infidelity or in ignorance), lead to a falling away from true humanness or true human realization.

Cross-culturally, cross-temporally (under differing modalities of particular social structures and historical frames), humans find themselves in a condition of incompleteness, of being unfinished. This incompleteness is expressed in a striving for, a being driven to, the realization of our potentialities in a mutuality of knowing and loving. Conditioned and limited goals or goods serve not as final satisfactions for our striving so much as they constitute continual reminders of its apparent insatiability and inexhaustibility. The dynamics and structure of consciousness indicate that our very "being" is a calling out for fullness, a "being-toward," a grand historical longing, a stretching out beyond the mere givenness of our limits. What is, is surely often lovely, but never enough. Thus, men and women question. And in doing so, they posit the quandary that is one with their identity as persons: Why are they not sufficient to themselves?

What is more, we can be present to or aware of ourselves as contingent and incomplete—as painfully unfinished. We are aware of our history, of our environment, of our relatedness to both. Finally, we are aware of the prospect of death. Our self-consciousness introduces the possibility of achieving a partial distance from the conditions of our history and cultural milieu. We need not blindly accept what *is*. We can at the very least fashion an attitude of life-stance toward what is. The world is not *given* only for our immediate obsessive response; it is also, and most critically, presented to us as *problematic*. Thus, again, when our world becomes a problem for us, our physical and ontological incompleteness is expressed in a cognitive form of incompletion: the question. It is the emergence of wonder.

Persons not only question who they are in relation to one another, but they question what they must do, who they might be, what they could hope for. And thereby, moral, religious, and valuational realms enter the human's experimental world. Each person is an embodied life statement, a self-saying which is uttered out of each one's finitude. Such an election or self-definition is spoken to the future in an unfolding project-career of self-creativity. This life statement is made explicit in and through the structures of culture and history. Consequently, as beings consciously open to the future, as knowers cognizant of possibilities beyond necessity, as self-knowers aware of realities beyond the immediate, men and women are not only problems. We are, as Gabriel Marcel reminds us, mysteries.

Within the mystery of human reality, however, there is profound ambiguity and ambivalence. It lurks in the incompleteness which reveals both our fulfillments and our radical sense of absence. This ambiguity is discovered in the unfolding nature of a life-project which is in many ways "already" and still painfully "not yet." It is rooted in the question which is our being—a self-aware reaching outside of our centers because that self-centeredness is profoundly insufficient. In other words, we are aware of ourselves as precariously contingent and unfinished, with a frightening and irrevocable task of forming, individually and together, self-defining life commitments.

Unfortunately, upon the discovery of our precariousness and insecure contingency, we seek to ground ourselves, to finish and fill ourselves, by running away from the fragility of our personhood. We submit to the blandishments of threat and domination, the pathological inversion of our drive to know and understand. In languishing for security, we enter into patterns of ultimate competition and accumulation, the pathological inversion of our affective potential. If we consume, collect, or produce enough, we seem to think we could eliminate the risks of being human, of trust, of intimacy. But we find instead the emptiness of a closed, monadic world that turns upon itself in violence. Finally, we seek escape, refusing to commit ourselves in the face of our own frightening unfinishedness. At times, slavery seems less terrible, and certainly more safe, than freedom.

All of these phenomena are fraudulent methods of self-validation. They are rejections of the conditions of our humanness, refusals of our scary finitude, avoidances of our freedom in the face of death. Thus we refuse to be who we are, by refusing the grandeur of freely knowing and loving, by avoiding life itself as much as death. In this way, each human person has possible self-negating dimensions. We can reject our destiny and personhood through violence which is self-hatred, through retention which is encapsulation, through self-maintenance at all costs, through hedonistic escape from committed love. Such is our fall. This is the underlying struggle of sin's drama: the rejection of our very humanity, the negation of our personal creaturehood. We refuse to accept ourselves as lovable creatures, who are not and need not be God. Ashamed at not being enough, at not being finished or self-sufficient, we seek a false completion in idolatry.

All of this is not to say that humans are basically evil or egocentric (in the restricted sense of that word), for what I have been describing is only one aspect of the ambivalence of being a finite person. There are, as matters of experience, natural "epiphanies"—moments which Abraham Maslow has called the "peak experiences" of transcendence, harmony, self-realization, and ecstatic love. Human possibility is momentarily revealed within the experiences of cognitive unfolding, when we find ourselves defenselessly open before the mystery of the "other." At times not subject to our control or strategy, we discover ourselves integrated and realized, in loving self-acceptance and self-donation, and in self-possessed commitment. This is the emergence of our true destiny as loved and loving creatures.

These "epiphanies," however, are tenuous, fleeting, and subject to disillusionment. The seduction of dominance and appropriation continually threatens to enthrall us. Our insatiable and inexhaustible desires seemingly never are fully realized. And our own resources—even those offered by a loved one—are often too frail, too fragile, and too far beyond our control. The human person is indeed, as Sartre has stated, an "infinite passion," a pressure toward the fullness of personhood—but a passion which, if it clings to and closes upon itself, is terrifyingly groundless and ultimately absurd.

CULTURES, HUMANS, AND FAITH

There are surely hundreds of ways to define or approach the meaning of culture—historical, psychological, and anthropological, but let us make simply an etymological rumination. Here, the Latin is suggestive.

"Culture." *Colo, colere, colui, cultum. Colere.* To cultivate, to tend and till. *Colere.* To dwell and inhabit as Tacitus and Livy used it. Cicero used the word to indicate a "fostering" or "study." Finally, and our own cognate of the past participle suggests it, the word "culture"—*cultum*—has something to do with the realm of religion. Vergil and Cicero used the word in the context of worship and honor—as in cultic objects.

A culture is a cult. It is a revelation system. It is the entire range of corporate ritual, of symbolic forms, human expressions, and productive systems. It quietly converts, elicits commitments, transforms, provides heroics, suggests human fulfillments. The culture, then, is a gospel—a book of revelation—mediating beliefs, revealing us to ourselves.

A culture is a cultivation. Humans tend and till themselves through nature into culture. When culture has an independent reality of its own it reciprocates and tends and tills us. We become cultured. Thus, although culture is *made* by humans, it in a special manner makes us—to some extent in its own image.

A culture is our corporate symbolic dwelling place. We inhabit, our consciousnesses inhabit our culture. The culture is a human tabernacle, the incarnation of corporate spirit. It is the living expression of men and women. Culture is *of* psyche and psyche is formed *by* culture. Hence, culture is problematic for any "theory of the human person," for any approach to spirituality and faith.

The word "culture" indicates the entire expanse of the ways that a group expresses and embodies its reality. It is the product *of* men and women. Thus it is part of the human totality. It is *of* the human. The human is not *of it* in any reductionistic sense. The purpose of a culture is to reveal and confirm us in our humanity. Like any expression of conscious labor, it must be a servant of our humanness, if it is true to itself.

It is true that culture is most aptly spoken of in the realm of meaning, intelligibility, formalization—the structuring and ordering that is appropriate to the tilling and cultivating of nature and our nature. But our understanding of culture must extend beyond those categories.

A given economic system, a political system, a constellation of the relations of production, a network of power relationships can all be considered part of the cultural reality. They are in a true sense as much symbolic forms as are human artifacts and literary expressions. They are expressions of values, carriers of values, teachers of values.

A spiritual and psychic problem emerges when the culture, which is a *part* of the human, achieves an independence from living humans, expresses only one part of their humanity, and dominates the humans who produce it. People then serve culture. Culture no longer serves them.

A religious and faith problem emerges when our very categories of ultimate meaning, significance, purpose, or fulfillment are dictated more by one form of cultural expression (i.e., an economic or mass media technology) than by human need, human purposes, or by the revelation of God.

It is important that any given culture be subjected to examination and criticized from the viewpoint of the human and of human potentialities and not from a fragmented perspective representing only *part* of our meaning. When men and women examine the context of their lives and labors, it is a fruitful undertaking to measure the authenticity, the humaneness, and the spirituality of a culture as expressive of and responsive to integrated human needs.

The identity, needs, and capacities of human nature call out for a culture that sustains, communicates, and enhances human relations.

Thus, the etymological beginning of this reflection might be concluded in this fashion: as *alienation*, culture is a frozen artifact against which the newness of human imagination is rigidly measured and against which the persistent human hopes for fulfillments, rights, and values are dashed. It is an estranged house—protecting not persons, but fragmentary forms of human life. In this sense, culture does not teach; it propagandizes. It is not a sacred expression of the human. It is an idolatry—in whose fabricated image humans are recreated and diminished.

As authentically human, culture is the tilling of history by humane self-expression. It is also the friendly symbolic dwelling place of the human spirit, whereby new generations are cultivated rather than repressed. It is, finally, sacred: a revelation of Spirit in time.

It is possible to focus on our human reality. This is the fact of what we are, our species-wide potentialities that can be identified in any culture and that differentiate us from the nonhuman. This is a received reality, what we are by reason of being human. It is created, but not by culture. It transcends culture and is not reducible to any particular culture. This is our personhood: our identity is rooted in the unique ways we are capable of knowing and loving.

We may also speak of the *expression of* our human reality. This is the way we embody our humanness in different historical and spatial dimensions. This is active, the way we express and reproduce ourselves in a broad variety of forms. This is culture.

When we speak of faith, we can mean at least two things: first, faith is a human *act* in history. It is an exercise of human

freedom, of commitment, of covenant. This act and the capacity to place such an act is not given to us by any culture,
although it is expressed and embodied in culture. Second, we
can mean faith to be a specific *content* of belief. This (like the
act of faith) is a two-sided reality. Faith in this sense is the content of our beliefs about our identity as human persons, our
purpose, our meaning, and our fulfillment. This is given to us,
revealed to us. We do not make up this content, we receive it.
And yet our reception is always historically and culturally embedded and conditioned; it is culturally expressed.

The Christian makes an *act* of faith covenanted to God in
Jesus with respect to a certain *content* of faith that concerns
the truth of our human condition and our purpose, with respect to what it means to be truly human and truly Godlike.

There are some cultural systems of human self-expression
(including institutions, economic relations, social patterns,
power relationships) that *foster* the act of faith (the covenanting of oneself in freedom) as well as the content of faith (love,
service, equality, cultic practices, sexual integrity, peace, sharing, reconciliation, the recognition of creaturehood, the acknowledgment of sin, and the need for forgiveness).

On the other hand, it is possible that some cultural systems or parts of those systems *inhibit* and threaten the free
placement of the act of faith (through propaganda, restriction
of religious liberty, psycho-social manipulation) as well as the
content of faith (by teaching competition, fear, violence, envy,
avarice, lust, hedonism, injustice, egoism).

If we are to presume that, like Christ who is God incarnate
in space and time, faith emerges in and is exercised through the
ambient of culture, our problem of faith and culture becomes
this: how can we have a faith that is truly historical (incarnate),
speaking to us and others in and through cultures, and yet be
a faith that is not reducible to cultural imperatives or cultural
immanence? How can we concretely live a faith that is not domesticated or intimidated, a faith that is not confined to cultural relativism, a faith that can challenge cultural ideologies
and idolatries, a faith that is not wholly acculturated?

We must always ask ourselves: How does culture liberate, engage, and actualize our faith? This is the question that most of us always presuppose.

But we must also ask ourselves: How does culture threaten, confine, compromise, and betray our faith? This is the question we most frequently forget.

HOSTILE CULTURES

Our history, our fragility, and the high stakes of our lives are all further complicated by the fact that we produce. We express ourselves in acting, in making, in thinking, both corporately and individually. Humans are embodied and embodying beings. In labor, play, and expression, we embody ourselves as individuals and group; in language, art, and societal patterns, we culturally exteriorize ourselves as community or species. In our culture we find the deepest symbolizations of life. It is our fundamental corporate task; and it takes part in all of our existential reality—our incompleteness and contingency, our brokenness and ambiguity, our sin and grace, our pathologies and peak experiences.

In its fullness, culture can be the free undertaking of communities and peoples in world-building; and as such, cultural structures can be invitational to the individual, offering us a world of patterns and values which serve as a communal critique for our subjectivity and perspective. In this way, culture emerges from the freedom of the human person and at the same time fosters human liberation.

Culture, on the other hand, exhibits a dynamic which can be an expression of dangerous human potentialities. As the exteriorization of human consciousness, cultural products can acquire the characteristics of an objective, pre-existent reality, and as a result are apprehended as an external force "over against" the demands of human freedom and open inquiry. It is true that objectified culture provides a patterned world of intersubjectivity; but it is equally true that its fixity can inhibit emergent human values. To a closed cultural value system, the novelty of human freedom and questioning becomes a threat. Such a system interacts with situations and persons exclusively in terms of *its own* objective reality.

A culture that is sustained by and sustains the Commodity Form of consciousness, for example, will relate to personal reality as a hostile, deviant, or heretical force. Thus today, many Christian values—chastity, pacifism, family life—are seen as deviant, mysterious, or strangely primitive. Consequently, those who embrace such values often find themselves under such great pressure that they must either accept the reality of the dominant commodity values or acquiesce in their own lives as laughably deviant.

When a cultural system reaches a point where the options offered to the individual demand either rejection or complete absorption, the system can no longer be authentically human, can no longer be invitational, can no longer serve the individual as a corporately embodied basis of critique. For it is now a closed system. It is ideological because its universe of discourse cannot be called into question. It is idolatrous because it enslaves persons to an objectified, non-covenantal reality. Cultural critical self-evaluation becomes impossible, since there can be no appeal to a set of criteria which are not reducible to the criteria of the culture itself. Culture is no longer the expression of humanity. Humans have become mere expressions of culture.

Any culture, as a particularized human embodiment, is of necessity limited, concrete, and perspectival. This is even more evidently true of the various value systems within a given culture. Precisely because it is a cultural value system, its reality criteria and survival criteria are intrinsically limited by its own concreteness and perspective. Consequently, once its particular languages, educational and political systems, academies of art and music, and "worldviews" achieve status as realities "out there," they (through human adherents) accept, judge, or reject other perspectives in terms of their own perspective; and any "newness" tolerated is only in terms of self-proliferation, quantitative growth, subtraction, addition, and multiplication of what already *is*. Any novel form of communication, artistry, learning, or belief must be either "co-opted" by what is, be assessed as revolutionarily counter-cultural, tolerated as inconsequential deviance, or, if the threat is great enough, eliminated. Faded jeans, hairstyles and street talk are easily enough absorbed by Madison Avenue to its own profit. Hysterical militants can eventually be rounded up. Religious sects and enthusiasts, if they have not bought all of the American Dream, can be accepted on the fringe with a bemused smile.

But what do you do with the powerful human drive toward personal love, personal knowing, faith, hope, love, and commitment in fidelity? They have to be explained away, negatively enforced, or denied legitimacy in terms of the Commodity Form. The first half of our investigation has been an attempt to describe such denials.

A culture, when it is sustained by a monolithic worldview such as the Commodity Form, is particularly adept at reinforcing the pathologies of knowing and loving. It is the nature of idolatry and ideology to call persons away from the precariousness of their unfinished free condition. The Commodity Form's ideology is solidified. It is closed, complete, finished. The only newness is repetition. The ideology of the commodity is not open to invitation, free commitments, or questioning. It relates to men and women in terms of demand, manipulation. It relates to other social systems in terms of pragmatics, utility, domination, and aggression.

An idolatrous ideology channels affectivity and choice into adaptation, assimilation, encapsulation, and servitude. It is a culturally systemic rejection of human freedom and contingency. But, in the flight from human frailty into the arms of pseudo-security and false fulfillments, the repression of our ontological poverty explodes into domination, explodes into violence within society and violence against other societies. In our cultural gospel, as in all idolatry, relief from the anxieties of personhood is pursued; but it is further bondage which is found. We encase ourselves in a denial of our authentic humanness, of openness, of invitation, and of risky vulnerability.

Certainly, I have been discussing "culture" only in its most hardened form of ideology. But it must be noted that the only force which could *prevent* such a hardening would be a fidelity to culture-transcending values, values not reducible to any specific cultural system, values grounded in the very nature and structure of personhood. These culture-transcending values have been the objects of a most relentless and systematic attack in the world of the Commodity Form. The values rooted in personhood are apparently on the decline, subject to a new form of planned obsolescence. The second half of this book suggests how their last defense resides in the traditions and lived practice of Judaism and Christianity, as well as in any authentic faith which might lead a man or woman to embrace and embody the Personal Form of existence.

CHAPTER SEVEN

THE GOD OF THE JEWISH SCRIPTURES:
IDOLATRY AND COVENANT

I cannot claim the Jewish Scriptures entirely as my own or for my own as a Jew might, for it is his or hers, both as a personally complete revelation and as the living expression of a people. Nonetheless, I can stand before what Christians call the "Old Testament," accepted as a prophetic figuring and actual part of the revelation we find in the person of Jesus Christ. The God I believe in is incarnate and historical, and I cannot approach God's revelation outside of Jesus' own historicity as a Jew or outside my own history lodged in and nurtured by the Jewish tradition.

Still, any approach I may make has to be limited, not only because I am not a Jew, but also because of the intrinsic limitations of my perspective. Although I trust it is not entirely idiosyncratic, my reading will necessarily be *my* reading. In facing and reflecting upon the revelation of the Jewish Bible, I dispense myself from scientific, historical, and textual research, from a full explanation of how the "Old" Testament is related to the "New." Consequently, I will approach it in a simple way—reflecting upon what unavoidably strikes me as the message of the story, the Law, and the prophets. While I admit it is incomplete and schematic, I find such an approach yields significance and challenge.

One of the most striking dimensions of the story includes the fact that men and women are made in the image and likeness of a freely creating God and that no other image of God is permitted than the human image which is the product of God's own loving handiwork. Everything that is created is pronounced good, even the man and woman who turn away from their very being in an act of disobedience to their personhood and their Lord. They would be like gods, in the promised security of controlling their fate and their call. They would trade covenant for domination. And the consequence was a falling against each other in violence or falling apart in disunity and fragmentation. Nonetheless, the continual promise of a God beckoning men and women into free covenant persists. Great figures emerge, willing to respond to the *invitation* and command of our being to enter into a life of relatedness. But more significantly, an entire people is called.

The history of Israel is a history of liberation: of being freed from political and economic oppression in the grip of their conquerors; of being released from the impersonal gods of nature, land, gold, or wood; of being saved from a mindless "behaving like the nations" in their self-destruction, their injustice, their lack of compassion for the poor and dispossessed.

On a more profound level, Israel seems to be called out of the most sophisticated forms of personal slavery: enslavement to the law, to the land, and even to the nation. Their history of covenant with their Lord is a history of purifications. The land, of itself, does not and cannot save; and that truth seems only to be existentially felt when they are deprived of the land. Nor does the power of nation save. It is not the power of armies, but the electing love of their covenantal God that protects them. But their trust in armies seems to be shattered only with the shattering of the army itself. Without land and army, the covenant is reborn and survives in the Law, the people, and its cult. Yet Law and cult themselves, if cut off from the covenantal Lord, can become as idolatrous as a golden calf. And so, in final poverty, Israel must be purified of an idolatrous law that has blinded them to their own humanity. It is compassion, not sacrifice, which is asked of them by their God. It is the law of the heart, not of stones or parchment, which the prophets promise and elicit. The covenant with God, the law of the heart to which God invites humans, yields not only a fidelity to covenant, but also the mutual recognition of one another's dignity and freedom.

> What is good has been explained to you, man:
> this is what Yahweh asks of you:
> only this, to act justly,
> to love tenderly,
> and to walk humbly with your God [Mic. 6:8].

Mere holocausts and the easy blood of animals are worthless offerings which are more a displacement of humanity than an expression of it. This God wants not the debasement of persons, not obsequiousness, not slaves, but free men and women, who recognize their dignity in their freedom of covenant and express that dignity in their recognition of each other's worth. Thus Amos rails against the trampling upon the poor, the extortion and exploitation of the oppressed, and the loss of justice while vile sacrifices are offered as magical atonement. Jeremiah (Chapters 7, 22) calls for justice and equity as the expression of a new interior covenant. Habakkuk (Chapter 2) warns against the treachery of wealth, the insatiable bondage to greed, the plundering of peoples, and the exploitation of the poor while towns and empires are built over their spilt blood. And Isaiah calls for a covenant that must be expressed in fidelity to human dignity.

> Is not this the sort of fast that pleases me—
> It is the Lord Yahweh who speaks—
> to break unjust fetters
> and undo the thongs of the yoke,
> to let the oppressed go free,
> and break every yoke,

to share your bread with the hungry,
and shelter the homeless poor,
to clothe the man you see naked
and not turn from your own kin?
Then will your light shine like the dawn
and your wound be quickly healed over.
Your integrity will go before you
and the glory of Yahweh behind you.
Cry, and Yahweh will answer;
call, and He will say "I am here."
If you do away with the yoke,
the clenched fist, the wicked word,
if you give your bread to the hungry
and relief to the oppressed,
your light will rise in the darkness
and your shadow become like noon.
Yahweh will always guide you,
giving you relief in desert places.
He will give strength to your bones
and you will be like a watered garden,
like a spring of water
whose waters never run dry [Isa. 58:6-11].

Thus, while the free covenant with the living God is a call out of bondage and idolatry, the people of God are at the same time and by that very reason called into a new life of relatedness—not only with God, but with their fellow human beings. This call to justice is the very embodiment and expression of relatedness with the living God. It is a relatedness, moreover, which presupposes freedom for persons. The Lord of the universe will pursue humanity with the persistence of a lover, a spouse, a father and a mother, but it will be a pursuit that insists upon a free response on the part of the human. God will not exact of us a blind acquiescence or subjugation. God waits for the free self-gift. As Martin Buber has put it in *I and Thou*: at the bottom of our identity, we are called to life in relationship.

The *Thou* meets me through grace—it is not found by seeking. But my speaking of the primary word to it is an act of my being, is indeed the *act* of my being.

The *Thou* meets me. But I step into direct relation with it. Hence the relation means being chosen and choosing, suffering and action in one; just as any action of the whole being, which means the suspension of all partial actions and consequently of all sensations of actions grounded only in their particular limitation, is bound to resemble suffering.

The primary word *I-Thou* can be spoken only with the whole being. Concentration and fusion into the whole being can never take place through my agency, nor can it ever take place without me. I become through my relation to the *Thou*; as I become *I*, I say *Thou*.

All real living is meeting.

Such is the call of men and women. Out of slavery and domination into the covenant of intimacy with a God who wants them only to be free in their self-gift. This God is Absolute Person, and invites forth the personhood of men and women fashioned in the divine image. God calls us to a dependence upon nothing other than the exigencies of our own humanity and its reaching out in trust, faith, and love for Yahweh.

The revelation of this God, consequently, is at the same time an exaltation of the human person, of human relationships, and of the capacity of men and women to freely enter covenants of intimacy, exercising their freedom in fidelity, hope, care. All other gods are unworthy of the human, for they demand not freedom and personhood, but submission, blindness, slavery, and the worship of unworthy objects. Thus God is a jealous God. There can be no division of our final allegiance. In God alone, in God's love, is our final identity, realization, and hope.

This is the Isaian love, which calls us by our first name, which has branded us on the palm of God's hand, which cannot ever allow God to forget us, which would not have us fear. This is the Hosean love, in which Israel's God would lead us with strings of care, teaching us to walk, holding us close, finding it impossible even to consider being parted from us. It is the love expressed in the Psalms which would set us free in the openness of life itself, which would never abandon us, which would hold us with a mother's love for her child.

Only when we understand the covenantal and loving dimensions of this God can we see the power behind the Ten Commandments—the dignity, the elevation of humanity, the prizing of every true human relationship it reveals. No image or artifact is worthy of our final allegiance and worship: only the covenantal Lord, in whose image we are fashioned, is worthy of and appropriate for our ultimate and free self-donation. The covenant must be reaffirmed and remembered and relived—as any other covenant which is to sustain life must be re-enacted and re-embodied. Fidelity to the great human covenants—family, loved one, parents, neighbor—is called forth from men and women. Sexuality is pronounced blessed, the sacred sign of our love and longings, an expression of our life choices, commitments, and identity. Human life is held sacred—without conditions. Trust is established as the protector of corporate life and community; envy and jealousy are branded as humanly divisive and fragmenting. The great laws of God are not, then, some list of frustrations delivered against the human person. They are the expressions of personhood in its fullest exercise and aspiration. These are imperatives for the realization of humanity, not the denial of humanity. They are advocates of freedom, not inhibitors of it.

There is so much more, of course, to the Law and the prophets that I might suggest here. But any reading of the Jewish Scripture will, I propose, yield a deeper realization that the revelation of men and women is found in the covenantal relationship. It is persistently a document affirming the unconditional value of the human person. It is a declaration of independence from all idolatries which would enslave or demean humanity. And it is the record of a painstakingly evolving education of a people toward the freedom of a most profound faith, constituted by love of and for persons.

CHAPTER EIGHT

READING THE LIFE OF CHRIST

THE CHILD

What is it like to read some time-worn text with new eyes and with a new principle of investigation? If I really begin an earnest inquiry, seeking out what kind of God, what kind of human, is revealed as Truth, what will I come up with? Or what will be my findings if I take up the Scripture with a fresh understanding of the Commodity Form and its gospel upon my mind? What might be my result if I asked what I could find in terms of cultural values?

I believe the answer is inescapable. The Gospel is the most counter-cultural and the most significantly revolutionary document one could ever hope to find. It reveals the meaning and purpose of human life in terms which are close to being absolutely contradictory to the form of perceiving and valuing human persons in our culture.

The gospel presents an image of God which shatters most categories that both atheists and believers employ; and it offers a model of humanity which is wholeheartedly personalistic, liberating, and ultimately exalting of human life. But let us just begin, and allow the story and text to speak for themselves. I will, only because of the limitations of space and the desire not to be tedious or repetitious, confine myself, for the most part, to the Gospel of Matthew, in order to get at least a general sense of how one rendition of Christ's life and message is presented.

If we keep in mind that we are looking at the way Christ reveals both the nature of God and the meaning of human persons, what are we to make of the fact that he is the son of poor people? A poor God? A poor humanity? There could have been so many other options. Why not enlist the elite who could really change society? Why not use the benefactions of power and prestige, choosing a Roman family, or a different time, or some place other than Israel, especially Nazareth, Galilee, Bethlehem, or a stable? Why should it be Mary on whose lips Luke places the Magnificat?—stirring words not of mere interior piety or submissive quietism, but of exultation in the God of Justice and of the poor:

> He has shown the power of his arm,
> He has routed the proud of heart.
> He has pulled princes from their thrones and
>   exalted the lowly.
> The hungry he has filled with good things,
>   the rich sent away empty [Luke 1:50-52].

At reading this text, one is tempted to ask if Christians have ever taken seriously enough the ringing "social justice" words of their gentle Mother; but it is more important to ask what is revealed about the God we say we believe in, God's revelation and God's predilections.

Luke, in his more extended development of the infancy narrative, announces the coming of a Savior to a poor man and woman with the words, "Be not afraid" (1:31), words also delivered to poor shepherds (2:10). The sign of his coming is the poverty of manger and stable, a poverty which, like the call to fearlessness, is reiterated throughout Jesus' life. The child is revealed to the entire world and seemingly all classes, yet his allies seem to be concentrated in the wise men, the poor, and, significantly, the blood of innocent, defenseless children. He has enemies from the start: the armies of a King Herod's pomp and power.

THE TEMPTATION OF HUMANITY

Matthew introduces Christ's public life with the proclamation of John, a man of ascetical simplicity who preaches repentance, a conversion, or turning around, a revolution of the mind and heart. After Jesus is baptized and pronounced beloved of the Father, we find him led by the Spirit into the desert in his first adult encounter with the power of darkness that threatens his destiny.

The three temptations are particularly instructive in that they present appropriation, magic, and domination as alternatives not only to Christ's mission from the Father, but as flights from his humanity, as escape from the risk of inviting men and women into free covenant.

> And the tempter came and said to him, "If you are the Son of God, tell these stones to turn into loaves." But he replied, "Scripture says: Man does not live on bread alone but on every word that comes from the mouth of God."
>
> The devil then took him to the holy city and made him stand on the parapet of the Temple. "If you are the Son of God," he said, "throw yourself down. . . ."
>
> Next, taking him to a very high mountain, the devil showed him all the kingdoms of the world and their splendor. "I will give you all these," he said, "if you fall at my feet and worship me."
>
> Then Jesus replied, "Be off, Satan! For scripture says: You must worship the Lord your God and serve him alone!" [Mt. 4:3-10].

Thus are established the themes of Jesus' life and message and redemptive work. It is not by the promise or sustenance of mere bread that his kingdom will be achieved. Nor is it through the magical machinations of escape or spectacle. And most of all, it will not be effected by turning away from the covenantal Lord and worshiping the Power of mighty kingdoms. No, rather it will be established by service to the God beyond humanity for the sake of humanity, a service that never turns from Christ's own human frailty and radical dependence upon the word of God. Thus, the three temptations reveal at least two significant things early in the Gospel of Matthew: there is the suggestion of a model for human action, a morality which is rooted in our covenantal relationship to God; and secondly, there is a revelation of our true personhood in the acceptance of our ontological poverty rather than in a trust of power, security, escape, magic, and their seductions.

THE ALTERNATIVE KINGDOM

After the calling of four not entirely impressive fishermen as his disciples and the releasing of men and women from disease, possession by demons, and paralysis, Jesus delivers the great Evangelical Discourse in Matthew, Chapters 5, 6, and 7. The themes can only be highlighted: graced and happy are those persons who are poor and gentle, those who mourn, who hunger and thirst for justice, who are merciful, single-mindedly pure in heart, those who make peace—even those who are persecuted in the cause of right. Nietzsche seems to have understood the Sermon on the Mount better than many Christians. Christ reveals that human fulfillment is found in the *opposite* of riches (whether spiritual or, as Luke more directly says, material), the *opposite* of mere good times and absence of suffering, the *opposite* of being powerful, unforgiving, the *opposite* of war-making, even the *opposite* of victory. Nietzsche found this doctrine scandalous, and attacked it as the demeaning of the will to power. Christians often find it equally scandalous, and ignore it in a life surrounded by power, wealth, and military might. "His words are mere metaphors," we reassure ourselves, "pious thoughts too gentle for this world and the business of our lives." But these reassurances are the words of a gospel other than Jesus Christ's. He would have his followers not be assimilated by "the earth," but be the salt of it, the light for it.

While Jesus presents his doctrine as the fulfillment and realization of the Law, he surpasses the Law in the application of his doctrine. Not only killing, but even unreconciled anger is condemned; not only adultery, but even the deceptive desires of the heart. Christ calls not for a "balance of power" or deterrence, but for a turning of the other cheek (we now make fun of that statement, as if it is some form of idiocy which shamefully embarrasses us as having been uttered by our own God); he wants not only equity, but giving to anyone who asks.

> You have learnt how it was said: "Eye for an eye and tooth for tooth." But I say this to you: offer the wicked man no resistance. On the contrary, if anyone hits you on the right cheek, offer him the other as well; if a man takes you to law and would have your tunic, let him have your cloak as well. And if anyone orders you to go one mile, go two miles with him. Give to anyone who asks, and if anyone wants to borrow, do not turn away [Matt. 5:38-42].

I have heard Christians quote "an eye for an eye" as justification for capital punishment, just wars, and preemptive strikes, so distant are they from the actual message of the gospel which precisely denies such a position. I have seen Christians rail against abortion, the use of contraceptives, and premarital sex as "un-Christian" (three activities which I oppose on gospel and traditional grounds), even though nothing in Scripture can be found to condemn them as explicitly as the commands in the quotation above; but the words of Christ above, so direct and concrete, are wished and even sometimes laughed away by some of these same Christians as being "non-pragmatic"—the acculturated line of argumentation used against any moral position. Quite simply, we must love our enemies; and nowhere by the wildest flights of imagination can it be found that such love could be expressed in death rows, nuclear warheads, and defoliation of countries. Such is the blindness which the Commodity Form can induce in human reasoning and, yes, Christian conscience.

After stressing the interior attitudes of almsgiving and prayer, Christ teaches prayer through the "Our Father"— expressing our relationship to God in terms of great human intimacy. His prayer aspires to the kingdom of God and the embodiment of it on earth, not just in heaven; it expresses radical trust in the love of the Father, it calls for human forgiveness, and it expresses final trust that our God is not some tyrant or trickster but a guide, a parent, a protector.

"Do not store up earthly treasures" (Matt. 6:1). "You cannot be the servant of both God and of money" (6:24). Trust in providence, not in production. You are of inestimable beauty and worth which you cannot earn but which is yours by birthright. And again: "So do not worry" (6:25,34). But what or whom, we must ask ourselves as Christians here and now, do *we actually trust? Where indeed* is *our* hope and security? Success? Money? Armaments? Nation?

We hasten to remove the splinters in the eyes of the rest of the world, in other nations, in derelicts, drunkards, prostitutes, homosexuals, drop-outs; we will not take the plank out of our own. Jesus calls forth from us not the mere words of "Lord, Lord," but the solid foundation of action in love—admittedly a narrow gate, but one which can be entered when we trust his love for us. "Ask, and it will be given to you; search, and you will find" (Matt. 7:7). The question is whether the search has been given up.

Christ's kingdom is then acted out and preached. He asks people what they might most deeply desire, and responds to them. "Of course I want to cure you," he says to a leper (Matt. 8:3). He is startled, not by power and prestige, but by the stunning ability of persons to freely believe. It is the centurion's faith that amazes him—and brings about the healing of the man's servant (Matt. 8:5-13; cf. 9:22, 9:29, 20:33). He calls disciples to a life wherein they have no security other than in following him, himself "having nowhere to lay his head" (8:28-29). He calms storms, hoping to disarm the fright of people, expecting of them, again, only faith (8:26). He forgives men and women, dissolving their paralysis so that they may walk as free persons (9:1-8). He eats with tax collectors and sinners, proclaiming that he has come for those who have recognized and accepted their needfulness, not for those who think they have no need of being saved. And he tells the Pharisees: "Go and learn the meaning of the words: 'What I want is mercy, not sacrifice'" (9:13). He is a person moved with compassion for the crowd, those harassed and without a shepherd (9:37).

What might these passages mean to a person who has been taught by and convinced of the gospel of our culture?

FOLLOWING AND FINDING HIM

The middle discourses, narratives, and parables in the Gospel of Matthew reveal to us the nature of discipleship. The followers of Jesus must give freely and give to the least person—healing, cleansing, giving not gold but their very lives. And it will be their lives which will be asked of them by an uncomprehending world. They will even be hated on his account and because of his message. But he charges them to proclaim the truth boldly, fearless and straightforward, solely because of their confidence in his fidelity to them.

Thus, it is not some pacifying homeostasis or legitimation of the given order which his followers will bring to the world, but an option which strikes so deeply at the heart of men and women that they will have to choose between ultimates, they will have to be "either/or," and they will find themselves confronting each other in this fundamental choice. Christ's call is to an ultimacy in belief, to a wholeheartedness without qualification or conditions. It is as simple as clinging to one's small life and losing it in the suffocating isolation of idolatry, or losing that life, giving it away, and seeing it expand and bring new life (10:39).

These words are for us, now. Thus we today must confront ourselves. We must ask ourselves the question whether
such words have any meaning in our present world. We must
ponder them in such a way that we will be forced to either
own and admit the Gospel of Christ seriously or merely entertain it as a metaphorical reality.

But how do we know where Jesus is to be found, or how
he might be apprehended? How do we see or recognize him?
He himself answers to the disciples of the Baptist:

Go back and tell John what you hear and see; the
blind see again, and the lame walk; lepers are cleansed
and the deaf hear; and the dead are raised to life and
the good news is proclaimed to the poor, and happy is
the man who does not lose faith in me [Matt. 11:4-6].

He asks us to believe in the possibility that our senses may be
reclaimed, that we may see and hear again, that we may walk
and come back to a human life, that the poverty of humankind may hear, just for once, good news about itself. Such
is the way in which the Gospel of Luke has Christ announce
his ministry to the world: "This text is being fulfilled today
even as you listen":

The spirit of the Lord has been given to me,
for he has anointed me.
He has sent me to bring good news to the poor,
to proclaim liberty to captives
and to the blind new sight,
to set the downtrodden free,
to proclaim the Lord's year of favor.
                    [Luke 4:18-20; quoting Isa. 61:1-2]

Jesus proclaims liberating news in the midst of our very
poverty—not by denying our poverty, but by setting us free
from the oppression and blindness which would have us deny
it and enslave ourselves. Like his own generation we can re-

ject him, just as we can reject our humanity, our neighbors, our very selves.

The full acceptance of Christ, however, and the full acceptance of our true humanity, is not the terror that it may first seem. When we place our security in the appropriation of things that may so easily be lost or taken away, freedom looms ahead as the greatest threat. If we have identified our very being and purpose with the idol we hold in front of our faces, the breaking of that idol in the act of liberation will at first be experienced as harrowing abandonment to our contingency. But the letting go, the painful parting, is the letting go of oppressive fear, the unclenching of the hand to embrace what we finally are. The burden of this truth, and humility before it, is not heavy.

> Come to me, all you who labor and are
>   overburdened,
> and I will give you rest.
> Shoulder my yoke and learn from me,
> for I am gentle and humble in heart,
> and you will find rest for your souls.
> Yes, my yoke is easy and my burden light.
>   [Matt. 11:28-30]

Who do Christians believe is speaking these words? Can we ever comprehend that this is God's self-revelation to us? God is being revealed to us not as some tyrant and judge over against human beings, but as a humble God, wanting only our liberation, our fullness of life. This is the God-Man describing himself as gentle. The Law, the Sabbath, and even humanity itself, are gifts for humanity and to humanity. The problem is in accepting them—even accepting ourselves in the frailty of our knowing and loving, the risk of our faith and hope. To yield to the goodness of created humankind, even in its poverty, is what God asks of us. To do so is to be obedient, in the highest sense of the word, to the Father. And to do so is to become Christ's brother, his sister, and his mother (Matt. 12:50).

The parable discourses, after a brief statement of the Sower's story, are introduced by a quotation from the prophet Isaiah:

You will listen and listen again, but not understand,
see and see again, but not perceive.
For the heart of this nation has grown coarse,
their ears are dull of hearing,
and they have shut their eyes,
for fear they should see with their eyes,
hear with their ears,
understand with their heart,
and be converted
and healed by me [Matt. 13:15].

Men and women, with their senses dulled, their perceptions clouded, become hardened to the word of God precisely because of their loss of basic human capacities. Thus the word of freedom cannot take root in them. It is blown away with the first wind of challenge. It is choked off by "worries of this world and lure of riches" (Matt. 13:22). And no one can perceive the power and promise of the mustard seed, the yeast, the treasure.

It is the desire to empower men and women, to help them recover their senses and their very selves, that leads Jesus to heal and preach, to feed and challenge, to dismantle their fears with "Courage! It is I! Do not be afraid!" (Matt. 15:28). He calls them beyond the magical divination of mere human regulations (15:9) into true whole-heartedness, beyond the mere externalization and ritualization of morality: "For from the heart come evil intentions" (15:18). Jesus is more interested in who the individual person standing before him says he is, than in what people in general say or think he is. Peter's commitment and profession of faith elicits from Christ the entrusting of the keys of his kingdom (16:18-19) even though the weakness of Peter will be made immediately evident in his rejection of Christ's future passion. Like him, all followers of

Christ will have the continual struggle of fully accepting their humanity, their poverty, and their authentic power.

> If anyone wants to be a follower of mine, let him renounce himself and take up his cross and follow me. For anyone who wants to save his life will lose it; but anyone who loses his life for my sake will find it. What then will a man gain if he wins the whole world and ruins his life? Or what has a man to offer in exchange for his life? [16:24-5]

The nature of such renunciation will be articulated in Christ's "Eschatological Discourse" and his own Passion, but he embodies it in his discourse on the church and the following narrative: those who are like a child will be greatest in his kingdom (Matt. 18:1–4); those who are not single-minded enough to turn from all idolatrous security, even their own talents and gifts, will not enter (18:8-9); his people are called to be willing to forgive unconditionally (18:21-22). And if such forgiveness is expected of men and women, it will also be given them by God—expressed not only by the unconditional love found in the story of the Prodigal Son, not only in the loving acceptance of the humble publican or the woman who has sinned, but also in the endless pursuit of one lost sheep. "It is never the will of your Father in heaven that one of these little ones should be lost" (18:14).

Christ calls his followers to a life of continuously desired fidelity and wholehearted commitment. Our very God is found in the committed covenant of marriage (Matt. 19:6). God's presence is in a person's continence offered for the sake of the kingdom (19:10-12,29). But God is not present in any idolatry or in any ultimate temporal securities or personal riches. God can be encountered only in the free covenant itself. To choose securities, wealth, or riches which do not rest in dependence upon God's fidelity to us is a choice against freedom and love and personhood. This is why it is so difficult for us when we are "rich," not in touch with our poverty as men and women, to enter into his kingdom. And this is why even the rich young man, somewhat confident in his following of the Law, goes away yet sad—unable to yield everything in his following of Jesus (Matt. 19:16-24). It is not an easy thing to do. We would rather win salvation with our holdings, earn it with our riches; but salvation, like love, cannot be appropriated in this way. It is impossible for us of our own power. But it is not impossible for God to beckon it forth from us—as God's own gift (19:26).

God's is a profligate love, indiscriminately given to any of us—not on the condition of our achievement, but on the condition of our free acceptance. Even the latest of the laborers will be accepted and graced; and in such a dispensation, even the last can be first (Matt. 20:16). To bring this love to men and women is Jesus' mission and purpose. It is his service. He came not to be ministered to, not to be placated, not to be won. He came quite simply to give and serve (20:27-28). This, indeed, may be utterly confounding—even embarrassing—to an acculturated way of life. Such is our need for its freeing truth.

HUMANITY'S SELF-JUDGMENT AND END

If people are held under the thrall of achievement, competition for supremacy, domination, and self-justification, such a message, such a gift, will be difficult to receive. The invitation will be difficult to hear. It is in this context that the great struggles of the last chapters in Matthew's Gospel can be fully understood. Like the Pharisee offering his prayers of self-praise, the most difficult person to speak the words of love and salvation to is one who "has it made" on his or her own. If I have won and accomplished, if I am a "self-made" person—what need have I of gifts? I have proved myself and justified my life. What need have I of anyone to say I am loved no matter what my lack of accomplishments? It is only when I stand, without pretense, in my naked humanity, in my utter incapacity to earn love and worth, that I can hear the lover be-

stowing the free gift of love. It is only then, unlike the Pharisee, that I can be compassionate, that I can give true love to
others.

Yet this is impossible when religion becomes the business
of expiation and the buying of salvation, or when the temple
becomes a den of thieves (Matt. 21:13). The human fruitful-
ness of love and giving becomes barren (21:18-19). Lip service is paid, but not the allegiance of the heart. Even tax gath-
erers and prostitutes, so aware that they cannot and could not
justify themselves, can believe the bestowal of love more trust-
ingly than the evasive, the idolatrous, the secure, and the
skeptical. Such slaves would rather pay homage to Caesar, to
the logic of results, or to exterior propriety. But Christ would
demand that the self be rendered to none of these.

The strongest indictments in Scripture are delivered by
Christ against the Pharisees (a title not so important for indi-
cating a historical school of the Jews as it is for an image of
the kind of behavior Christ found recalcitrant to salvation).
The center of our attention in reading his charges to the Pharisees should be: What dimension of our own lives is resistant
to truth? What kind of person does Jesus so harshly judge? It
is those closed off to loving or being loved, those so established in power, prestige, and security that they have neither
need of love's grace, nor intimacy enough with their own
human poverty to gaze upon their fellow men and women
with compassion, those who think they can save themselves.

They tie up heavy burdens and lay them on people's
shoulders, but will they lift a finger to move them (Matt.
23:14)? They demand places and titles of honor, seeking to be
served rather than serve. They would have themselves exalted
at the expense of others. They are blind guides. Hypocrites.
Frauds.

You who shut up the kingdom of heaven in men's
faces, neither going in yourselves nor allowing others
to go in who want to [Matt. 23:13].

You who travel over sea and land to make a single proselyte, and when you have him you make him twice as fit for hell as you are [23:15].

They make gold, offerings, even the holy place of God more important than the offerer or the God offered to. Titles and tinsel are held to be more significant, than the "weightier matters of law—justice, mercy, good faith" (23:23). Straining out gnats and swallowing camels, they, as we continue to do, make mercy and justice less important than uniformity and ritual. Thus, the outside is clean and impressive, while the interior is "full of extortion and intemperance" (23:25). Whitened tombs, filled with dead bones and corruption within. Will the Pharisee in us resist being encountered by such words?

Christ's indictment is one final attempt at revelation in the name of all those whom he would gather to himself "as a hen gathers her chicks under her wings" (Matt. 23:38). "And you refused." It is our refusal which is our condemnation. Even in the case of hardened hearts, it is not that this loving God seeks to punish and be proved right. God's love remains—but in the midst of our refusal. God's forgiveness is continuously offered, but ignored. Thus condemnation cannot be escaped, because it is a condemnation which is gripped in the hardened heart itself. The all-powerful God, committed to covenant with human persons, cannot force us. God has been made willingly powerless and poor by allowing us to be free.

And so we bring our destructions upon ourselves. Closed to being loved and forgiven, we close ourselves to loving and forgiving. We bring the "end times" of tribulation and destructive self loss upon ourselves and one another. Wars, betrayal, deception, lovelessness and lawlessness become normative. False prophets, false saviors run rampant. Judgment will come: a self-imposed judgment upon humanity in the light of Humanity's Truth (Matt. 24). The facing up to our own humanity, to our radical contingency and incompleteness, to the fact that we are not God, cannot be postponed to some far-off distant hour. For it is only in the present, the now, that we live, and seek to find ourselves revealed: either in God and the fullness of human personhood, or in idolatry. We must be awake, for we do not know the hour. We cannot put off choosing. The hour is now. This is a spiritual reality. This is a communal reality. This is a socio-political reality.

In Matthew 22, Christ gave the greatest commandment of the Law, the commandment learned from his own traditions as a believing Jew:

> You must love the Lord your God with all your heart, with all your soul, and with all your mind. This is the greatest and first commandment. The second resembles it: You must love your neighbor as yourself. On these two commandments hang the whole Law, and the Prophets also [22: 37-40].

It is a stunning text, a request for wholeheartedness. God's is an invitation not to bargaining the wager, not to paltry oblation, not to earning a tyrant's pleasure or benediction, but to a gift of your self in love. The foundation of such a gift—and the condition of its possibility in the first place—is a gift of God to you; and thus the primacy is placed on the reciprocal law of *returned* love. But the second commandment is "like unto the first": loving your brothers and sisters as you love yourself. A most simple, and yet, paradoxically, difficult commandment. You do not fulfill the law or yourself by *just* loving God—or at least protesting that you do. And it is not sufficient to love yourself alone—as if that were even possible. But in the full realization of truly loving yourself, you love your neighbors; and doing just that resembles loving God. Yet it is also suggested that you cannot love your neighbor unless you love yourself; you must trust that the gift of yourself is even worthy of being and loving, if you are to risk giving it away. There is no final exclusion between self, others, and God. To love one is to love all. They are interpenetrating aspects of the same total act of self-donation. Again, our life in God is personal, is mutual, is social.

These supreme commandments are most dramatically fulfilled and explained in Chapter 25, when Christ is speaking of the Last Judgment. Here we find Jesus' own evaluative basis for what it means to be saved or lost as a human being. It is noteworthy here that when Christ is speaking of death, judgment, heaven, and hell—the "four last things," which have been and often still are important focuses of sermons and retreats—he does not base his judgment upon the criteria which many Christians have settled for. His is a strikingly different approach to "hell-fire" and "damnation."

> The virtuous will say to him in reply, "Lord, when did we see you hungry and feed you; or thirsty and give you drink? When did we see you a stranger and make you welcome; naked and clothe you; sick or in prison and go to see you?" And the King will answer: "I tell you solemnly, insofar as you did this to one of the least of these brothers of mine, you did it to me" [25:37-40].

Marx in his wildest dreams, humanists in their most articulate flights, secularists in their most vaunted claims, cannot approach the revolutionary, the humanistic reaches of this statement. Nowhere has humanity been more highly exalted. The *least* human person—the dregs, the poorest, the least attractive or productive, the least wanted, the most homely, unintelligent, or unappealing, the most neglected or forgotten human person, is identified with Jesus himself, identified with God himself. The identification is stronger than even that of our most important eucharistic texts. And recognizing the sacramental presence of Christ in the poor demands as much the eyes of faith, if not more, than seeing Christ's sacramental presence under the sign of bread.

Empirical observation, measurement, or description will not penetrate the appearance of bread to see the person of Christ. Nor will they yield the face of God in the eyes of the poor. What is exacted of us in both cases is committed faith and hope in the promise of God.

Thus, the last text before the Passion narrative is one that clearly delineates the conditions of salvation, the expression of faith, and the intimacy of God's presence in our lives. Note that it is not tithing, not sacrifice, not church-going, not even the most meticulous fidelity to sobriety, continence, or obedience, that Christ insists upon: it is our response to the least of human persons, to the poor, the sick, the old and abandoned, the hungry and thirsty, the naked, the imprisoned and unattended.

What strange gaps of history, conscience, and understanding, therefore, have been at work in us to trick us into calling world hunger a mere question of politics, not religion; into calling basic human equality and food-drink equity a phantasm of bleeding-heart liberals; into calling prison reform a plot of communists and muddle-headed professors; into calling the aid of refugees some mighty beneficence above and beyond duty or even human respectability; into calling the distribution of clothing and other of our earth's wealth unfashionably utopian.

It is the Christian, the church-going believer, who must face the words of Christ and then try to continue in conscience ignoring the poor, the dispossessed, the hungry, the imprisoned, and the homeless. For if Christians turn away from the "least of these" in the name of pragmatics, hardheaded realism, or, the worst blasphemy in the name of religion, they are turning away from none other than the Christ they profess to believe in. They are turning away from the greatest commandment. They are turning away from God. They are ultimately turning away from themselves. It is not so much that our compassionate God condemns us. We condemn ourselves—clinging now and eternally to the smallness of our logic and our fears, to a shriveled hope and self-consciousness defined by the lords of culture; to feasibility, affluence, and the commodity.

Thus, the greatest tragedy for Christians happens when they sell, ignore, or explain away the heart of their belief itself, of their very God, to the dictates of practicality, helplessness, self-defense, consumption, and marketability. Yet it is not as if the living of this truth has ceased to be. Perhaps the greatest benefactions of the churches is that they have provided the soil for continual witness to the actual values of Christ. The institutions of hospitals, leper colonies, old-age care, even education (though often lost in the massive dimensions of corporateness), have to some extent been testimony to the values of Christ. And often the greatest saints, declared or otherwise, have lived—sometimes often in opposition to established power—such a truth. Even today, Christ's witness and Christian testimony continue to move hearts, nudge wills, and compel minds into the direction of wholeheartedness, compassion, and service.

But the overwhelming fact is that the values of culture so often seem to take deeper hold, strike deeper root, on our everyday perception and self-expectation. The message of loving even the least human being has been lost in the din of commercialism, in the clamor of anti-communism and racism, in the fears of external aggression and the loss of our world predominance, in the panic of over-population, and in the cost-benefit analysis of how to deal with the old, the poor, the criminal, the unborn, the politically neutral.

THE CRUCIFIXION OF HUMANITY AND GOD

Such a fate, it seems to me, was not lost to the consciousness of Christ himself. In his own life he was victim of betrayal, conspiracy, denial, and failure—even by those who professed to love him and act in his name. At the foundation of this denial and betrayal is actually the turning away of men and women from themselves as well as from God.

Sin ultimately is the rejection of one's very personhood and purpose. It is only in this respect that Christ differed from other human persons and is fully one with God—so radically open and obedient to his humanity and to the covenantal unity with the Father that he is without sin. It is in his full acceptance of his human poverty and precariousness that he is the full revelation of God, because he is, in the utter emptiness of his abandonment and trust, utterly filled with God.

The word of God is something alive and active; it cuts like any double-edged sword but more finely; it can slip through the place where the soul is divided from the spirit, or joints from the marrow; it can judge the secret emotions and thoughts. No created thing can hide from him; everything is uncovered and open to the eyes of one to whom we must give account of ourselves.

Since in Jesus, the Son of God, we have the supreme high priest who has gone through to highest heaven, we must never let go of the faith that we have professed. For it is not as if we had a high priest who was incapable of feeling our weaknesses with us; but we have one who has been tempted in every way that we are, though he is without sin. Let us be confident, then, in approaching the throne of grace, that we shall have mercy from him and find grace when we are in need of help.

Every high priest has been taken out of mankind and is appointed to act for men in their relations with God, to offer gifts and sacrifices for sins; and so he can sympathize with those who are ignorant or uncertain because he too lives in the limitations of weakness . . . During his life on earth, he offered up prayer and entreaty, aloud and in silent tears, to the one who had the power to save him out of death, and he submitted so humbly that his prayer was heard. Although he was Son, he learnt to obey through suffering; but having been made perfect, he became for all who obey him the source of eternal salvation [Heb. 4:12-5:9].

The passion of Christ, the passion of his life and his death, is the passion of humanity—a standing face-to-face with our own poverty and fragility. Our frailty, the passing of friends, the erosions of time, the risks of commitment, the unfinished and insecure dimensions of faith, trust, and love, are so easily avoided by our clinging to the security and deadness of things, by the mechanics and magic of idolatry, and by the fantasy of escape. But such a flight from our poverty is a betrayal of the true power to which we are called. It is a denial of ourselves, a conspiracy against the source of our loveliness and our dignity. It is a flight from freedom into the slavery of secure sinfulness, of unredemptive death.

Jesus feels this temptation with his whole being. But rather than run from his humanity, with its pain and its promise, he abandons himself in faith to the promised covenant of the Father. His agony, his sorrow, his suffering, bring him to the brink of abandonment, to the darkness of radical insecurity and dependence upon God alone; to the precariousness of believing in himself, in humanity, and in God, of hoping without the certitude of logical necessity, of loving without the assurance of payment. But he yields at the depths of his humanity's darkness, in the face of Dachau and My Lai, of millions starved, of love and life refused, of hatred between brothers and sisters. God's revelation in Jesus is not a blessing from afar. It is a witness to the fact that our very God loved the prize of creation enough to be one with it, to embrace our tears and sighs, to feel our hungers and pains of unfinishedness, to drink the cup of our longings and unfulfilled desire.

Thus the Crucifixion. Not so much at the hands of the people's refusals or Pilate's crudity and indifference; not so much before the powers of Caesar and Mars; but at the hands of humanity itself—in the rejection of men and women who deny their very personhood; who, convinced of their worthlessness and submissive to idols, cannot conceive the possibility of their actually being freely loved in and through their poverty.

In every cultural or historical frame, Christians must face up to the crucified God. We must ask ourselves anew: What kind of God does this reveal? Can this God who is most frequently represented as a defenseless poor baby in a manger and as a defenseless man on a cross be a tyrant? Can God be possibly understood in terms of retribution, of punishment, of fear, force, threat? Can the Gospels which have God constantly telling us not to fear be a message of terror? Or have we transformed God into such travesties by the machinations of our own idols, when we bear faith to our children and the rest of the world? Can this be the God of fright and tricksterism that we have so often entertained? Or has it been the gospel of the world, of slavery, of the Thing, and of Death which has contaminated our very understanding of the Lord? If we do not face and answer these questions, individually and corporately, we stand in danger of denying the crucifixion.

We also deny the crucified God if we ignore the invitation of Love's cross to us. Quite straightforwardly, can it really be construed that Christ on the cross would institute Inquisitions, Crusades, forced conversions, racism, the blessing of tanks, and "killing a commie for Christ"? Are we called to follow him, or the received wisdom of our culture? Is it he, or is it our "civil religion" that reveals what we might be as humans, indeed as Christians? Or is he a harmless image that conspires with the powers of darkness, convincing us of our lack of worth, our loss of compassion, and our impotence as persons? "Who do you say that I am?" he addresses to each of us. This is a gentle God, a God who would wipe away every human tear, who would rather suffer the terrors of created freedom than leave us bereft of our highest destiny.

A final way that we deny this crucified God is by insisting that we save ourselves. Christianity is a belief about what God does in and for humanity, not about what Christians do for God.

> We were still helpless when at his appointed moment Christ died for sinful men. It is not easy to die even for a good man—though of course for someone really worthy, a man might be prepared to die—but what proves that God loves us is that Christ died for us while we were still sinners [Rom. 5:6-9].

The spirit too comes to help us in our weakness. For when we cannot choose words in order to pray properly, the spirit himself expresses our plea in a way that could never be put into words, and God who knows everything in our hearts knows perfectly well what he means [Rom. 8:26-27].

We are only the earthenware jars that hold this treasure to make it clear that such an overwhelming power comes from God and not from us [2 Cor. 4:7-8].

He has said: "My grace is enough for you; my power is at its best in weakness," . . . For it is when I am weak that I am strong [2 Cor. 12:9-10].

I have been crucified with Christ, and I live now not with my own life but with the life of Christ who lives in me [Gal. 2:19].

As for me, the only thing I can boast about is the cross of our Lord Jesus Christ, through whom the world is crucified to me, and I to the world [Gal. 6:14].

It is by grace that you have been saved, through faith; not by anything of your own, but by a gift from God; not by anything that you have done, so that nobody can claim the credit. We are God's work of art, created in Christ Jesus to live the good life as from the beginning he had meant us to live it [Eph. 2:8-10].

Here is a saying that you can rely on and nobody should doubt; that Christ Jesus came into the world to save sinners [1 Tim. 1:15].

. . . Relying on the power of God who has saved us and called us to be holy—not because of anything we ourselves have done but for his own purpose and by his own grace [2 Tim. 1:9].

This is the love I mean: not our love for God, but
God's love for us when he sent his son [1 John 4:10].

And so, again and again, it is no shame to be a frail and contingent human being. In fact, it is priceless to be so. It is, necessarily, to be loved into existence.

Denying our sinfulness as church and Christians, insisting
upon our success, our power and pomp, our greatness, as the
proof of our being saved, we reject the cross as well as God's
love made manifest in Jesus Christ who died for and with us.
Earning salvation, winning salvation, proving that we are
good, competing for salvation, marketing salvation, selling
salvation, guaranteeing salvation, are not only common expressions of the commodified gospel. They are rejections of
the Gospel of Jesus. If I honestly ask, "Where is my security,
whom or what do I trust and believe in?" And I reply, "Jesus
Christ, in whom the inseparable love of God is revealed"—I
must then fully face the implications of believing in him and
his gospel.

The agony and the death of Christ is the agony and the
death of God, if we are to believe that Jesus is true God. It is
as if God, beyond all human imagination, when deciding to
create men and women capable of rejecting themselves and
life itself, when deciding to give them the capacity to love, also
decided to die. God would be a suffering God. In God's desire
that we freely relate to creation and love, God was delivered
into our hands. Thus, Christ's abandonment is the abandonment of God on behalf of the beloved. Not only would God
love us; God would choose to trust and have faith in us—
surely not in terms of God's very being, yet nonetheless surely
with respect to us as the created expression of infinite love.
God entrusts life and truth to us by making us free. God suffers the dying within our love which will not subjugate the
beloved, but which will enable us to reach the ecstasy of highest joy: free reciprocation. The agony and death of God is not
confined to Gethsemane and Golgotha; it is the measure of
creation itself.

Christ undergoes the suffering and death of humanity—not so much or merely by identifying with the millions untimely taken, or the numberless starving and abandoned, but most crucially by fully embracing and being faithful to his human freedom. It is almost as if our God may have expected something too great of us in desiring that we be free, something too difficult and high. We cannot face the dying to ourselves that love or trust or faith would elicit. Better to pursue the securities of idols. Better to seek the unfeeling deadness of things than the mysterious dying to our smallness in a free gift of ourselves. Better to possess the cold but sure completion of machinery than to say "Yes" to the promise of a person.

And yet in Christ, both God and humanity yield to love. God suffers the risk of infidelity and love's rejection. Jesus suffers the insecurity of Truth itself; the acceptance of his humanity and his fidelity—even in darkness and incompletion—to the covenantal longing of his heart. And it is to the Fashioner of that covenant, to the One who beckons him in his deepest desires, that Christ yields and commends his spirit. In acknowledging his weakness, he finally reveals his greatest strength—the life of God living in his precarious faith, hope, and love.

Our yielding, our commending, our entrusting of ourselves to the living covenantal God, is the rebirth of our truest selves out of sin and death. Trusting in our God made manifest in one of us, we can finally hear the words of the Reborn when he says "Fear not," when he gives us the power to forgive, when he unveils our true history and promise on our way to Emmaus, when he makes the greatest of believers out of Thomases, the greatest of lovers out of Magdalens, the greatest of leaders out of Simons. We "refind" ourselves, not as mini-gods scrambling for the thrones of power and dominance, but as God-like brothers and sisters in a community of unfinished free beings called to the mystery of fullness. We discover who we truly are not by overcoming others, but by serving them.

CHAPTER NINE

CHRIST AND THE IDOLS
OF CAPITALISM

THE REVELATION OF THE PERSONAL FORM
IN JESUS

We have reflected upon one account of Jesus' life and revelation. Such an inspection was necessarily selective and partial, concentrating for the most part on the Gospel of
Matthew and a few texts of Saint Paul. But we could have just
as easily concentrated on the writings of the School of John,
with its emphasis upon the Christian's stance in opposition to
the darkness and unfreedom of the world. The ways of violence, deception, and slavery belong to a kingdom intractably
alien to a life of suffering love and self-donation. The Gospels
of Luke and Mark, as well as the early letters of Paul, also
yield an integral portrayal of Christ and the Christian life
standing in striking opposition to what we have called the
Commodity Form.

I examined Matthew not so much as a mustering of proof
texts as an attempt to be present to the broad and recurring
lines of revelation. I tried to avoid both excessive literalism
and the metaphorizing-away of the unavoidable challenge. In
this way I hoped to show how an ordinary person asking the

119

questions "How is God revealed?" and "How is humanity revealed?" and "How am I revealed?" will at every turn find the
God who elevates and exalts human personhood.

It will now be worthwhile to review the revelation of
Jesus at a higher altitude, reflecting more theoretically upon a
general understanding of Christian anthropology, and then
showing how such a view of human life and purpose contrasts
to the view of the human person found in our own cultural
anthropology.

As I have suggested earlier, in a philosophical view of our
human nature the most that we seem able to do of ourselves—
if we do not embrace domination, appropriation, or escape—
is hold out our hands and our lives to the unconditional answer of our being's question. To be a human person is to call
out for a response, a revelation of our fullest mystery and purpose as capable of knowing and being known, of loving and
being loved. In the scripture of the Jewish Bible the Mystery
of human fullness reveals itself as the covenantal Lord of the
universe in whose image the human person is formed. Each of
us is called into free covenant, to interior fidelity, and to a
risk-laden life of trust in that Lord and in ourselves as our
Lord's handiwork.

In the Christian faith, Jesus Christ is the full and definitive
revelation of God to humanity, for he is the point where God
and humanity coalesce. Revelation in Christ, consequently, is
not merely the unfolding and making-known of what it means
to be God; it is at the same time the full revelation of what it
means to be a human being. Jesus Christ reveals not only the
divinity to human persons; he reveals humanity to itself. He
himself embodies the delicate interpenetration of human contingency and full Godlikeness. And in revealing both, he re-
deems the broken passion of created freedom.

When the Godhead is revealed historically in Jesus, we are
witnessing a divine insistence upon the free response of the
human person. It is a benediction upon humanity and personal freedom. God, in becoming one with humankind, does
not manipulate, force, or dominate us by power or munifi-

cence. Quite to the contrary, in becoming fully human, God invites persons into a freely entered covenantal relationship through Jesus and their own humanness. It is in this act of invitation, this act which calls forth a freely given trust and fidelity from persons, that God makes the fullest revelation of divinity and of human dignity.

Consequently, Jesus Christ, the enlightenment of humanity, is God's self-giving response to the calling-out of the created universe, now made aware of itself in human persons. God does not stop and complete human personhood in such a way that the participatory freedom of men and women in their own destiny may be extinguished. Rather, God's revelation in Jesus is a beckoning to me to accept my contingency and to transform the question of my being into freely uttered exclamation: I freely believe! I freely trust! I freely give! These are exclamations whereby men and women realize themselves in their relationship to each other and in relation to God. For just as the revelation of God and humanity is realized in the one Jesus Christ, men and women are realized in the one dynamic of believing, trusting, and loving one another, themselves, and God. Herein lies our utter uniqueness as individuals and our irreplaceability as free covenanting beings.

To believe or trust in one's self, to believe in another person, and to believe in the personal God, are analogous activities—just as the two great commandments of love are alike. Each is difficult. Each makes us face how precarious our existence is. Each has its nights of darkness, misunderstanding, and sense of absence. Each involves an unfolding and risking in the donation of persons. Each demands a vulnerability, even a dying to ourselves, in the admission that we are not our own ultimate center, validation, or purpose. Each act brings us out of our smallness and limits, our historical and special confinement, into the fourth-dimensional world of personhood. For what we have revealed in Christ is that faith, hope, and love are the very life of our God, communicated to and living in contingent human reality. Faith, hope, and love are the divine calling-forth of freedom from men and women.

They are the patient, persistent eliciting from human persons of the irreplaceable basis of their dignity: their capacity for free covenant. They are the exclamations of consent to their human poverty and authentic strength.

The model for these existential exclamations is Jesus Christ, who reveals the fullness of the human person not in domination or escape, but in a yielding to one's own humanity and a breaking out of encapsulation into intimacy with the other. *Human knowing* is revealed not as manipulation, control, and mere external observation, but as the medium of full experiential participation in the mystery of one's humanness and an openness to the other. And the affective drive to do something—*human willing*—is revealed not as appropriation and competition, but as the inherent human exigency to give one's self away in love, in service, and in the joys of covenant.

Jesus did not flee from the tragic dimensions of human existence. He lived in the limitations of our weakness, as Paul says, offering up "prayer and entreaty, aloud and in silent tears," being tempted in every way that we are. Thus he did not flee the transcending passions of our life and longing; nor did he flee from the face of death, so harrowing to our frailty and desired security. Rather, he embraced both, in embracing his humanity, and he entrusted both his life and his death to a loving, absolute God beyond all human fragility.

The Incarnation, as well as the entire life of Christ, is a testimony received in faith that we are redeemed by a God-made-vulnerable in loving creation, and that we are fulfilled only in our irreplaceably unique self-donation. "Man only is," Karl Rahner has said, "when he gives himself away." It is the very poverty of our humanity, our precarious contingency and unfinishedness, our openness, our frail capacity for the risks of living and loving, that is our strength and beauty. It is precisely this poverty, so terrifying and at the same time so lovely, which Christ so whole-heartedly yields to.

The revelation of God in Jesus is the developmental unmasking not of a terrible God, but of a God who would "wipe away every human tear," of a God who is radically personal and communal in knowledge, love, and free creation. God would have us "fear not." God is within and beyond us, calling us to ourselves, but only on the condition of freely entered covenantal life. God is, consequently, Absolute Being—or better, Absolute Personhood—in whom we partake by the exercise of our personhood, to whom we are beckoned by the exigencies of our being human.

Such are the foundations of the Personal Form, through which men and women are revealed as irreplaceably free persons. Seen from this more general altitude, and complemented by our reflection upon the scriptural revelation in Matthew, the Personal Form can now be placed in greater contrast with the Commodity Form and the choice of a god and human revelation found therein.

THE CHOICE OF GODS AND GOSPELS

What is the nature of the fundamental choice that people make in our country? The choice, under different forms, is ever present to us—and it is made willy-nilly. There must be a bottom line to the lives of each of us. We are all driven to ask: "Where finally is the truth?" Humans will seek out and demand a god or gospel no matter what. The question is: What god or gospel is worthy of humans?

Earlier we have seen how in our own culture the Commodity Form of consciousness makes claims upon our final allegiance, how it penetrates our self-perception, our values, our hopes, and our purpose. We can now see more clearly how the characteristics of the Commodity Form stand in relation to human reality and to the revelation of the Personal Form in Jesus Christ. Experiencing ourselves as incomplete and open freedoms, we often seek completion in thinghood and the commodity. They are idols to which we offer our freedom and personhood in exchange for the spurious securities of domination, appropriation, and escape. In the process, the most precarious aspects of human life are compressed into objectness. And thus our subjectivity, which exercises itself most fully in commitment, faith, hope, and love, is lost. With the evaporation of human risk, we experience the evanescence of freedom. The terrors of incompletion are denied, but in the denial our very selves are lost. And yet the pain remains, because no thing can ever deliver on its promises to frustrated personhood.

Christ would have us penetrate to the depths of our human personhood. He calls us to embrace and affirm our incompletion in acts of believing, trusting, and caring for ourselves, for each other, and for the God beyond us who completes us only in our freely given covenant. Our incompletion is indeed our poverty, but it is only in touching and living at the edge of this poverty that we may reach the fullness of our true power and destiny. Thus defenses against that poverty must be broken down.

THE COMMODITY FORM	THE PERSONAL FORM
Value Grounded in Thinghood	*Value Grounded in Personhood*
Marketability of the person	Intrinsic value of persons
Production: worth as what you do	Worth as who you are
Consumption	Self-gift
Thing-Knowledge	*Personal-Knowledge*
Observation and description	Faith: self-consciousness and interiority
Measurement and control	Understanding and trust
Quality as quantity	Human quality as non-measurable
Emphasis on derived knowledge	Immediate experience
How-questions	Why-questions

THE COMMODITY FORM	THE PERSONAL FORM
Thing-Willing	*Personal-Willing*
Determinism	Limited freedom
Escape	Self-investment
Non-commitment	Covenant
Passivity	Engagement
Deadness	Aliveness
Thing-Behavior	*Person-Behavior*
Violence:	Peace:
Domination	Acceptance of weakness
Manipulation	Respect of freedom
Retaliation	Forgiveness
Punishment	Healing
Defense	Defenselessness
Devaluation of life	Exaltation of least person
Demand	Invitation
Competition	Sharing
Retention	Giving
Thing-Like Affectivity	*Personal Affectivity*
Sexuality as mechanics	Sexuality as sign of person
Body as machine	Body as temple— sacral presence
Fear/threat	Fear not
Non-commitment	Covenant—committed devotedness
Retention of self	Self-donation
Technique	Telos
Externality	Interiority
Replaceability	Uniqueness
Coolness	Tenderness
Hardness	Compassion

THE COMMODITY FORM	THE PERSONAL FORM
Thing-Like Affectivity	***Personal Affectivity***
Accumulation	Detachment
Invulnerability	Vulnerability
Exchange	Prodigal love
Hedonism: immediate self-gratification	Generosity: suffering love
Thing-Reality	***Person-Reality***
Having	Being
What is	What we can be
Human skepticism	Faith and fidelity
Human paralysis and doubt	Hope and trust
Individual isolation	Love
Unfreedom as final condition	Freedom as final condition
Death	Life
Thing-Life	***Person-Life***
Flight from the self	Recovery in solitude
Fragmented relationship	Rediscovered community
Addiction to things	Simplicity of life
Degradation of persons	Commitment to justice
Fear of the vulnerable	Open to the wounded

The Gospel sets before us the values and vision whereby such poverty can be lived and felt. They are values inalterably opposed to the values of the Commodity Form and its insistence upon our self-validating securities. They are linked, moreover, to specific models of human knowing, human willing, and human behavior, just as the values of the Commodity Form are linked to thing-knowledge, thing-willing, and thing-behavior. At each stage, we find the values of the Commodity Form and Christ in opposition. And underneath all opposition is the fundamental choice: men and women are either revealed as things or revealed as persons. They are either secure but dead, or insecure but living and free.

I have tried to show how values, behavior, self-consciousness, and reality-perception are interwoven into entire fabrics. The Commodity Form and the Personal Form stand in opposition to each other on every level. They solicit from men and women, whether they are conscious of it or not, a final and totalized allegiance. Each presents itself as the ultimate explanatory principle, as the revelation of what we are and can be. Consequently, what we must do is first *face* this choice, consciously, and know that we are dealing with an option concerning what god to believe in.

In our culture, if we aspire to live in the Personal Form, especially as revealed in Christianity, we have to realize how the cultural gospel is not only an alternative to the Gospel of Jesus, but also a metaphysics of humanity, a philosophical worldview. As a worldview, as a theory of human realization, the cultural gospel perverts the fundamental exigencies of human identity into a denial of humanness and a denial of God. It offers a practically lived atheism and antihumanism, insofar as it is an embodiment of the most fundamental of human sins: idolatry.

The power of this idolatry, of our original sinfulness, lies in its underlying rejection of our creaturehood, of our precarious created freedom. At the same time, it perverts the core of our identities as knowing and loving beings. To set up a god for ourselves more secure and less demanding than a God who would have us free and responsible, to set up a god-on-our-own-terms, a god who would fashion us not free but enslaved, is at the same time an act of self-alienation, a disenfranchisement of ourselves and of our true identities, and a rejection of love. It perverts our potentialities for knowing and loving into their opposites, and fragments our human community into an aggregate of isolated mini-divinities who claim to be the cause, source, and finality of being.

The Commodity Form, which serves as an undertow toward thingification, also channels our self-consciousness, valu-

ing, and interpersonal behavior in the direction of dominance
and self-aggrandizement. We are drawn into conflict among
ourselves, and are led to believe that we will fulfill our insatiable longing for completion and self-realization on our own.
If we can just collect enough, produce enough, or win enough,
we will be god. We will have gotten rid of our painful incompletion. The paradox is that, as in every idolatry, we eventually entrap ourselves after the image and likeness of the idol—
the thing we have created and trusted—the commodity:
replaceable and obsolete, only quantifiably valuable, and
bereft of freedom or qualitative growth. Thus the law of sin is
indeed death. It is the death of our selves.

The Personal Form also beckons us to be godlike, but by
reaching down into the full meaning of our incompletion, not
by running from it. Incompletion is one with being on-the-
way, with being in process, with being a created freedom. It is
one with temporal loving and choosing. It is one with the created project of collaborating in our own realization, not by
self-aggrandizement and violence, but by yielding to who and
what we are: free beings longing for the unconditional mystery of love.

Such "divinization" is effected only in freedom—in freely
loving, believing, and trusting, in giving ourselves away and
thereby finding ourselves. It is on this level that we discover
and accept our destiny as being created in the image and likeness of a covenantal and freely creating God. The denial of
our destiny as persons in this culture is nothing other than an
ontological lie. The Commodity Form is the form of untruth,
the sacred canopy of human obscurity and darkness, concealing us from ourselves and perpetuating our self-alienation. It
is culturally legitimated pretense.

Perhaps now we can see that the Commodity Form and
the Personal Form are at odds at their very foundations, as
well as in the particularized opposition of the specific values
we listed earlier. It should not come as a surprise that a follower of Jesus might find himself or herself to be an outsider
in a culture dominated by the commodity. It should be no

shame to feel different, even to feel a bit disjointed and out of place, in a civilization which divinizes the thing.

A Christian's values, if they have not been fully acculturated, are bound to be different. If we do not feel different, even embarrassingly different, something is wrong. Madison Avenue-land, television, rock radio, advertising, will trigger constant reminders of our almost displaced existence. We will feel like strangers. The facts that life is cheapened, that retaliation and competition are conceived as ultimates, that familial consent and commitment seem alien, that armament and defense are so universally accepted, that fidelity in marriage seems strange—are thus not so dumbfounding as they might first appear.

I have heard Christian couples ask quizzically if *they* were the "weird" ones, so little does anything in this culture seem to agree with their deepest beliefs. They should not be distraught. They have merely come into contact with their faith as a lived, historical option. They have discovered that atheistic communism is not the greatest or only threat to their belief. It is lived atheism—whether capitalistic or communistic—which assaults their faith. And they have finally discovered the closeness of the danger—not in some different land, but in their own culture and its idolatrous belief system.

Such people, however, are not alone. Once having discovered the true issue of their lives, they will find out that there are countless other men and women who have made the same discovery. They will find that they can enter into communities of people who try to sustain their belief and aspirations in opposition to a powerful cultural gospel, people who attempt to come to grips with a culture they may in many ways love and desire to live within, but never ultimately succumb to. They will also discover how in their own belief as Christians they have a corporate life, a web of traditions, and a living basis of community that can support them in their choice for the Gospel of Christ. It is this dimension which I will now investigate.

In doing so, I would like to mention again that I do not consider Catholic Christianity, or even Christianity, the only source of resistance to the Commodity Form. Too often Catholics and other Christians collaborate and compromise, rendering not only taxes but fidelity and conscience to Caesar. Too often I experience how the values and dogmas of the Commodity Form insinuate themselves into my own self-understanding and evaluation of persons. I am too aware of my own collaboration to deny the corporate collaboration of our churches.

Yet, the Catholic tradition and faith is the one which I know most intimately and which has both sustained and challenged me. I judge it to be the truest and most fruitful way to live in resistance to a commodified culture. Otherwise I would not attempt to live its faith or invite others to it. At the same time, I do not consider it to be the *sine qua non* of Truth itself.

I am convinced that if Christians, Jews, and Humanists penetrate to the depth of their commitments, longings, and beliefs, if they enter that depth with a painful honesty and an integrity open to the fullest mystery of their human personhood, they will find themselves, at the bottom of those depths, indelibly and eternally brothers and sisters.

CHAPTER TEN

LIVED CHRISTIANITY
IN AN IDOLATROUS CULTURE

If the revelation of Jesus Christ is an unequivocal testimony to the divine possibilities of men and women as open to mystery, to self-gift, and to covenant with God and other persons, then the spiritual community which bears his name could be expected to extend and embody that testimony of his life, death, and resurrection. Christ is God's response to humanity's calling out, an invitation to our fullest possibilities, a calling back to our essential vocation. Just as Christ's revelation to us was in terms of continuity and identification with the human family's truest identity, so also the presence of Christianity to culture must be one of such identification and invitation. The revelation of God is, in its deepest sense, the revelation of humanity. This should also be the foundational characteristic of those persons and communities who wish to embody such revelation in history.

Consequently, Christianity is at its heart a service of humanity and human fulfillment. As a historical and human reality, Christianity lives in and through cultures and is sustained by culture. To the extent, however, that a Christian church aligns itself with the pathological cultural values of appropriation and domination, it stands in need of self-purification from

131

within—self-purification in the name of the very values it professes to believe in. A church can be unfaithful to itself and to the truth that it carries within it; it is not exempt from idolatry or sin. The Book of Revelation makes this quite clear in addressing some of the early Christian communities:

> Write to the angel of the church in Ephesus and say, ". . . I know all about you: how hard you work and how much you put up with . . . Nevertheless, I have this complaint to make: you have less love now than you used to."
>
> Write to the angel of the church in Smyrna and say, "Here is the message of the First and Last: trials you have had and how poor you are—though you are rich . . . Do not be afraid of the sufferings that are coming to you. Even if you have to die, keep faithful, and I will give you the crown of life for your prize."
>
> Write to the angel of the church in Sardis and say, ". . . I know all about you: how you are reputed to be alive and yet are dead. Wake up; revive what little you have left; it is dying fast!"
>
> Write to the angel of the church in Philadelphia and say, "Here is the message of the holy and faithful one . . . I know that though you are not very strong, you have kept my commandments and not disowned my name . . . Because you have kept my commandment to endure trials, I will keep you safe in time of trial . . . Soon I shall be with you. Hold firmly to what you already have, and let nobody take your prize away from you . . ."
>
> Write to the angel of the church in Laodicea and say, "Here is the message of the Amen, the faithful, the true witness, the ultimate source of God's creation; I know all about you; how you are neither cold nor hot. I wish you were one or the other, but since

you are neither, but only lukewarm, I will spit you out of my mouth. You say to yourself, 'I am rich, I have made a fortune, and have everything I want,' never realizing that you are wretchedly and pitiably poor, and blind and naked too . . . Look, I am standing at the door, knocking. If anyone of you hears me calling and opens the door, I will come in to share his meal, side by side with him . . . If anyone has ears to hear, let him listen to what the Spirit is saying to the churches" [Rev. 2:1-3:22 passim].

I have used such a long citation because it is crucial at this point to recognize the ways in which a church can be idolatrous, enslaved, and unfaithful to its very calling. Thus our reflections here cannot be interpreted as a justification or legitimation of all the practices in the Christian churches. In fact, the evidence is ample and clear that many in the name of Christ have not preached his revelation but have prevented it.

One of the factors in such a deviation from a church's witness may well be the conflict between what has been called the "natural institution" and the "sect" models of Christian life. If Christianity is conceived as a natural institution, immersed in world and culture, its visibility and power in communicating Christ's message are enhanced; but there is the danger that in becoming "natural," acculturated, or secular, the actual message is itself distorted. In the sect model, the Christian community is not seen as a natural institution, and the purity of Christ's revelation is insisted upon; however, the sect has less social power, less influence in communication, and it is easily ignored or lost in the huge dimensions of other cultural institutions. The problem, then, is how to maintain one's identity while at the same time immersing oneself in the world by living in and through a culture. Some observations may be helpful in illustrating how internal infidelity can be faced and purified.

AGAINST THE IDOLS WITHIN

1. Self-Critique: Christianity is composed of social and cultural embodiments which are perspectival, incomplete, and unfinished. As a historical embodiment it consequently has the potential to become idolatrous or ideological and thus unfaithful to its vocation. It can become committed more to its own self-justified "sinlessness" and power than to the service of men and women and itself as loved sinners. Thus, the church has often read the Hebrew Scripture's prophets as a critique of Judaism or the world around, but not as a possible indictment of its own tendencies to idolatry and enslavement and oppression. In such a way it sets itself up beyond criticism and self-reflection in terms of its own values and scripture.

More dangerously, a church can become so acculturated and powerful as a natural institution that it finds itself in bondage to its own historicity. Thus we have seen painful and perverse identifications with the Holy Roman Empire, the Crusades, the Inquisition, the National Folk religion of the Third Reich, the aristocratic tendencies in Latin American Catholicism, and the co-option of "middle class" Christianity in the United States so often identifying God with country or even with free enterprise. In all these cases, the particular cultural milieu in which the Christian life is to be preached becomes the center and foundation of belief, rather than the life of Christ himself becoming that center and foundation. As a result, the church serves as a powerful source of cultural legitimation. It is identified with the interests of the culture and its most powerful institutions. As such, it can easily collaborate in the enslavement of men and women rather than in their liberation.

For example, the criteria of success which we found in the "American Fairy Tale" of production and consumption frequently appear in our culture as the measures of faith and religiosity. Achievement and wealth become endowed with redemptive, even salvific, power. Poverty and marginality, which should serve as signals of grace, are inevitably interpreted as the just deserts of "those lazy people who cannot take care of themselves." Thus the substantive teachings of Christ concerning justice, compassion, and generosity lose their clarity and power in a web of slickly spiritualized, but still racist and class-oriented, marketed myth.

Nonetheless, due to the very nature of faith, with its whole meaning rooted in a recognition of one's own poverty, Christianity has a perduring intrinsic basis for self-critique— of its own historical perspective, of its cultural embodiment, of its ideologizing, of its members. Faith must be lived or it is not real. It is the primary labor or "work" of the Christian, the Gospel of John says, to believe that we are the beneficiaries of a loving, unmerited redemptive act. The testing out of this faith is precisely whether it bears "fruit"—love of others, compassion, and equity. Thus, the only way to suppress the true Christian's sense of justice and compassion is to repress the very content of the Christian's faith.

It is true that at times such a repression may have been partially achieved, but never fully or else lived Christianity would have disappeared, there no longer being any fruit borne. But such fruit has always been borne—in individuals, in movements, in reforms, in mendicants, in men and women who have lived only to serve.

The impulse for self-critique and reform is felt by any believer who, conscious of his or her massive capacity for pretense, stands encountered by the Scripture. It is experienced by any Christian who has felt the distaste of being preached to about poverty and humility in the midst of power and pride, by any priest who has called his people to a life which he himself is too fearful or reluctant to live. It is exhibited in the endless questioning of children who feel the inconsistencies of our lives, and in the soaring feeling of adolescents who discover the Sermon on the Mount for the first time. The Gospel of Christ will always be ineffectually preached to any unjust social system if it does not first confront the church itself, and if, indeed, it is not a judgment and challenge for the individual believer.

2. *Interiority and Action:* The Christian faith is communicated by a witness and invitation which are encountered only through personal interaction and lived experience. Liberation, most fundamentally, is not a political, economic, or sociological phenomenon. It can be found—or accepted—only when we are made present to ourselves and our possibilities, only when we are in touch with our deepest humanity. Faith is not limited to class, not inaccessible to the poorest or the richest (although, as we have seen, it is more difficult to discover faith if we have entrusted ourselves to a spurious wealth covering up our interior and ontological poverty). At the same time we must recognize that liberation and faith are events that happen only in time, and as such are nourished or inhibited by certain kinds of economic, political, and social structures. Consequently, Christian action reaches out and extends itself to the environmental conditions of the culture—for there is no private realm which is not somehow touched and influenced by the public realm.

Social action is not the preserve of some special-interest group. It is an imperative of faith. This is true not only because of the content of the New Testament and the nature of the vocation to which Christ calls men and women; it is also true because there are social conditions which minimize the very possibility of experiencing love, hope, and faith. Destitution, degrading prisons, world hunger, and armament are affairs of spirituality. The human spirit is at stake, not "just" the human body.

Material poverty, as well as the addictions to consuming, accumulating, and winning, make the gospel difficult to speak and painful to hear. Thus, organized deliberations and resistance must be entertained, planned legislative change undertaken, and collaborative social service enacted by Christians themselves. The relationship of parts to totality holds. When a Christian couple works for peace, for food distribution, for legislative controls on advertising, they are enhancing the lived faith and joy of their children. When the same couple practices justice, fidelity, and compassion with each other and to their children, they are bringing about a change in their society.

3. *Moral Consistency:* In a given culture, there are many "language value-systems" and methodologies that can be used in the communication of a liberating faith. In a cultural ideology, however, the methods and languages become extremely restricted if a Christian is to retain any integrity in offering the Gospel of Christ to others. The most blatant examples have been to use the power and fear tactics of a totalitarian state to make "conversions," or to torture people into conversion.

In American culture, the conflicts are far less blatant, even though they are significant. As we have seen, many of our socially accepted moral values and methods of action are founded upon a worldview and philosophy of the human person that is both antihuman and, *a fortiori*, anti-Christian. Principles of Christian activism, consequently, cannot embrace moral "language" or techniques which intrinsically violate the content of faith itself. Manipulation and deception, the Madison Avenue approach to religion, uses of dominance and intimidation, the appeal to violence are all language methodologies which violate the content of Christian faith, whether they are practiced by a corporation, a revolutionary, a striker, or the pastor of a parish.

I have seen university students recoil from an "absolute Christian pacifist" who professed that he would kill Melvin Laird if he thought that that action would end the war in Vietnam. I have read Catholic "letters to the editor" in which convicts (like Gary Gilmore before his execution by the state of Utah) were described as vermin and beasts to be "wiped out." If Christians are going to be selective in their application of gospel values (e.g., we can facilely articulate "just war" theories in which thousands of innocents will be killed, but we cannot tolerate anyone who might speak of a "just abortion"), they will have to articulate honestly the distinctions which enable them to approve certain forms of murder and not others.

Perhaps this inconsistency was most incisively pointed out by Father Guadalupe Carney, a Catholic missionary in Honduras, who was asked to leave the Jesuits if he remained a chaplain to the People's Revolutionary Army there. During the last retreat he would make as a Jesuit, just months before he would be killed by the Honduran army, he relentlessly challenged my own pacifism and the "double standards" of Christians and their religious communities. "Why is it that we allow and praise chaplains for big armies, chaplains for the Pentagon, chaplains who are paid thousands of dollars a year and live in great prestige and comfort, but we will not allow a chaplain for a poor army trying to defend its peasant people?"

He chose to work with his poor: baptizing them, regularizing their marriages, offering them Eucharist and Reconciliation, until he would die with them. But we remain, ambivalently, with his question unanswered.

A second compelling example of the problem of inconsistency has been the way that Catholics have responded to the life and words of Pope John Paul II. Invariably, throughout the years of his pontificate, one would find a resistance to the integrated vision of his message. In my own journeys to Europe or Africa, Australia or Central America, I would find "liberal" or "conservative" Catholics responding in a fixed pattern. The liberal group would love what the pope had to say about social justice and capitalism, but hate what he would have to say about human sexuality and spirituality. The right wing group would celebrate his documents on sexuality and sacrament— and totally ignore or explain away everything he had to say on economics, the poor, capitalism, or warfare.

Wholehearted consistency has often been lacking in the past, and it has made Christian witness ineffective and seemingly dishonest. It is a strange contradiction to condemn the values of materialism and at the same time to measure a church member's love for God in terms of the money he or she contributes to the building of a church. These are all examples of the selective moralizing which has made Christian preaching seem deceitful and meaningless within the churches themselves.

4. *Unity in Diverse Expression:* It will be important to develop a viable philosophy of Christian action. Human activi-

ties, because they are placed in space and time, are necessarily partial, perspectival, and incomplete. Consequently they are intrinsically ambiguous in some way, somehow conditioned and limited. To accept ambiguity, to realize that the full range of Christ's revelation cannot be expressed in its entirety through historically conditioned action, is not a justification for compromise with death, aggression, or idolatry. Rather it is an admission of the human inadequacy of being in one space and time. No one of us can do all things, nor can all of us do the same things. What is needed, as a result, is a tolerance for the diversity of Christian actions, which unify and intersect in a common faith and longing but which ramify into a variety of methodologies and styles.

Opposition to armament or to abortion can be exercised in a legislature, in tax-resistance, in journalism, in jail, or in the pulpit. Resistance to racism or injustice can be practiced on a picket-line, in a classroom, through a newspaper, or within the intimacy of a home. The unity of the vision and faith is more important than the diversity of expressions. The interpenetration of diverse Christian approaches complements the singular incompleteness of each one. Unification of specific actions in a greater totality prevents the reduction of the partial methods into the culture as a totalizing ideology. It also prevents any one method, style, or action from assuming the role of *sine qua non* in Christian life and faith. At its doctrinal basis, Christianity is a religion of embodiment and incarnation. It must remain so in the realm of action as well. Some Christian radicals may live and talk as if they were somehow separated from their cultural ambient in some pure "ahistorical" state. But such is not the case in reality, nor is it desirable in terms of the very principle they profess. For their principle is a Person, a covenantal God embodied historically and culturally and communicated through the limitations of language and temporality.

5. *Freedom and Structure:* The tendency to ever-intensified "pure" positions of Christian witness may be linked to the fol-

lowing phenomenon. On the part of many, the recognition of the pathological condition of social systems has led to an obsessive reaction to external structures, to the past, and to all institutional value-frames. For the most part, the disaffected have sought refuge either in the negation of all structure and values (historical embodiment) through utopianism, or in a flight from all structure through a noncommittal and debilitating tentativeness. Both alternatives seem naive and ineffective. The organic and evolutionary nature of change and growth is ignored in favor of anarchic structurelessness and an ahistorical romanticizing of revolution. Moreover, the mere polarization of forces, without a complement of understanding and love, cannot ever bring about the quantum leap into human realization. All the revolutionary inversions and permutations of the Commodity Form together cannot yield the Personal Form. Forms of perception and valuing can be apprehended only in terms of our own human historicity and its limits.

The second alternative—that of flight—is symptomatic of a hopelessness and a cynicism which emerge from our fear of "being burned" by fires of rapid change. In the actions of commitment, taking a moral stand or making life promises, structure is avoided because life is seen as too unsure and limits too confining. Young persons often talk of losing their "freedom" when they commit themselves to the structure of marriage. In actuality, they are operating out of a concept of freedom which makes any choice—self-limitation in history—impossible. You cannot choose without embracing structure. To insist on no structure is to exclude commitment. And that negates freedom. Thus, when freedom is mistakenly held to be exclusive of any structuring or stability in one's life, the whole self is never given with any passion to a person, an ideal, or even the future.

This paralysis in commitment, of course, enhances the hegemony of the Commodity Form. There is nothing real or true of itself, nothing worth living and dying for. The names for that condition are anomie and hopelessness.

It is a difficult and precarious undertaking to live a life of structured freedom. But it is the only struggle worthy of humans. We need to see and experience lived examples of men and women who have a third alternative to (a) pure structure, where people resist any change and openness to the future, where newness is feared and fled; and (b) pure freedom, which is an illusion of ultimate non-committalness, an escape from self-defining responsibility, a flight from the past and a dread of the future. Moreover, the living resolution of the freedom-structure dualism will assist us in terminating the other fruitless dualisms which hinder both Christian thought and practice.

World against heaven, action against prayer, technique against spirit, marriage against celibacy, initiative against authority, experimentation against tradition, conscience against law, community against individual—all of these polarizations result from a fragmentation of the vibrant totality of faith. Any choice between these polarities will be fruitless, for each pole is actually constituted and realized in its relationship to its so-called opposite.

Heaven has its intelligibility *in* and gives intelligibility *to* this life. Action is short lived and fruitless without the centering of prayer, prayer is sterile without the fruit of the action. Spiritless technique and omni-directional enthusiasm are either impotent or deadly. Traditional authority lives in and is sustained only by experimentation and initiative. And morality is not the choice between conscience and law; it is the dialectical interrelatedness of both. Morality—committed human action in history—takes place only when the subjectivity of conscience collaborates with the objectivity of law and fact. In each of these spurious oppositions, the mutuality of freedom and structure is forgotten. In each of their resolutions, we will find people of faith and action who accept the delicate relationship between human structuring and freedom without rejecting either.

STANDING BEFORE THE IDOL

As we have already suggested, the Personal Form is not reducible to the Christian churches and the Christian churches are not exempt from the Commodity Form. In some ways, the Christian churches have helped generate and continue to support the imperialism of the commodity. Nonetheless, I have been maintaining that if a Christian were to honestly face the gospel of the commodity and the Gospel of Christ, he or she would be driven to choose between ultimates, between final and authoritative interpretations of the meaning and purpose of human life.

The listing of the values of the Commodity Form does not necessarily lead to an increased burden of guilt for the Christian. Neither is the generating of some new program necessarily hoped for. Rather, of greatest importance is the attempt to focus our search for radical dependency on the redemptive power of God's love for us. Our reflections have been basically a method of being present to what or whom, at rock bottom, we believe in, trust, and worship. Who or what saves us? Is it our securities, our accomplishments, our achievements, the rewards of culture and nation, our role as business persons, priests, professionals, even our own fidelity? Or is it the prodigally loving act of redemption in the reality of Jesus Christ? Is it his way, his truth, his life that we subscribe to and believe in or is it the catechetics of capitalism?

If we say Jesus Christ, then we are called by him to a life of simplicity, a life without racism or vengeance, a life of compassion and trust, a sharing of our goods, a consciousness of and attention to the world's poor, and a committed covenant in faith, hope, and love. In a culture increasingly demanding the thingification of human life, we are called to struggle for the personalization of the universe. In a world made ever more mechanical, threatening, and alien to personhood, we are called to render reality benevolent.

True moral conflicts arise, however, when, in our well-founded and sane recognition that things, production, consumption, technical reason, even competition, cannot and should not be ignored in the building of human life, we accept these values as ultimates. In our witnessing to the world, in our participation in "culture-building," the world has come to be too much with us. We Christians compromise with the "powers that be," with wealth, hedonism, nationalism, and economic ideology. We become too comfortable with Caesar.

Having faced the dominant gospel of our culture and compared it to the Gospel of Christ, we should arrive at a growing recognition that our relation to this culture can be only as people apart. Christianity at rock bottom conflicts with American culture, even subverts it. The last thing that Christians need is to become more secularized.

In recent years, attempts of Catholics to release themselves from the Roman and ecclesiastical appurtenances of the past have introduced the danger of being too fully identified with the cultural imperatives of the present. Thus the easy talk of secular cities, religious hedonism, Christian fulfillment, and sacred national pride have seduced many of us into yet another form of cultural support rather than cultural critique. This is the very thing that has happened in more traditional "acculturated" lifestyles of Christians—only the traps were in the form of superfluous and conspicuous wealth, a legitimation of social classes and pacification of the poor, a predominant association with cultural and national power brokers, and a refusal to take stands against social inequity or armament programs.

In a culture of lived atheism and the enthroned commodity—whether in its traditional forms or in its pseudo-liberated surrogates—the practicing Christian should look like a Martian. He or she will never feel fully at home in the commodity kingdom. If the Christian does feel at home, something is drastically wrong.

To feel like a freak in an alienating society, however, is not to be sundered from the people of that culture. The deepest longings of men and women, even in our culture, have not been so efficiently repressed that the desire for truth has been extinguished. All humans yet long for something to believe in, Buick notwithstanding. They yet desire community—even if it is a group of friends who, as Camus suggested, spend their lives telling each other that they are not God. Persons still yearn to live lives of integrity. They yet yearn for mystery that is not magical but personal. Service still beckons them. They feel the suffocation of a closed materialistic universe, and in their pain search for something and someone beyond. They bridle at the enforced skepticism about their most primal hopes. They have felt the bankruptcy of the secular gospel and its divinization of the market.

In this context the situation of contemporary Christianity is not entirely unlike that of the very early church—huddled in frail expectancy, newly aware of its own sinfulness and capacity for self-betrayal, painfully conscious of its inadequacy. Even in the context of the writings concerning the apostolic and pentecostal church, we can sense the atmosphere of divisiveness which had threatened the community, the threat of rupture between particularists and universalists, between Peter and Paul, between Jew and Gentile. And this community felt the ever present possibility of being swallowed up by the powerful cultural forces of Eastern religions and the Roman empire.

In so many ways, Christian men and women today are huddled together in their basic longing, in their experience of powerlessness, in their sense of sinful searching for false power and the security of idols. They have experienced divisiveness within the Church, within religious orders, within the realms of cult, moral practice, dogma, and life style. And they feel oppressed by the present Roman empire, the lived atheism of the Commodity Form, in which life, human sexuality, labor, love, and human dignity itself are subject to alienation. The new forms of slavery—relativism, skepticism, and selfishness—are bewilderingly omnipresent.

Twenty years ago the problem appeared almost insurmountable—not because of the power of the Commodity Form, but because of the fissures within Christianity itself. Conservatives clung to the past, to militarism and to nationalized faith, as relentlessly as radicals baptized mindless change, revolution, and hedonism. Today, however, after probing to the depth of our own poverty as humans, and yielding to it and opening ourselves to the possibility of rebirth, Christians seem to have discovered a new interest in Scripture, a commitment to interior depth through prayer and retreats, and an openness to communitarian movements. In some instances they have seen a reborn parish strengthening a lived, rather than nominal, Christianity. In other cases, Christians are experiencing a regenerative return to evangelical radicalism—leading not to American chauvinism and displays of wealth, but to gospel simplicity and pacifism. Out of the individual and shared acceptance of sinfulness and poverty has grown the common experience of standing in radical covenantal relationship in Christ. It is a relationship sustained by his promised Spirit of peace, forgiveness, strength, and fearlessness, aware that it is consecrated not to the world, but to the truth preached in faith and lived in trust. It is Jesus—not any privileged group, not even any Christian group—who has conquered the world of darkness and death.

The foundations of Christian unity are so profound and so desperately needed in this fragmented culture, and the stakes are so high, that it would be a tragedy for both faith and society if Christians were to be paralyzed by their differences and embrace spiritual isolationism. United in the essential faith of one Lord, one covenant, one history, a shared sinfulness, a shared promise, and a commitment to the kingdom preached by Christ, Christians can call each other not to their differing partialities, but to the only totality worth living and dying for: freedom in Jesus Christ.

If Christians are able to give themselves in wholeheartedness to the life and promise revealed in the person of Christ, if they are willing to be encountered, "judged," and called to a consistent living of the gospel, then they will be able to stand before the world, before any culture, and speak their variety of tongues. They will prophesy, heal, interpret, and live a life of freedom in faith, hope, and love. They will stand against darkness, against idolatry, and against slavery, as they embody living resistance to the claims of the Commodity Form. Their resistance will be rooted not in self-righteousness or a posture of sinlessness, but in the truth which they carry in faith. Recognizing the deepest values which they share with all men and women in their most profound longings, conscious of their poverty and dependence upon God, they can bring the Personal Form into fuller realization. What the powers of culture have deemed impossible, they will live.

The reception of the revelation of Christ, however, as well as its profession to the culture, takes place in history and relationship. Consequently, the ideals to which Christians find themselves called will have to be sustained in the arenas of common history and societal life. This is most important today, since it is so frequently on the corporate level of life that the power of the Commodity Form exercises its greatest influence on individuals. In order to more fully respond to the invitation of the Personal Form, Christians must consider the practices of their own tradition as well as possible models for communitarian and corporate embodiment of what they believe.

CHAPTER ELEVEN

CHRISTIAN PRACTICE
IN THE PERSONAL FORM

COMMUNITY: RESPONSE
TO CULTURAL ISOLATIONISM

A life of faith and of hope and of love rises in contradiction to the values of the Commodity Form in our culture. Faith, hope, and love are the three human activities deemed most impossible by the cognitive and behavioral standards of commodity consciousness. In Catholic tradition, one believes that these three human acts are "theological virtues"—the highest exercise of our human personhood, wherein we participate in the very life of God. Thus, not surprisingly, the anti-humanism of our culture is at the same time a lived atheism.

Lived belief, the lived practice of these theological virtues, must conflict with the received conditioning of our social, political, and theoretical systems. It is this conflict, as well as the facts that we are intrinsically social beings, that we are intrinsically inter-subjective, and that the revelation of God is in and through a community or a people, which lead us to a recognition of our need for community. Our faith vision is received only in terms of our history and psycho-social development; if it is to be nurtured and purified and sustained, it will also have to be in terms of our historicity and sociality.

Traditional religious communities (which we will briefly discuss later in this chapter) have been, despite the lapses, enduring focuses of shared communitarian faith and witness aspiring to the revelation of Jesus Christ. But today there are a number of newer emphases upon Christian community life: from a growing sense of a priest-brotherhood found in *Jesu Caritas* communities, to the Focolare movement, to the Jean Vanier communities of the handicapped, to counter-cultural Christian communities modeled after the Catholic Worker. The Cursillo movement and Christian Life Communities continue to develop, with regularly shared prayer and faith sessions, ongoing communication, and long-range commitments. The Charismatic Renewal movement also emphasizes the communal dimension of praying, of healing (memories, physical and psychological suffering) in the context of community, of greater emphasis upon continuing personal contact and support within chosen or parish-located groups. The Marriage Encounter movement likewise stresses the communal sharing of faith, prayer, and some goods, and the mutual support of families in their commitment. The Sojourners, the New Jerusalem, and peace communities of activists all offer witness to faith, and service to men and women. Inner-city pastoral and justice groups undertake regular communal prayer and meetings of shared faith. Groups of informally gathered married couples study and discuss their vocations. Christian professional groups cluster in families for the confirming of life, ideals, hope, and plans. These are all examples of the movement among Christian people for a new sense of corporateness and communality.

All of these groupings are based on the discovery that a Christian, in the face of our culture's dwarfing and isolating of the individual, must turn to a community of shared life-experience which both fosters committed faith and enables the individual to criticize and challenge the programming of the culture. The most effective means by which both goals are achieved is in a communally shared Christian life.

Physical growth, both individual and social, is cellular; the same principle applies to the life of faith. Christian cell-communities should be formed which will call forth (a) an internal fidelity of the members to a life of prayer, shared faith, and mutual encouragement and correction, (b) an internal critique of personal and community actions, apostolates, and goals in the light of faith, (c) an opening of their shared life of faith to others by hospitality and encouragement in the Christian life, and (d) external critique and planning with respect to changing the social and environmental conditions that inhibit personal integrity and growth within the local community, the city, the nation, and the Church.

In each of these areas, the community will have to be present to itself: as fundamentally Christian in commitment and orientation; as counter-cultural in its advocacy of the Personal Form; as non-competitive in its encouraging, sustaining, and challenging; as corporately conscious of its most fundamental choices in faith and specific life options; as unified in its orientation to service, freedom, and the work of justice.

Such a communitarian life demands a commitment of time, energy, and sacrifice. Its mutual support system cannot take place outside of a commonly recognized commitment of persons to each other in the name of their shared vision. A community of this kind must be (a) consciously choiceful, (b) explicitly committed to and willing to be called to the life of the Gospels, (c) open to change through the authentic living-out of its principles, and willing to be challenged to fuller Christian praxis, and (d) prepared to confront the patterns of the Commodity Form—injustice, manipulation, domination, dishonesty, escape—not only as they appear in the culture at large but also as they surface within the group itself.

In the process of sharing and deepening a living corporate faith, a Christian community will recognize that if it is not possible for a group of mutually committed men and women to struggle honestly with their own propensities to injustice, competition, and non-responsibility, they will hardly be justified in challenging those same patterns in the society at large which they criticize. They will realize that there is something fundamentally unjust in indicting other people or institutions for failing to do what they themselves refuse to undertake. This is the meaning of internal and external critique.

One's personal life, as well as the life of the community in which one lives, has social and political dimensions. That is true both in the sense that the communitarian life is in itself a stance and a witness against the Commodity Form, and in the sense that the same behaviors of domination and violence in international, national, and urban groups are potentially operative in a group of men and women who come together to foster and deepen their own Christian lives. If they are able to face and purify the patterns of injustice in their lives together, they will be able to bring greater compassion as well as insight to those patterns which are found at broader social and political levels.

PRAYER: FORMATION OF A CHRISTIAN IDENTITY

When a Christian community acknowledges its own brokenness and poverty, and also brings its vision of the Personal Form to society, it will need to call upon resources other than its own. The basic resource, of course, is faith in Jesus Christ as the revelation of God and humanity, and through Christ, his community in history—a freely entered church. The ecclesiastical dimensions of dogma, faith and morals, cultic practice, and universalism are crucial aspects of the individual and communal search for self-identity and continuity.

It seems to me, from my own experience as well as from the history of many communal movements in the church, that any Catholic community which is to survive cannot test its relationship to the Catholic community of believers in much more than one area of dogma, morality, cult, or universality without seriously jeopardizing its identity as Catholic or its potential for speaking to its fellow believers out of a commonly embraced union of hearts. While it is a painstaking and risk-laden enterprise to call into question or challenge traditions in one area—e.g., cultic formalism, the ministry of women in the church, the particularities of moral practice in social life or sexual life, the investigation of the meaning of dogma or Scripture's inspiration, or the possibilities of indigenization—the strain of unity becomes considerably heightened if more than one of these areas are challenged. This is not so much a question of critique as it is one of identity. For example, it would seem that the depth and longlastingness of Dorothy Day's witness to her fellow Catholics in the area of social justice and gospel simplicity are directly proportional to her unequivocal orthodoxy in the other areas of dogma, cult, and universality. To the extent that her continuity with the praxis of Catholicism was unimpeachable, the fruit of that faith borne in loving service and pacifism has often become irresistible to the mature Catholic conscience.

The power of the charismatic movement, likewise, and its striking impact on the Catholic church in introducing a radically different form of personal and corporate prayer, is clearly linked to its continuity with the universal and historical church as well as with the Sacred Scriptures.

But to be a community which calls into question celibacy, a male clergy, permanent commitment in marriage, the Trinitarian formula, transubstantiation, traditional prayer, and the church's social positions, all at once, is to be a community with no solid identification in itself, no clear lines of continuity with the historical community of believers, and no foundation for witnessing to *commonly shared* values and beliefs. Any hoped-for prophetic action or witness is lost because the shared universe of signs, values, and beliefs has been diminished and dissipated into relativism and subjectivism. And this relativizing of universal faith, in turn, abets the cultural forces that form our identity and claim our allegiance.

If any relationship, any person, any community is to grow, it will *develop out of its totality* and its historical continuity. At a certain point, when too many factors of continuity are displaced or lost, the person or relationship will experience not growth, but fragmentation and eventual dissolution. Consequently, as it understands and appropriates its own development, it will be important for a community to have means whereby a centering of identity and continuity with history can be supported.

In this context of centering and grounding one's historical identity, there are two special means and traditions practiced in the Catholic church which are worthy of extended discussion and consideration. These are prayer and the sacramental life; and we will consider them, for our purposes here, precisely in the light of their relationship to the Commodity Form, the gospel of culture, and the rooting of identity within change.

Prayer is a social and political act. It cannot be considered otherwise when we reflect upon the societal and political revelation of human life that we find in the Commodity Form. We have seen its underlying themes of idolatry, the denial of covenant, the flight from intimacy and interiority, the insistence upon control and manipulation, and the absence of freedom in faith, hope, and love. Prayer, on the other hand, is most fundamentally a covenantal relationship with another person—God—and it partakes of all the risks, struggles, joys, and darknesses that attach to any personal intimacy.

As an act of interiority, of entering into solitude, prayer demands the major effort of extricating oneself from the patterns of behavior which have become normative in commodity consciousness. Centering ourselves in prayer is an exercise in being present to our identity and purpose as persons, in locating the desires of our being which cannot be fulfilled by the false promises of the thing. The very act of being consciously present to ourselves is a mammoth undertaking in resistance to facile externalization, to cultural pressure, and to social expectation. This is a crucial reason why prayer can be so difficult—especially if we are people under the thrall of cultural imperialism. It feels just too strange even to locate ourselves as persons. There is no empirical payoff, no immediate guarantees of success, no way to measure or control, no way to evaluate competitively.

Silent solitude is filled with risk. It lacks pragmatics. It is hopelessly unmarketable. The centering of prayer is an exercise in honesty, in getting in touch with our needfulness and poverty so shrilly denied by commercialism and materialism. It is an exercise in self-revelation rather than self-deception. Prayer is an assault upon the fraudulence of mere roles, of social and cultural pretense, of the idols we cling to and are enslaved by. As such, it carries with it all the existential terror of any act of intimacy with another person. Afraid of being "found out," we avoid the intimacy. We cannot speak to another person from the depth of our being. Thus it is not only prayer to God which is found to be so impossible; any prayerful communion with another person seems equally inaccessible.

Yet we long for personal communion. Somehow we do long to be found out. To be seen as we are—to be accepted as we are. This is what takes place in the intimacy of prayer. We discover that the God who is revealed to us in Jesus Christ has "found us out" already and not rejected us. Thus the news at the bottom of our identity is not despicable and desolate. It is good news. The declaration of our poverty, of our dependent needfulness, of our incapacity to save ourselves through idolatry, of our ontological incompleteness, is not a shameful discovery, but a discovery of our being loved for what we actually are. We need not hide our fragility in order to be loved.

This is the message of prayer. It is the message of any personal love—achieved not by a few minutes' method, or a crash course or a renewed physical glamour, but by the risks of placing faith and hope in another person. It is a life task. It is a commitment. We disengage ourselves from the universe of values and possibility legislated by the demands of culture.

The moments of prayer are (1) a freely-entered presence to one's self, to one's deepest longings, and to the personal God one professes to believe in—involving, at the first step, acts of faith, hope, and acceptance of oneself as one is; (2) a recognition and truthful acceptance of one's poverty and needfulness in the presence of God, and a crying out of one's ontological contingency; (3) a listening to God's response (such a listening is possible only when one accepts one's own incompleteness) not only in Scripture but also in the movements within oneself; and (4) a giving thanks and returning of one's self to God when one recognizes that one is loved into being and loved for one's very being.

Consequently, the whole process of prayer—its quieting, its truth, its centering in being rather than in having—is characterized by profoundly counter-cultural activities. Contrasted to commodity living, prayer seems inaccessible, impossible, remote. It is beyond our power (of course) and control, and hence unmanageably fearful. What is most intimate to us is felt as most alien and frightening. And so we stay away— from our selves, from intimacy. Thus prayer is not only a counter-cultural act. It is a reappropriation of our personhood and identity. It is a dealienation, a decommodification of our very lives.

Corporate prayer exhibits similar structure, even though it is experienced at a different depth. Charismatic prayer manifests similar patterns of acknowledging poverty, of healing the perverse forms of idolatry, of admitting and accepting creatureliness, and of breaking into praise founded upon radical trust, acceptance, and the experience of saving love. Shared prayer, when it comes from openness rather than from obsessiveness, talkativeness, competition, or quantification, exercises our openness in faith before the other. It is a declaration of intimacy not only with God, but with the others in whose presence we reveal our poverty and aspiration. It overcomes the isolation and separateness that cultural values impose. It demands a recognition of our common frailty, breaking through the covering masks of self-subsistence, independence, and self-justifying idols which construe being loved as both threatening and unnecessary.

Perhaps we can see, then, the political and social *content* of prayer. Prayer is not somehow a realm separate from or untouched by the cultural milieu. In fact, it is precisely the cultural, the social (and psychological) dimension of prayer which makes it seem so impossible to undertake. But just as entering prayer is a breaking of bondage to the cultural gospel, so also the fruit of prayer is an empowering of the person in freedom, discipline, and commitment to stand before the gods of culture and yet to live otherwise. Prayer thus yields one of the most dramatic and sustaining forces for authentic social action and for long-term social commitment.

SACRAMENTALITY: FORMING
THE LIFE OF PERSONS

Among the traditions and practice of the Catholic church, the sacramental system has played a crucial role in calling Christians to themselves. Even in their most formal historical expressions, the sacraments, with their use of Scripture, have served as continual sources of interior renewal and self-criticism, and of the development of deeply committed men and women. It is as if the power of the sacraments has been greater than any of the corporate deviations from Christ's life, greater than the destructive possibilities of full inculturation, greater than the blandishments of magic or the blandness which comes with the loss of the transcendent and the mysterious. The sacraments have been a constant focus of the transcendent and the immanent, between the God "beyond history" and the God of space and time. *The New Catholics,* a book of autobiographies presented by men and women who have found new faith over the last generation, reveals the great power of this integrated vision of Christianity. It is wholly committed to this world and the value of human flesh and blood; it is wholly given to the transcendent God who enters and transforms and challenges this world.

With the arrival of Christian secularism's fashionableness, much of the sacramental system has been called into question. This acculturated devaluation of the sacraments has been compounded by the turbulence of much needed changes during the past decade. In the past, the heart of sacramentalism had surely often been neglected in an over-concentration upon externals; but advocates of changes have just as often depended merely upon modified formalities as the hallmark of truth and growth, and in the process the full power of sacramental life has often remained untapped.

Nonetheless, the sustaining influence of the sacraments persists. It can be discovered in the countless elderly men and women who are able to see the faith of their ancestors in the faith of the young, and in the young who have come to discover and embrace not only their renewal, but the best and deepest of their past. For my purposes here, I wish only to highlight the social and cultural dimensions of sacramental life; but I believe that this will touch upon the very identity and power of sacramentality.

Sacramentalization is an elevation, an exalting and celebration of the most intimately human aspects of our lives. Sacraments retrieve and make holy the critical moments of growth and human development. They celebrate and embrace the truly human. Each sacrament is a centering, a recovering of humanity to itself through the inviting power of a God who pronounces what is deepest in human persons as something irreplaceably good. Thus while all of the sacraments are a remembering and making present of the life of God in the life of humans, they are also a revelation of, a remembrance of, humanity for itself.

Personhood, commitment, and covenant are the hallmarks of sacramentality. So also is memory. The sacraments are personal and corporate affirmations of the Personal Form. They are rememberings of who we are: rememberings of our humanity, of our frailty and needfulness, of our covenants, of our power for commitment, of our social nature, of our creatureliness, of our marvelous destiny. Every key concept in this paragraph is a concept of the Personal Form. Centering, commitment, personhood, faith, hope, love, needfulness, and human fulfillment as persons are missing from among the conceptual categories of the Commodity Form. It is my suspicion that the Commodity Form's prominence in advanced industrial societies has in great part devaluated the sacramental life among Catholics—not because sacramental life itself is under attack, but because human personhood has been reduced to a commodity by its criteria of what is real and valuable.

While the Commodity Form dulls us into forgetting our truest identity and so separates us into isolated competing units, the Personal Form engages the memory of our personhood and so establishes our unity in that personhood. The sacraments are rememberings: rememberings of our creaturehood, in birth, sickness, and death; rememberings of our history, of our being saved, of our being called; rememberings of our covenantal life choice; rememberings of the precious *present* which we take for granted and so often forget. Since the opposite of remembering is not only forgetfulness but dismemberment, the sacramental life is also a celebration of our *unity* in covenant and our destiny as persons called forth by God. A sacrament *re-members* us, puts us back together, heals our individual and corporate fragmentation. As such, sacraments are crucial, even in the specific forms they take, for our effort to embody the universality of our personhood in a way that transcends culture, countries, class, society, and temporal history.

Infant baptism, as it is presently practiced, is a celebration of birth, of community, of life. It is the corporate invitation extended by a community of faith to a new human being—not in order to predetermine his or her life, but in the consciousness that the stakes of life and choice are too high for indifference. Thus the community wants and claims the child for its life of covenant, freedom, and faith.

At the same time the community calls itself and its families to a renewed commitment, in covenant and promise to the child and his or her future. Baptism is a corporate and familial recognition of our human poverty—not as something to be escaped, but as something to be embraced in the recognition that we are chosen precisely in our frail humanity for the self-transcending life of knowing and loving. As a corporate act, as an affirmation of commitment and covenant, as a recognition of human dignity and mystery, it is profoundly counter-cultural.

Just as the Commodity Form of life touches the full range of our experience as men and women, just as it is a "form of being" and a "formation system" for acculturating persons throughout their lives, so also Baptism is the initiation of a person's entire experience of faith in God. Baptism is the beginning of our corporate and social formation in the realm of the Personal. It suggests, moreover, how the sacramental life itself is a Personal "formational" system that challenges cultural formation, in life crises, in service and covenant, in our ways of reconciliation, even in our manner of dying.

Baptism is the family's and the community's commitment to a "counter-cultivation" of our individual development. A culture *cultivates* us—educates, tills, and tends us. A culture is also a *cult,* a religious value and behavioral system that fosters and nurtures us, that can easily claim and engulf us in a world/life vision. To baptize our children, then, is in a sense culturally subversive: it is a commitment to cultivate and give a cultic vision to our youngest loved ones, which is a radical alternative to the social-economic "cultivation system" that is the Commodity Form. It is also, and more significantly, the incorporation of the child into the very life of a triune, covenantal, personal God.

The Sacrament of Confirmation, while not historically instituted and practiced as such, can be considered to be a celebration of mature commitment after a period of years of formation in Christian practice. It is a commission, in the form of a covenantal profession, that our vocation—our being "called forth"—is through the Spirit, who establishes us in the truth of Christ which the world itself may not only misunderstand but may even condemn. Just as Jesus in the Gospel of John returns to the Jordan, the source of his baptism, when during the feast of the reconsecration of the Temple he experiences the resistance of the world and its rejection, so also our adult rededication is made in the face of our knowledge of the cultural gospel and its blandishments.

Reconsecrating ourselves to the task of fashioning our lives in the manner of Jesus' living and dying, we follow his Spirit in our life-choice of service rather than domination, healing rather than violence, and redemptive love rather than hate. In reciprocity, our community of faith and resistance sends us forth to the praxis of Christian life and strengthens us with the very power of our covenanting God.

From this point of view, we can see how Confirmation could be fruitfully regarded as the sacrament of the mature single life—surely a life-choice quite distinguished from Marriage and Orders, even though those more specified life-choices may be embraced in later years. In our culture, which so often reduces marriage to a rite of passage into adulthood, Confirmation in the Christian community more deeply identifies the patterns and commitment of a freely chosen Christian life of sexual integrity, generous service, and personal fidelity.

The sacraments of Orders and Marriage (both of which we will discuss more fully below) are further covenantal celebrations of life-commitments as ministers to the Christian community and as spouses in the shared intimacy of mutual sanctification. At the heart of each of these sacraments is promise-keeping—the recognition that the only irreplaceable gift, to the world or to an individual, is the gift of one's self.

Within this self-donation is the equally counter-cultural value of permanence in commitment. Stability of life-forms and intimate relationships, constancy of moral values and promises, are both powerful supports for the formation of men and women of conscience and solid identity. Instability and impermanence, certainly, are most conducive to the passive acceptance of external power, environmental control, and social engineering.

Penance, or the Sacrament of Reconciliation, is the remembering of our need to forgive and to be forgiven, the acknowledgment of our sinfulness, the owning of our desire to heal the fissures in our lives, our practices, our relationships. It is a compelling sacrament, one most difficult for contemporary people because of the cultural pressures not to recognize our ontological poverty, not to face our contingency, not to give up the idols we grip for false security.

The Sacrament of Reconciliation is especially hard, not really because of the embarrassment of self-revelation to a "mere human," but because the objective honesty which such a revelation requires is painfully real to the penitent. It is intersubjective; my sinfulness becomes communally and socially known to another person. Such a socially acknowledged need for forgiveness and repentance is boldly contrary to our privatized inclinations.

Indeed, it has to be admitted by church people that the failures of past confessional practice, the compulsions and obsessiveness associated with the Sacrament of Penance ("religious scruples"), the frequently induced fear and lack of compassion, the distorted focusing of all morality upon sex, and the scandalous inadequacies of priests have often diminished the healing power of this sacrament. But the tragedy is that in a time when the actions of self-revelation, acceptance, honesty, and forgiveness are so desperately needed, it is this sacrament which is least practiced. Its full reconciling force will never be experienced unless we ask for and grant forgiveness for past mistakes and sins and proceed to see its social, political, and cultural significance for the present. To confess one's sins is not only the beginning of a change of heart: it is a liberation from servitude to cultural pretense.

The forgiveness of sins, surely founded upon the saving love of God, is essentially a *communal* reality. One of the reasons confession has been so ineffectual in the past is no doubt the neglect of this fact. The "unrepentant penitents" could continue to hate, to be racist, to be unjust and unreformed, as long as there was no social claim made upon their consciences, and privatized sins of selfishness, pride, and impatience went unchallenged. Any attempt to give pragmatic reality (by suggesting a "penance" of corporal works of mercy of forgiving someone or telling the offended person about the lie or calumny) would have been met with powerful resistance. Much of the "rote" character of sin-telling was precisely an act of avoidance. Much of the selection of confessors was made precisely on the basis that there would be no socially objective acknowledgment and challenge of sinfulness. My own school, twenty-five years ago, had two favorite priests: one who couldn't hear and one who couldn't speak. Deadly serious as to guilt and compulsion, people were often completely repressive of the possibility for true repentance and change. So it will be with all exercises of penitence that fail to take seriously the communal and social nature of faith and sacrament.

The Sacrament of the Sick is the ultimate victory over the gods and idols and fears of our culture. In a civilization that systematically represses the actuality and implication of our creaturehood, that covers over the natural dimensions of dying with technique, circumlocution, and the empty smiles of Sunday morning religious hucksterism, this sacrament admits that death is real, but proclaims that it is not the last word.

We affirm faith's power over sickness and mortality. We say that there is more to us than material monuments and things, that our indestructibility is intimately related to our covenants, and to our capacities for faith, hope, and love. We affirm the efficacy of faith not only in a loving eternal providence, but even in our physical and temporal dimensions, as in God's power we heal our interior sufferings and often our physical distress.

The Sacrament of the Sick stands directly in confrontation with our dominant myths and values. It is a reliance in faith that we are loved creatures. It is a final embrace of our humanity, an entry into the very dying of Christ with trusting abandonment. Our "last" sacrament, then, stares even death in the face and empowers us to be fearless.

I mention the Eucharist last because it is the sacrament most fully embodying the Christian life, the Personal Form, our ways of communal resistance, and the act of remembering. The very structure of the Eucharist recapitulates the other sacraments in so many ways. It relives the life of Jesus. It embodies our corporate mission as a people of service. First of all, in the Eucharist we acknowledge that the only way we can come into each other's presence and the presence of God is as sinners. A great divestment of our egoisms and our claims to self-righteousness is the precise moment of entry into the mystery of God and communal life. It is an act of unilateral disarmament, a declaration of peace to be recapitulated throughout the entire eucharistic celebration. It is a request for mercy.

The Eucharist is, secondly, an act of listening. It is uncommon in our society that a group of people would open themselves to be called and judged by the word of God. Not only is the listening posture uncharacteristic of a civilization compelled to make noise and distracting clatter, but the willingness to be moved and changed by the testimony of something other than profit, self-interest, or pragmatics is truly remarkable.

In the sacrament of Christ's redemptive sacrifice, we also celebrate and consecrate our own gifts. We identify our lives, our labors, our passions, and our joys with the body, blood, history, and person of Jesus. It is an attempt to reconfirm our choice of loving and life-giving service, as we reproduce in ourselves not only the manner of Jesus' death and resurrection, but also the very substance of Jesus' reality as food for his brothers and sisters.

Recalling our history and salvation, becoming mindful of our own need for the healing action of God in our lives, remembering our sinfulness and reliance on a covenantal God, and making Jesus our own life and sustenance, we give thanks. Seeing the face of our God in food that sustains us in our poverty, we are sent forth to minister to our brothers and sisters in poverty, through whose faces, again, we will encounter the living God. The "sacrament of the poor" reminds us of the poor.

This is not theory; this is reality. In my own experience as a priest, I have found two people who receive the body and blood of Christ as no others. They are Teresa of Calcutta and Jean Vanier. There is only one other time in their lives that they can be seen to respond to the world with the same rapt intensity: when they are receiving a poor person into their lives, or when they are receiving you as a guest.

The Sacrament of the Eucharist is the celebration of the redemptive act of God in human history. It necessarily engages the personal realm in us—unless we are able to repress its essentially social content. In that case it will not change us, it will not transform us. It will only have the effect it has had on two people who have walked to the same Mass for fifteen years, and during the same fifteen years have refused to speak to each other.

The Sacrament of the Eucharist is corporate, interior, covenantal, and celebrative in its exercise of freedom. This sacrament elevates the commonplace, the symbolic, and the communal to the very life of our Trinitarian—interpersonal, social—God. It is an exaltation of our humanity, because in the Eucharist we are involved in the life and gift of Jesus as the unifying focus of God and humanity.

Each sacrament, which is a participation in the life of Jesus-God-and-human, is a revelation of the personhood of God in which our own personhood partakes and is ultimately realized. Each sacrament belies and resists the gospel of the commodity. Each, even the Sacrament of the Sick, confirms and embraces life in the midst of a civilization that has enthroned dead things. Each declares independence from and liberation from the chains of culture and its confined universe. Each sacrament is an act of freedom and covenant, in a society that declares both impossible. Each is exercised communally in a nation where community is dead. Each embodies faith, hope, and love in a world of minimalized risk and marginalized care.

Thus the sacraments are at the same time the engagement of human persons and divine Persons in covenantal relationship. They are prayer. They are politics.

MARRIAGE AND CELIBACY: COUNTER-CULTURAL LIFE CHOICES

Two dominant aspects of the gospel of commodity, as we have seen, are the erosion of permanent commitment and the

thingification of human sexuality. While the media supposedly celebrate sexual liberation, sex in the media has no linkage with the full human person or human covenant. In this
cultural ambience it becomes evident that the sexual life of
Christians has considerable importance not only in their personal adherence to the Gospel of Jesus, but also in terms of
witnessing to human personhood.

The only intimacy recognized in the Commodity Form is
physical proximity. Knowledge of the other person as a person is painfully absent for many couples who enter marriage
even though they may have considerable physical knowledge
of each other. With the heightened hedonism of our culture,
moreover, the pains of suffering and sacrifice are considered
as impenetrable evils to be avoided at all cost. The continued
intimacy of a shared life which is open to new life, however, is
one which necessarily entails the suffering of growth and of
daily dying to immediate gratification, to the satisfaction of
one's clamoring ego, and to one's defenses against self-revelation. It is precisely in the fires of this struggle for love and
commitment that marriages either fall apart or achieve more
powerful union.

The high incidence of divorce cannot be separated from
the dominant values of our society. The breakdown of familial covenant is part and parcel of the commodified universe,
with its values of competition, hedonism, non-involvement,
non-risk, loss of faith, and hopelessness. Many, even the most
idealistic, enter the life choice of marriage with skepticism
about their love, with paralyzing fears that it cannot last, and
with lurking suspicions that they cannot give themselves
unconditionally. And the very conditions and reservations
they bring to the commitment actually determine the instability of it.

It is my belief that the institution of marriage (as well as
the institutions which support its indissolubility against intense cultural propagandizing in the media) is one of the last
bases for resistance to the Commodity Form. The family provides a primary sphere of human life where the deepest expe-

riences of fidelity, of trust in other persons, of self-acceptance, of growth in intimacy, can occur and can offer data that belie the absolutes of capitalism. When families are broken apart, the incursion of the Commodity Form into the life of the child is even more far-reaching than otherwise. For a family-less child, the *only* data about life and love comes from media, social pressure, and cultural expectations. If covenantal marriage dissolves in this culture, the Personal Form may well disappear.

Part of the devaluation of the institution of marriage derives from the devaluation of human sexuality. The continually increasing incidence of pre-covenantal sexual intercourse among a majority of young people serves to separate the fullest expression of bodily intimacy from the interiority of total commitment and personal intimacy. Sexual intimacy receives both its intelligibility and its deepest eroticism from the intimacy of persons. Divorced from personal intimacy and the commitment upon which it is founded, sex itself becomes a social and personal lie. It is transformed into an object of immediate short-range gratifications, in avoidance of the self-investment appropriate to a life-long covenant and profound self-revelation. It is again quantity, often in different combinations and different packaging, which is substituted for the more fundamental longings of the human person.

In a culture which portrays life-commitment as impossible and undesirable, which inhibits the flowering of true intimacy, which deems a suffering love and sacrifice to be negative values, men and women who enter into a personal covenant by mature and free consent are taking a radical stance.

In an environment that intimidates persons who face risks made in freedom, that has reduced human affectivity to aggression, domination, and control, a life of marriage will be both terrifying and, at the same time, a profound source of liberation from the dialectic of domination and appropriation. It is a learning how to die, to accept one's finitude, to accept another person, to be stretched toward unconditional love, to share truly not only one's goods and gifts but one's poverty and life-grace.

In a society dedicated to "holding on to" everything, a life of marriage entered in the Personal Form is a schooling in how to give oneself away.

Sexuality and commitment as they are perceived through the Commodity Form provide the context wherein the issue of celibacy may be most fruitfully discussed. It is not surprising that in a culture which systematically attacks the covenant of marriage, the devaluation of other forms of chastity (I mean an integration of one's sexuality with one's whole personhood and life commitment) prevails. Chastity is impractical, out of date, undesirable.

The mutually sustaining forms of chastity in marriage and in the single life are yet to be fully investigated—especially the ways in which the struggles of celibate love are enhanced and nourished by the witness of faithful married love, and how the purifications and "dyings" of married love are complemented and sustained by men and women who live lives of celibate love. Both forms of chastity witness to the human condition and its full promise—one under the form of committed intimacy to another person and the risk of openness to new life, the other in a dimension of non-possessive loving and non-privatized care that is considered to be unacceptable foolishness in the canons of acculturated sexuality.

A celibate who lives a warm and affective life of intimacy which is not reducible to genitality, and a life of hope which is not reducible to the blood of offspring, says by this life-choice that human happiness, tenderness, compassion, and passion are made possible by our very humanness and a caring life of faith and hope. Such a life, of course, is more difficult in the doing than in the saying. It is true that there is great power in the witness of celibate love, in its implicit affirmation that one's personal choice has no intelligibility without eschatological faith and hope in Jesus Christ. In our culture especially, people have found it dumbfounding that someone might find human intimacy and compassion while forgoing physical fatherhood or motherhood and choosing to love without lover, spouse, or sexual gratification.

But it is also true that many celibates fail to give the ideal witness of the celibate life. The pains of relinquishment can be frequent and intense. The physical incompletions felt in intimacy without genital orientation or expression are filled with difficulties, purifications, and an aching vacuum close to the bottom of one's physical life. Care and carefulness are difficult to express in an integral way, and the sequential struggles found in a life of celibacy are as trying as the struggles in married love. There has been failure—not only in the high incidence of men and women who have rationalized their vowed public commitment in compromise and deceit, not only in those who have tried to change their commitment in openness and integrity, but also in the more culturally acceptable (and dangerous) forms of infidelity to celibate love. So often celibates have merely displaced their affective life rather than transforming it. Love and care are directed to things, possessions, games, professionalism, achievement, and the collection of trifles. A loss of tenderness and compassion, of affection and passion often seems to accompany the vowed celibate life. The concentration of all of one's moral sensitivity in moralistic sexual preoccupations may also be a by-product of a celibacy not grounded in love of Christ and of other human persons.

All of these risks and dangers, however, are worth taking, not only because of the intrinsic value that a life of celibate love can embody, but also and especially in the light of our culture's sexual gospel. Chastity, both in the marital and celibate forms, stands as a rare testimonial to human integrity, to the symbolic and actual importance of being embodied selves, to the pre-eminence of personhood and covenantal life. In a hedonistic culture, moreover, chastity is a most effective critique of fulfillment through immediate gratification. It is a living refutation of the reduction of persons to either machines or animals, to progeny or to pleasure. The contradiction is well known. This is why sexual integrity is under such relentless attack in advanced Western societies, why it has to be explained away as deviance, repression, or frustration. It is a scandal to Madison Av-

enue, Hollywood, and the halls of academe and Rockdom. Yet
it exists, and as a phenomenon within our culture, the life of
married or celibate chastity can be a most subversive lived force
today. It is truly counter-cultural.

The blind acceptance of the Commodity Form is especially
evident in the realm of sexuality. Somehow we are led to believe
that there is a sexual liberation going on—as if, mysteriously,
human affectivity and sexuality were exempt from the hegemony of the thing. But if we look at sexuality and its mechanized
commodification in our culture with any degree of honesty, we
will see that this is not the case. The so-called sexual freedom is
the affective erotic expression of the dominant economic and
philosophical "reality" preached by our cultural gospel.

The wisdom of our capitalistic society in its marketing of
sexuality and immediate gratification would have us believe
that sexual integrity and commitment, chastity and marital fidelity, are something dreamed up by celibates in Rome hoping to impede our gratification and increase their control over
us. The truth is, there is indeed a great deal of control over
and manipulation of our sexuality, but it is not exercised by
clerics. It is exercised by the market and the thing. There are
societies and civilizations which never heard of the Roman
Curia but which have insisted upon the importance of sexual
integrity. But they have not been in the grips of a commodified universe and its overwhelming promotional power.

THE VOWED LIFE IN COMMUNITY:
RESISTANCE TO INCULTURATION

In recent years most religious orders have been puzzled
and frightened by the drop-off in the numbers of people applying for admittance. The only communities which seem to
have grown are either those which have been heavily emphasizing traditional values, or those which, like Mother Teresa's
Missionaries of Charity, have also made the investment of
themselves in a life of unequivocal witness to the gospel and
service to the poor. In both of these cases there is an interest-

ing phenomenon which is not too often looked at: each presents to a young person a *real alternative* to the gospel of the "World," a real possibility of living in a way not dictated by the lords of culture. In the case of sheer conservative emphases, the motivation could of course simply be the superficial distinctiveness of religious uniform, a rigorous rule, and formal singularity. It may also be a mere flight from the world and even from one's self. But it is quite clear that a way of life *different* from *passive acculturation* is sought. Most of the orders and congregations which have lost great numbers, or have even been disbanded, seem to have been the ones that have also foundered in finding their new identity in response to the call of the church for renewal: in too many cases, change has been merely a move to further acculturation, secularism, and the adoption of cultural values.

I believe there are many alternatives to the superficial conservatism on one hand, and the panicky trendiness on the other. One powerful and often overlooked possibility is in the rediscovery of the religious life as a counter-cultural force. Men and women religious are called to be special Christian activists, who, by their subversive mode of life, invite other men and women to question the obsessions that dominate their social world and prevent them from being open to their own full potentiality as persons. "Religious" can live in the world, certainly, in continuity with the truly human, rooting themselves beneath and within various human projects—economic, educative, social, political, and ecclesiastical—with the aim of liberating themselves and others for mobilization into deeper Christian life. Nonetheless, by the quality and intensity of their prayer and shared communal lives, they will witness to the fact that the human condition is not reducible to social and political projects. Their lives will clearly point to values that transcend the limits of nation, race, class, or ideology, and that sustain their commitment to each human effort they undertake. A covenant with and in Christ remains central to their vows, but the very *evangelical* nature of their commitments leads them to be culturally radical.

In their openness to one another, in their fidelity to the Word of God, in their renunciation of dominating power—even though isolation might be less demanding, infidelity less precarious, and power more immediately satisfying—religious have the opportunity to bear unambiguous witness to *faith*, founded in the God who invites. They choose *obedience* to God's calling forth of their personhood, expressing it in fidelity to their Christian tradition, to their life promise, and to their common struggles.

In their relinquishment of private property and its accumulation, in their rejection of self-aggrandizement and all forms of psychological or economic possessiveness—even though extensive property is the aspiration of our culture and aggrandizement the promise of material fulfillment—religious have the opportunity to witness unambiguously to *hope*, grounded in the God who shares. They choose to be *poor* by letting go of final reliance upon possessions and by a trusting abandonment to the Lord.

In the risky gift of their lives and the vulnerability of their self-divestment in compassion—even though self-withholding seems the guarantee of security and dispassionate coolness the model of cultural isolation—religious have the opportunity to bear unambiguous witness to *love* grounded in the God who gives. They choose to be single-mindedly *chaste* in the passionate gift of their whole selves without reservation.

We can see, then, how the traditional vows of poverty, chastity, and obedience are not only expressions of a life of faith, hope, and love, not only fundamental commitments to human freedom, but also relentlessly counter-cultural stances in the three crucial areas of human action. It will be well to elaborate on this.

In the area of property, capitalist culture offers human fulfillment under the guise of infinite accumulation, appropriation, and competitive self-enhancement. The vow of poverty is a stance taken in freedom not against property *per se,* but against security and fulfillment in property. It is not a negation of things, it is an affirmation of their proper ordering in human relations: persons always before property. Men and women cannot be fulfilled, saved, or made happy by the production or accumulation of commodities. They are fulfilled only when they relinquish their idols, only when they see things as *expressions*, and servants of personhood. The vow of poverty emphasizes detachment, simplicity, sharing, and a celebration of the goods of the earth. In each emphasis, the vow then embodies a clear alternative to cultural dogma. At the same time, it is also a solid foundation for social activism, rooted in the conviction that the human person is primary in ethical, political, and economic life; thence follow the moral imperatives of equity, the fair distribution of wealth, the obligation to help the poor and dispossessed, and the desirability of communitarianism. The vow of poverty is the theoretical and practical controlling limit on our relation to property and things. Religious life demands it as a bulwark of its fidelity and promise. But our culture needs it even more desperately.

The second major area of human interaction is in the issue of power. We have seen how this issue is resolved by the cultural gospel, with its emphasis upon *laissez faire* marketing and morality, upon isolation and individualism, upon domination, control, and competition. The vow of obedience professes that isolation and egocentrism, as well as the violence that arises from them, will not rule one's life or one's community. It is a purification of the ego's demands for self-sufficiency. Obedience is a commitment to resolve human struggles not through domination, but through openness to the other and a yielding of one's "non-negotiable demands." Obedience is the willingness to be named, to be called, and to be held responsible as an interdependent social being.

The final crucial area of the counter-cultural stance of the religious vows is human affectivity. Not only is this area repressed in the Commodity Form; it is also displaced, by the reduction of human sexuality to mechanics and dispirited coupling. Musculature displaces passion. Love is a production, a making, a making it. It is a performance and a drive to legitimation. Commitment is evaded, as we have seen, and the purifications of our desires and affections never take place. Rather, they are channeled into the seductions of escape, violence, and manipulation. The vow of chastity, on the other hand, professes human interiority and the trans-cultural, trans-temporal sacredness of the human body. Letting go of the immortality of blood, it affirms the eternality of Love. It is an exercise of free disengagement from cultural imperatives; it is a declaration of independence from the devaluation not only of sexuality, but of personhood itself.

In each of these areas—power, property, and affectivity— the person who lives the vowed life finds himself or herself in radical opposition to the values of the culture. In each area, moreover, we have a social and political programmatic, an alternative model of human interaction and growth, a model for entering and changing the cultural ambient. Sharing. The primacy of persons over property. Responsibility in a mutually accepted interdependence. Human loving. The elevation of sexuality to a human act.

So many men and women who live the traditional religious life of the vows do not make such connections. Traditionalist groups fail to draw any relationship between the life they profess to live and its socio-political impact. They often present themselves as political quietists with personal and corporate financial security.

More reformed groups have succeeded only in passing themselves off as accomplished "men and women of the world." What special gift do they have to offer? They are not perceived as a challenge to or hope for the desperation of our society. And often, uninformed by prayer, asceticism, or passionate spirit, they perceive themselves as secularists with little to give or say. In both cases, the powerful content of the three vows is neither perceived nor practiced.

In this instance, religious men and women fail to touch the energetic sources of their vocation. And it is precisely this misconnection which underlies the ineffectual changes that have been attempted. Only when we see ourselves as social and cultural beings who have chosen a gospel other than the one offered by the culture itself can we discover our full vigorous potentialities and make the changes that are incumbent upon us. Only then can we see the necessity for a life of integrity in our sexual lives, a life of authentic sharing, simplicity, and detachment in our use of things, and a life of true responsibility and commitment in obedience.

We are witnessing, perhaps now more than ever, an increasing demand for a more explicit presence of Christian communities and their living of the life of the Gospels and evangelical counsels. The need is even more pressing when situated in a civilization that grows continuously more materialistic, individualistic, and consumption-oriented, more technologically trapped, more mechanistic in its affectivity, and more fragmented in its long-range life commitments.

If my reading of our culture is correct, the last thing desirable for religious people is an easy identification with such a culture. The last thing needed is another milieu-culture Christian or milieu-culture community. Christianity indeed must be lived in space and time within cultures—but always beyond the culture, transcending it and transforming it, and if necessary working against its values as a counter-cultural force. The life of the traditional vows is an attempt at an admittedly limited "unambiguous statement" about the fulfillment of persons in non-appropriation, in a love which is not reducible to genitality, and in a committed life of mutually shared risk and openness to the other.

We presently experience a growing awareness, on the part of many young persons, of the desirability of and necessity for a shared community of prayer, vision, support, and resistance to the idols of capitalism. Many young people are recognizing that their faith, hope, and love have to be made explicit and embodied in community consciousness and action. Yet these people find little of the direction and leadership they seek. They look for the encouragement of lived witness and invitation, but the lived witness is too often ambivalent, too often like the culture itself; and the invitations are too often hidden, too often timid.

At the same time, a considerable number of men and women who have embraced the life of traditional vows and community are experiencing a call to a personal and communal rebirth as Christians. They desire to have their faith and vows more radicalized and centrally focused upon the Gospels and the person of Christ. They experience this call not so much as a judgment upon the past as a judgment upon their own future.

Moreover, there is a growing need for mediation in the church and in society, due to increasing polarization, incapacity for tolerance, and the instability of men and women in their life promises. It has to be questioned whether the present structures of the parish and religious houses are truly capable of meeting these polarizations and challenges. Perhaps a more intense communal life of prayer, celebration, and service is the most appropriate response. But there is little leadership available and few viable models of community life are offered. In response to such a situation, it would be well to consider whether traditional communities could see their mission as providing models for corporate living and sharing which are less culturally ambiguous and more open to the larger church around them.

Many communities of religious in their training live in large buildings (even though they might be divided into smaller subgroups) that tend to separate their members from other people, because of environmental necessity or for the sake of efficiency or academic efficacy. Many undesirable possibilities emerge: isolated personal lives, irresponsible and dishonest attitudes towards poverty, anonymous security and abundance, unresponsiveness to communal needs or excessive waste, and assumption of leisure-class values and aspirations, with ignorance of critical social issues and decisions (racial prejudice, abortion, militarism, media exploitation, penal reform, urban decay). These are often the byproducts of isolation, suffocating comfort, and false security.

After the completion of religious formation a person often tends to find self-definition in terms of an institution, a school, or a professional task. Sharing frequently takes place on this level alone—students, classes, projects. Sharing of faith, doubts, communal strategy, decision making, mutual encouragement and correction become privatized and increasingly infrequent. What is neglected, because it is taken for granted and rarely made explicit, is the fact that faith and the life of vows rooted in Christ are the only sustaining bases of corporate identity and personal meaning.

Moreover, the institutional frames themselves tend to separate religious men and women from other people. A religious faculty as a community of service and faith rarely shares its life with the lay faculty even to the simple extent of sharing meals with them, Eucharistic or other. Rarely are outsiders regularly invited to pray with the religious community. The houses take on the appearance of closed fortresses; at least that is the way they are frequently—albeit sometimes unjustly—perceived. Community life can become so closed as never to have a basis for sharing lived faith with fellow professionals, students, friends, or even members within the community. What is shared is knowledge, professional competence, even ministerial powers—but rarely the intimacy of a life lived in faith and hope.

In some unfortunate moves toward smaller communities, none of the difficulties above are really transcended; rather they are transposed merely into another smaller, more private, more secularized, more comfortable environment. What we lack in these cases—as in our dying large communities—is a model of communal life that emerges from a cultural and social understanding of the meaning of the vows in a lived atheistic culture. What we lack is a vision of community life which is apostolic in the very offering to society of an alternative way of living and being together. What we lack is an insight into the dialectical relationship between faith and society.

Religious communities, in their effort to renew themselves, miss the power of their own traditions and the vows when they search for ways to make life more amenable and luxurious, or more isolated and rigidly formal, or more cozy and undemanding. An understanding of how the Commodity Form has insinuated itself into both the conservative and the modern models of community might serve to unleash the full potential of communities of men and women who openly testify to a personal and corporate living out of the Gospel of Jesus Christ. Too often religious life has been and remains a testimonial to affluence, financial survival, isolation, and individualism—the hallmarks of the Commodity Form way of life. It need not be that way. But it will be otherwise only if we so choose—newly conscious of the cultural and social context of lived faith.

CHAPTER TWELVE

LIVING LIFE
IN THE PERSONAL WORLD

There is already a real perceptible danger that, while our dominion over the world of things is making enormous advances, we could lose the essential threads of our dominion and in various ways let our humanity be subjected to the world and become subject to manipulation in many ways—even if the manipulation is often not perceptible directly—through the whole of the organization of community life, through the production system, and through pressure from the means of social communication. We cannot relinquish the place in the visible world that belongs to us; we cannot become the slave of things, the slaves of economic systems, the slaves of production, the slaves of our own products . . . [The answer] is a matter of the whole of the dynamisms of life and civilization. It is a matter of the various initiatives of everyday life.

John Paul II, *Redemptor Hominis*
(rendered into first-person plural)

When we consider the vast range of the Commodity Form's influence in our lives, whether it be in national policy, in our media, or even in the forming of our personal experience, the sense of its totalized presence can overwhelm us. Where to begin? How can one start to resist and not have one's beginnings be some futile fragmentary gesture? The variety of the ways of expressing commitment to the Personal Form might appear to be too much to handle. A resolution to this threatening sense of paralysis about so many problems and so many possible responses can be found only when we once again understand and apply the "principle of totality"— the fact that our personal lives, our faith, our labor, our prayer—are all intimately related to social, political, and economic reality.

Our understanding of the all-encompassing struggle between Christ and idolatry as competing total *worldviews* that claim our allegiance should impinge on all of the concrete choices and particular options before us, what John Paul II termed "the various initiatives of everyday life." It is our commitment in faith which vivifies and gives meaning to the partialities of isolated decisions and the various expressions of that commitment.

The totality—a life of faith in Christ—lives in and is sustained by the particularities of diverse parts; and the parts receive their life and meaning by their relationship to the totality which is at the center of our lives. This, ultimately, is the meaning of the Mystical Body, a doctrine which helps us articulate how the Personal Form can be embodied and enacted in our different lives and labors. We all have distinct gifts and life choices; they are a coherent organic whole by virtue of the common Spirit we share. The diverse ways we resist the Commodity Form are necessarily different for each of us; but the universality of our common allegiance to the Personal Form in faith unites us.

As a practical application, I will simply suggest how one might integrate one's life, embodying the unity of faith and justice and at the same time maintaining a vision of the whole.

The example I give will be that of a middle-class Catholic mother of three, but the schematic pattern is applicable to young persons in search of a way to resist consumerism, men and women religious—teachers, administrators, spiritual guides—to professional lay persons, to bluecollar workers, to old and young.

Each dimension, it will be noted, represents a response to the "life" of the culture and its "texts" which we examined in chapter one. The full integration of these different dimensions represents the Christian "return to the self in solitude," a recovery of relationship in covenant, a recommitment to the works of justice, a rededication to the simplicity-of-life principle that "things are for persons," and a compassionate remembering of the marginal and the visibly wounded in our world.

THE RICHES OF INTERIOR POVERTY

We must re-learn to be alone. It is a difficult lesson to learn today—to leave one's friends and family and deliberately practice the art of solitude . . . For me, the break is the most difficult. Parting is inevitably painful, even for a short time. It is like an amputation, I feel . . . And yet, once it is done, I find there is a quality to being alone that is incredibly precious. Life rushes back into the void, richer and more vivid, fuller than before. It is as if in parting one did actually lose an arm. And then, like the starfish, one grows it anew; one is whole again, complete and round—more whole, even than before, when the other people had pieces of one.

Anne Morrow Lindbergh,
Gift from the Sea

The "empty" interior life of cultural ideology is primarily resisted by one's willingness to confront oneself in the present moment, stripped of pretense and appearances, freed from the impulses to produce, consume or control, open to the simple reality of the here and now. What am I, when I am not planning tasks to be done, proving something by comparing myself to others, programming my information, or producing the things that seem to validate me?

For our mother of three, prayer will be crucial, as a regular method of centering her life, of bringing order to the constant demands and tasks that fashion a home and young family. Without this centering in faith, even if it be for ten minutes a day, the full reality of her life will never be brought to full attention. She will be lost in particulars which become duties exacted of her rather than expressions of love and choice. Without centering, she will be unable to see how the compassion, affection, care, and structuring she provides her children are important social acts, are furtherances of justice, and are profound methods of resisting the Commodity Form. She will be unable to see how the crucible and joys of intimacy with husband and children are actually the testing and living out of the revelation of Christ. She will miss seeing how the purification of her needs and demands is actually worked out in relationship, and as such is related to the suffering and victory of Christ.

Her centering in prayer is a declaration of independence from the thousands of culturally created pressures in her head pushing her around with threats and fear. Prayer liberates her from our culture's criteria of success. Daily centering is an "enabling" activity, whereby she becomes once again conscious of the irreplaceable present and extricates herself from endless tapes about the past and endless rehearsals of the future. She repossesses her life and mind and feelings. Prayer brings her in touch with her deepest identity, her most basic desires and hope, her poverty and her promise. This centering with her relationships of intimacy will be foundational in any human expression of the Personal Form in Christ. It will also be crucial to her resistance to the Commodity Form. If this does not occur in her life, all other procedures and tactics will be worthless.

The commitment to solitude and the rediscovery of our interior lives, however, is not an easy discipline to undertake. Not only is it difficult to disengage our selves from the noise of our culture's media; it is daunting, as well, to let go of the demands of our work and relationships, just to make time for quiet.

Moreover, there may even be a lurking fear to face ourselves in the simple truth of who we are before God, to let go of illusions, of control, or of the various external riches we think are central to our worth. There is no way a "self-made" man or woman can adequately enter the presence of God. All that we can bring, ultimately, is the poverty of our humanity and creatureliness. It is interesting that Jesus in the gospel story of the Pharisee and Publican contrasts a "self-made man," who thanks God that he is not like the rest of people because of his virtue and accomplishments, with the humble soul who can only offer repentance and trust. It is the Publican who goes home "one with God."

We often do not feel loved by God because we do not allow ourselves to be truthfully known by God. We are too often captivated by what we have done and what we have failed to do, whether for good or ill.

It is a great loss to us, for we never find out what it is about ourselves that makes us lovable, not only by God but by anyone. A prayer discipline of solitary witness to the truth of the Gospels invariably leads us to discover what it is that Jesus desired from those around him, what it is that God wants of us. "Never have I seen such faith." "Much is forgiven her because she has loved much." "Fear is useless; what is needed is trust."

The full riches of our personal interior world are best revealed in the Easter narrative where Jesus encounters Peter. Peter is someone who has had his successes and certainly tasted profound failure as well. When Jesus speaks, he is interested in neither wins nor losses. He is interested in one thing. "Do you love me?" What a vulnerable thing for the Word-made-flesh to say. Peter's response, moreover, can come only from the poverty of his vulnerable heart. In that moment, as well as in those irreplaceable moments of truth in solitary prayer, the power and the riches of personal existence are revealed. They are not what we have. They are what we are.

As Anne Morrow Lindbergh notes in the citation above, however, the discoveries of solitude enrich our relationships as well. Moreover, the same pattern persists: if we let go of our pretenses and the managerial control of our lives, we will find a truth that frees us in the covenantal world of persons.

THE POWER OF RELATIONSHIP

> It is not the desert island, nor the stony wilderness that cuts you from the people you love. It is the wilderness in the mind, the desert wastes in the heart through which one wanders lost and a stranger. When one is a stranger to oneself, then one is estranged from others too. If one is out of touch with oneself, then one cannot touch others. How often in a large city, shaking hands with friends, I have felt the wilderness stretching between us.
>
> Anne Morrow Lindbergh,
> *Gift from the Sea*

Solitude, of course, is not the whole story. As the great spiritual teachers knew, whether Teresa of Avila or Francis de Sales, prayer is tested and made most real in relationship. Family, community life, friends—our greatest joys can be the occasion of our most painful experiences. Dorothy Day wrote that the trials of interpersonal difficulties in the Catholic Worker houses were more harrowing than the intrusive guests at the door. Jean Vanier has said many times that getting along with the "handicapped" was easy when compared to getting along with fellow assistant volunteers. And Mother Teresa knew that the sacrifices of community life were more stressful than the asceticism of prayer and poverty.

In relationships of depth, we will find ourselves revealed. This is not always a pleasant experience. Allowing our selves to be known—especially our fears, our egoisms and pretenses—can be intimidating, especially when cultural clatter and amusing diversion are easy escapes. Work, projects, and possessions all offer a mode of relating that exacts nothing deeply personal from us. We need never be known. We need never be unmasked for what we are.

A woman about to be married worried: "What will he think when he finds out what I really am like?" The reluctant response was this: "If he doesn't know who you are, what do you think are the grounds for his loving and committing to you?" As in prayer, so it is in every relationship: if you do not allow yourself to be known, you will never experience being loved. What will be "loved" will be an illusion, a performance, a pretense, but your interior world will be opaque before others and, eventually, to yourself.

To be sure, there will be varying degrees of self-revelation in our relationships, depending upon the depth of our covenant and commitment in them. But any relationship that is authentic will involve self-disclosure. It will sometimes hurt. But it will be the only way we will experience being loved.

Our mother of three will find it important not only to foster and make time for her primal covenant, but also to enter into collaboration with other people, to share her family's strengths and struggles, to communicate her faith, to encourage and be confirmed in her choice. This will involve not only the formal relationship to a parish community, but also a more thoughtful interaction with other couples at the deeper level of faith for mutual challenge and support.

Taking a stand against the imperatives of competition and individualism in our culture, her participation in some kind of community will be most effective if it is marked by regular group commitments to prayer, discussion, celebration, and social service. This experience of community inevitably breaks through the isolationism that inhibits our capacity to form deep communal relationships.

These strategies, however, are merely ways of disposing ourselves to personal encounters with others. What cannot be planned or controlled or produced is the revelation of our power as persons. That requires not our productive efforts, but the acceptance of what we are gifted with—the very gifts of personhood that make each of us utterly unique and radically equal at the same time.

For that mother of three, it is only she who can give herself away. When she says, "yes, I believe in you, I hope in you, I love you"—all uttered out of the vulnerability of her heart—she has entered into her deepest personhood. She has also embodied, once again, the Trinity of Persons in the world.

PERSONALIZED THINGS: SIMPLICITY IN LIFE

For our use, humans have natural ownership of things, because through their reason and will, they can employ things for human benefit. They were made on behalf of persons.

It is against reason to be burdensome to others, showing no amusement and acting as a wet blanket. Those without a sense of fun, who never say anything ridiculous and are cantankerous with those who do, these are vicious, and are called grumpy and rude.

Saint Thomas Aquinas,
Summa Theologica

A critique of consumer society cannot mean a rejection of consuming. Nor does resistance to the commodity culture require a renunciation of things. As Martin Buber said, without the "It"—without things, without matter—we human persons could not live. In fact, the world of things and products, once transformed by the acts of love, creativity, and aspiration, is itself personalized, even divinized. Such can be the glory of any cultural production.

Obviously as well, without consuming, we're dead. Without things, we could have no embodied reality. The point of the critique is our *attitude* about producing and consuming. Are they extensions, revelations, celebrations of the personal world; or do they crush and repress it? Lovely clothes, a beautiful home, diverse cuisines, stirring art and play are, at their finest, the splendid embodiment and expression of personhood.

If we have no interior life or relational life, however, they can become our prisons. This is the message of Peter Whybrow's *American Mania: When More is Not Enough*, David Myers' *Spiritual Hunger in an Age of Plenty*, and Tom Kasser's *The High Price of Materialism*—only three of the latest studies demonstrating that the amassing of fortunes and distractions cannot fill the deepest needs of personal life.

Thus, our mother of three will do well to consider some personal asceticism in her relationship to things. Her interior dispositions and commitments, her most basic desires, must be *embodied* in practice. The fruit of the experience of authentic prayer is action at the most immediate level of experience, one's style of living. Everything need not be done at once, but something must be done as the embodied expression of her commitment and desire.

She will not let television be a surrogate life for herself or a substitute intimacy for her children. She will live more simply—not necessarily as some form of self-denial, but as an affirmation and appreciation of life and all the good it offers. She will treat Christmas less commercially and competitively. She will consume less alcohol, seek less after the appurtenances of comfort. No one of these expressions will be a *sine qua non* as an act of resistance to the Commodity Form, but some expressions must be made. Concrete practice, even if it is a simple thing, reminds us of who we are and what we choose. These changes in her style of life will enhance her ability to pray, will open her up to more people, and will heighten her concern for justice.

Restraint in our consuming and use of things is not a good in itself. Cut off from its personal roots—that all things are for the good of persons and the glory of God—such asceticism can become a bloodless ideology, as far removed from our truth as untrammeled hedonism. But connected to the integrating experience of solitude and relationship, it will invariably lead to an expansion of personal existence. Having traveled light enough to make time for the intrinsic gifts of our personhood in prayer and intimacy, we ineluctably begin to see the personal dignity of every mother's child, even those counted among the "least" of us.

THE AFFIRMATION OF PERSONS:
LABORING FOR JUSTICE

An English journalist, observing the Sisters of Charity in Calcutta, reasoned: "Either life is always and in all circumstances sacred, or intrinsically of no account; it is inconceivable that it should be in some cases the one, and in some the other."

Annie Dillard,
For the Time Being

In Annie Dillard's stunning meditation on the meaning of time and human significance, she recounts a litany of the great natural disasters which have devastated millions of people and then, more painfully yet, she presents a harrowing catalogue of destruction and degradation concocted by humans against one another. Whether the English policy that led to the starvation of a million Irish, Pol Pot's slaughter of one fourth of his fellow Cambodians, Stalin's tens of millions, Mao's thirty million, or the eight hundred thousand Tutsis killed by hand in a hundred days, in every case of such massive injustice, the underlying theme of depersonalization is inescapable. Humans are objects, things, numbers, all expendable for a good enough reason.

For the Time Being is a strategic reminder of the fact that contemporary American culture is not the cause nor even the primary expression of injustice, violence, or depersonalization in the world. The degrading of persons takes as many forms as

there are cultures, and it is incumbent upon each culture to discover and acknowledge its own patterns of injustice.

In earlier chapters we have noted how the consumer society
can reduce persons to mere objects, whether by making them
mere functions of economic forces or demonized "enemies" and
criminals or by excluding them from our "community" of moral
agents because of their undeveloped or diminished functioning.
"Blobs of protoplasm" and brain-dead "vegetables" are much
easier to render expendable than merely nascent or profoundly
damaged persons.

Thus, the fourth strategy for integrating the Personal
Form in this one woman's life will be an ongoing education in
issues of social justice, even if her family or professional commitment makes much activism impossible. The consciousness
of the relationship between faith and justice will not only
open her to the emerging issues of equity and human dignity,
it will also give her personal and family life a social and political content. Connections have to be made—not only among
the wide diversity of issues, but also between social issues and
her familial commitment—as resistance to cultural persuasion. Truly "being" a family and "parenting" children are as
much counter-cultural acts of justice as they are acts of faith,
hope and love.

A merely "general understanding," however, will not sufficiently embody her societal commitments. In addition, it will be
important for her to give some portion of her time and energy
to at least one movement for justice, whether by serving as as a
conduit for others, or being knowledgeable about an issue's implications, or by taking part in lobbying, group organization, or
public protest. Commitment to a particular issue, as well as the
power and resourcefulness of her commitment, will depend on
her capacity to integrate and concretize her "partiality" to the
wide variety of struggles against the degradation of persons.
Thus, critical consciousness of the spectrum of social problems
and how they are related to the underlying Commodity Form
will sustain and be sustained by her investment of time in one
specific person-commodity conflict.

A Christian's commitment to justice is not some merely political phenomenon. It is not a function of party or ideology, whether of the right or left. It is a matter, ultimately, of faith in the words of Jesus in the Gospels. Whatever we do to the least of our brothers and sisters, we do to him. Having identified his own body with the least of human persons, Jesus has revealed to us that our treatment of them is not only a matter of justice. It is a question of sacrilege.

EMBRACING THE WOUNDS OF PERSONAL LIFE

There are no ordinary people. You have never talked to a mere mortal. Nations, cultures, arts, civilization —these are mortal, and their life is to ours as the life of a gnat. But it is immortals whom we joke with, work with, marry, snub, and exploit . . . Next to the Blessed Sacrament itself, your neighbor is the holiest object presented to your senses. If he is your Christian neighbor, he is holy in almost the same way, for in him also Christ *vere latitat*—the glorifier and the glorified, Glory Himself, is truly hidden.

C. S. Lewis,
"The Weight of Glory"

The final integration of counter-cultural personal life occurs when we deliberately enter the presence of persons for whom the consumer and commodity ideology is not a dream, but a nightmare. These might be people of profound dependency on others, often at the margins of cultural life. Perhaps they are hopelessly unproductive or incapable of achieving anything. They may be so seriously handicapped, senile or wounded that nothing can be done for them except abide with them.

C. S. Lewis's observation that our God is "hidden" in the person next to us is intensified by Simone Weil's conviction that this truth is fully revealed only by those held of no account according to cultural standards. In her *Selected Letters,* after observing that Shakespeare's fools are the only people who tell the truth, she writes, "There is a class of people in this world who have fallen into the lowest degree of humiliation, far below beggary, and who are deprived not only of all social considerations but also, in everybody's opinion, of the specific human dignity, reason itself—and these are the only people who, in fact, are able to tell the truth. All the others lie."

The family woman we have been imagining will have many occasions to be in touch with the impoverishments of human life—in the utter dependence of her young children, the ever-present purifications of yielding their future to hope and trust, the sufferings and truth of intimacy. At the same time, however, it will be valuable for her to have some kind of continuing and regular contact with the very poor, the dying, the lonely, the handicapped. I mean by this not only organizational or support work, but immediate contact. What is at stake here is not so much something she can give them, although she will indeed be "giving." Far more important is what they allow her to see.

The ontologically and culturally wounded, as painful as their struggles are, have an unequalled power to educate us to our pretenses, our fears, and the rejection of our humanity. The handicapped often have no pretenses to cling to, and in their openness and necessary acceptance of their poverty they can disarm our greatest fears. They bear the wounds of humanity, visible before all, reminding us of our most dependent fragile beginnings, of our diminishment and dying, of our ultimate inability to manage and control either our bodies or our world. Thus, this woman will learn to see herself in the poor, encountering her own impoverishment, her own aging, fear, and sense of abandonment. In allowing her to be a part of their lives, the marginalized will engage and call forth from her greater fearlessness and love. They will empower her for fuller truth and compassion.

The struggles for social justice, the necessity for political change, the penetration of prayer into her life will take their most profound hold upon her only when she is in touch with her true poverty as a human being by identifying with those who have come to be called the dispossessed. Her initial fear and anxiety will dissolve when she yields to their presence, faces her humanity, and surrenders to her own neediness. She will find her commitments purified and deepened, her family life enriched. Her life of prayer will become more real. Her style of living will little by little change. And she will become aware of personal powers she never thought she had.

Dr. Ann Manganaro, a Sister of Loretto and neonatal physician, discovered this truth but a few years before her own dying from cancer. She had been taking care of a premature, abandoned infant for weeks in her intensive care unit. When all efforts to keep the baby alive failed, she took care of the burial. When asked by a friend what the point of the baby's life was— he had never seen his mother, never been without a ventilator, never tasted food or played, never spoken, never achieved any-thing—Dr. Manganaro's answer was this: "You forget some-thing. That baby had the power to evoke my love."

And so it would come to pass for Dr. Manganaro that she would fully realize that baby's power. In her last days, sur-rounded by family and friends who knew so well her great gifts of intellect and heart, now diminished, the very last gift she gave them was the power to evoke their love.

THE COUNTER-SYNTHESIS

Do you hate consumer culture? Angry about all that packaging, all those commercials? Worried about the quality of the "mental environment"? Well, join the club. Anti-consumerism has become one of the most important cultural forces in millennial North Ameri-can life, across every social class and demographic. Sure, as a society we may be spending record amounts of money on luxury goods, vacations, designer cloth-ing and household comforts. But take a look at the nonfiction bestseller lists. For years they've been populated by books that are deeply critical of consumerism: *No Logo, Culture Jam, Luxury Fever, Fast Food Nation.* You can now buy *Adbusters* at your neighborhood music or clothing store. Two of the most popular and critically acclaimed films in the past decade were *Fight Club* and *American Beauty*, which offered almost identical indictments of modern consumer society.

What can we conclude from all this? For one thing, the market obviously does an extremely good job at responding to consumer demand for anti-consumerist products.

Joseph Heath and Andrew Potter,
*Nation of Rebels: Why Counterculture
Became Consumer Culture*

You cannot *build* a counterculture, for that itself is a cultural product you've made. The only thing you can do counter-culturally is something that the culture cannot cause or you produce. It must transcend human production, the consumer society, the world of commodities. All of our efforts to construct a counter-culture are condemned to failure because they are our efforts. Our media exhibits the same enclosed paradox of self-creation, stuck in human narcissism. As Thomas de Sengotita notes in *Mediated,* "the bubble of self-regarding self-representation that has insulated us for so long from the suffering of millions in a world dominated by our interests and institutions . . . will reform around us, and cradle us again." Culture is inescapable if culture is all there is.

And yet it has been the contention of this book that there is another form of existence. The Personal Form of life is a reality in which we participate but something we have not created. It is something we have been given. This form of life, moreover, must animate every task we undertake as human persons, if we are not to be mere pawns of culture, society, capital, the media or any other of our "tasks."

If we wish to embody the Personal Form of existence in our culture, we will have to integrate our experience. Just as the Commodity Form makes its way into each arena of our lives—in our loss of personal focus, in our isolation from each other, in our personal manners of consuming and living, in the broad structural realities of social injustice, and in our repression of our consciousness of the marginalized poor—so the Personal Form must live in and permeate each experiential arena. One area alone will not be enough. Prayer alone will not work, unless it is tested in relationship and its fruit is borne in the works of justice and mercy. Community alone suffocates in self-interest if it is not sustained by individualized life-commitment, prayer, and the outreach to service. Style-of-life changes without a sense for justice and an ongoing contact with the poor are ineffectual and ultimately self-defeating. Tithing one's time for the marginal, for it to be an authentic and lasting commitment, can be maintained only by a life of prayer, community life, and the intimacy of centering and resting in the truth of prayer. The project of holiness in society is just as dialectical as the power of social and personal disintegration.

All areas of our lives interpenetrate each other, live in and through each other, and actualize the life of the totality. Such is the mysticism of the body. The integration of the parts enables the totality of faith to be concretized and sustained in our daily lives. Such an integration is the only enabling resistance to the idols of capitalism. It is also the only enabling response to the Gospel of Christ.

The Commodity Form of existence makes claims upon our lives through the systemic interpenetration of every area of our experience: the loss of solitude and personal identity, the dissolution of community and commitment, the insensitivity to the multifaceted occurrences of injustice, the insinuation of consumerism into our very manner of living, and the repression of our consciousness of "marginal persons."

We must allow the Gospel of Jesus to do the same, for the claim of the Personal God upon our hearts and lives is as systemic as the claim of idolatry—worshiping our productions.

The life of Jesus is not only that wherein we are saved, not only that by which we are instructed; it is also the very way, the very methodology, of Christian praxis.

In the early stages of Jesus' public life, as the Gospel of Luke presents it, we can discover how Jesus makes his own response to the call of God and the challenge of the world. After having fully committed himself to partaking in our humanity through his baptism, Jesus is led under the power of the Spirit into the desert (the poverty of solitude and personal prayer). He then emerges radically changed in his manner of living, having resisted the temptations to the pleasurable, the spectacular, and the powerful (style of life). He goes back to Galilee to announce the good news to the poor and set the downtrodden free (laboring for justice) before he undertakes a life of ministering and healing (tithing to the marginal and the "least"). Weary, he calls friends to himself to share in the apostolic undertaking of the kingdom (community life).

We see so clearly here that the integration of all five arenas in our personal world is not only a tactic for resisting cultural ideology. Nor is it merely some method for incorporating the gospel into our lives. It is the way of Jesus who is the Way.

And his Way is this. As opposed to every human effort, every culture ever built, every cultural product humans have fabricated by their skills, ingenuity, or marvelous means of production, there is a hidden reality embedded within the least of human persons and is utterly irreducible to culture. For it is not something humans can produce, manufacture or cultivate. Nor is it something they can "present" as their role or profession or public image.

This reality, moreover, is not a finite, non-renewable natural resource that, once expended, is lost. Quite to the contrary, it lasts only when it is expended. It is real only when it is given away. Finally, it is not something achieved. It can only be received as a gift: our endowment of personhood with its power to have love, hope and faith evoked from us and to call them forth from others. This is why God could be so in love with us as to become one with us, even in our humblest, most needy condition.

To be a human person is inevitably to be lodged in culture. But we are not made in the image of any culture. Culture is *our* image. We are the image of *God*. Such is the revolutionary nature of holiness.

CONCLUSION

REVOLUTIONARY HOLINESS

The practice of Christianity has too often been isolated from its social and cultural context. To the extent that it has been so isolated, faith has been ineffective—both in the impact that it has had on the lives of Christians and in the power of its witness to the culture in which it exists. On the one hand, Christians have been too uncritical of the ways in which the economic system and the political structure have influenced and even distorted Christian values. On the other hand, Christians have been unimaginatively dualistic in their understanding of how their faith might be of social and cultural importance.

Even in so-called "Christian" cultures like ours, the operative values and modes of perception have often been virulently anti-Christian and anti-human while people of belief persisted in pretending that such a social and political environment had nothing to do with faith. In its most distressing instances, organized Christianity has actually served to legitimate worldviews and political systems whose values are diametrically opposed to the message of Christ as found in the Scriptures. With the excuse that they were merely rendering unto Caesar what was Caesar's, Christians have not infrequently rendered unto him their consciences, their life purposes, their hopes, and even their children. The problem has been most intensified in those cases where Christian churches have been

closely identified with worldly or cultural power. The legitimation of that power soon displaced fidelity to the Gospel of
Christ as the foundation and guide of the Christian life.

Today, the situation of Christians in American culture is
paradoxical: although the culture is nominally Christian, the
values of our society are appearing as more and more anti-
thetical to those of the gospel. Reading the signs of the times
can jar us into seeing the striking oppositions between cultural wisdom and Christian wisdom. It is my belief that the
Commodity Form claims such ultimacy and takes so powerful a hold over our consciousness that we are obliged to make
a choice of final allegiance between contradictory accounts of
how humans might be served and saved.

A critical awareness of the Commodity Form and its pervasiveness in our values and perceptions is the first condition of
such a choice. It is only when we face up to the fact that there
are fundamentally opposite readings of the human situation
beckoning our allegiance that we can face the choice that is upon
us. This consciousness, moreover, enables us to see the pattern
of values that underlies a wide diversity of issues which so often
tend to separate and isolate us—values usually based upon prejudice, special interest, or selective application of principle.

Only when such consciousness is operative can a Christian
perceive that racism, abortion, militarism, are not questions of
mere politics. They are questions concerning faith in God and
humanity. It is not a matter of personal preference or privatized
morality that a person resist the legitimation of capital punishment and abortion, or protest the selling of armaments and Saturday night specials; it is a question of how that person views
human nature, its dignity, and purpose. There is a Christian
view. And it is unalterably hostile to the Commodity Form.

Our purpose here has not been to prove that capitalism is
essentially contradictory to the message of Christ. Even though
that could be the case, we have been more interested in showing how capitalism, if it is not subjected to standards of a
value system or vision of humanity outside of its own criteria

for truth, value, usefulness, and success, is inherently destructive of humanity, and *a fortiori* systematically opposed to Christianity. For, in the absence of any other belief system than itself, capitalism will fabricate its tyrannical idols and subject men and women to a bondage and spiritual destitution as devastating as any totalitarianism.

Atheist Marxism could not escape disillusionment and disintegration. Its institutions were not humanistic, not just, and not self-critical: class analysis and rigid state structures became the legitimation of violence, destruction and a metaphysics of fear. The terror of men and women who lived under totalitarian regimes only enkindled further their desire for freedom and integrity. What was finally discovered was the truth suggested 25 years ago, in the first edition of this book.

At the center of Marxism was a gaping hole. It is absence of spirit. There is little of compassion and hope. There is a lack of faith in the resilience and freedom of men and women. And most damaging of all, there are ultimately no good reasons provided for persons to be free and alive. People are expendable because, again, there are no controlling limits to ideology. Having no transcultural, trans-statist values grounded in the human person, men and women are the sacrificial offerings to the idol of the idea. Only in those Marxist countries where there was a thriving culture-transcending faith was the power of resistance felt and the dignity of the individual affirmed against totalitarian domination. In the case of China, having extirpated its ancient faiths and repressed openness to new ones, communism has yielded to capitalism, now in the service of totalitarianism. Those pundits who have insisted that capitalism is inherently liberating may have to rethink their presuppositions. They may also have to wonder what would happen to the earth if China ever consumed at a rate equal to our pre-eminent consumer society.

There are pressing questions, however, that remain for Christians, especially for those of us who are Christians in the United States and other Western and Northern countries.

Do we also have to face a gaping absence of spirit in our own political and economic life? Is there a lack of passion for human dignity and equality, an absence of moral outrage at the subjugation and demeaning of human beings? Have we unquestioningly accepted the "status quo" as the only real world that can be lived in and passed on to our young? Is our faith merely nominal and superficial—so much so that our children see no lived alternative to the lives of depersonalization which our culture offers them? Might it take us greater courage to resist, in word and action, the idolatry of consumerism than it has taken to resist the "evil empire" of the communist world?

At an international meeting of Jesuits in the mid-1980s, a group of us were discussing the problem of atheism in our various cultures. Aware that our faith was strongly influenced by our differing political and economic worlds, I mentioned to a Jesuit from Poland that while in his own country the greatest courage might be demanded of them to resist communism, I thought that in the United States the greatest courage was required to resist consumerism. He astounded me when he answered: "No, in Poland it takes much more heroism to speak out against the materialism of capitalism than the materialism of communism. Communism, we can identify; consumerism is so much more subtle and lethal."

If a man who lived behind the Iron Curtain could see it, why is it that we cannot? The great task of holiness and of following Christ in a consumer society is not a matter of right wing or left, of conservative or liberal. It is a matter of understanding the full message of Christ's redemptive mystery: that having been reaffirmed as persons in the full image and likeness of God, we must actually believe in God's redemption and see that love of one's self, one's neighbor, and God transforms every aspect of our lives and labors. The authentic disciple of Jesus is never pulled between a love of God and a thirst for human justice, is never seduced into the delusion that faith somehow has no connection with how we treat our sisters and brothers in this world, and is never presumptuous enough to believe that the great human struggle for justice can ever be resolved without the most profound humility before a God who has created us equal in personhood and destiny.

Christians, when they abandon the questions of justice and hunger, of poverty and militarism, to socialists, liberals, and Marxists, do as great a disservice to their own identity as to the human community. Quietism and passivity not only perpetuate injustices committed against humanity, they also undercut the central fact of Christ's life and message. Jesus called to the attention of the disciples of John that he is recognized and preached precisely *in* the actions of justice, compassion, and human liberation. Christ *identified himself* with the face of the poor, the dispossessed, the hungry, and the imprisoned. To exclude them and their oppressed condition from the content of the Christian faith is to exclude its founder and Lord.

Excluding the social, political, and cultural content from Christian faith debilitates the church in other ways. First, having left the questions of justice to social activists, agitators, and Communists, many Christians paradoxically see the movements of justice and liberation as the work of atheistic Communism and the devil. This is a profound perversion of their own religion, sadly compounded by the identification of all the evils in the world with communism.

Thus externalizing evil, the church suffers a second debilitation in the absence of interior self-criticism. Critics within the church are seen, and often perceive themselves, as the enemy; thus they often leave the church or are forced to leave it. Any hope for an increased fidelity to the revelation of Jesus Christ is shortcircuited when the church denies its own sinfulness and need for conversion. Only the "others" have to be converted. And we forget that having denied our sinfulness, we may also ignore the beckoning of the Lord who came to call sinners.

Finally a further debilitating aspect of the faith/society dualism is that the church fails in its mission to its own culture. The values of a culture are somehow written off as being "out there," as being neutral to faith and spirit; thus the most powerful impediments to faith, embodied in the Commodity Form and the Idols of Capitalism, go unchallenged. And not only are they unchallenged, they are legitimated.

Social change, social criticism, and cultural growth have been largely ineffectual in American society and in the American churches because of the dangerous separation of spirituality and faith from society and justice. Social activists, bereft of the sources of spirit, commitment, lifestyle, and resilient faith, most often fail to bring any total vision or long-haul commitment to social programming and change.

Thus the liberated of one generation become the oppressors in the next. Values are not communicated; the balance of power is. A standard of living is raised; but so is the sense of alienation and depression. For the human spirit has not been touched. And the universe of discourse established by the Commodity Form is never transcended. Social change and institutional restructuring, separated from the life of spirit and faith, lead either to passionless disenchantment or—more frequently—social domination. This domination epitomizes the tragic failure of communism: born of the longings of the human spirit for integrity and joy, communism became a de-spirited and ruthless ideology, pragmatic and manipulative, closed and confining, as demeaning to humanity as the czar or imperialist it had hoped to replace.

On the other hand, when interiorized or ritualized spirituality has isolated itself from the concrete aspirations of oppressed men and women, our dualism has yielded merely passivity and compromise. Acquiescent before injustice, devoid of compassion for fellow human beings, people who have faith without just and loving action are bloodless spirits. And thus, while slaughtered millions are piled upon the altar of history, disincarnate faith dulls its human senses in narcissistic contemplation and self-fulfillment or the formalities of a self-justifying ritual. Men and women, as if in a daze, can continue to approach the Holy Table, breathe in lotus postures, or contribute to collection baskets, while starvation, institutionalized violence, and oppression of the poor become the accepted "ways of the world."

If only we Christians might realize the heights to which we are called by our incarnate, covenantal God. If only we might remember the utter newness and brilliance of what our faith implies. No longer would we have to search for some identity, some justification in the vast mountains of things. No longer would we clamor for some new savior or seducer. No longer could we even conceive of a fake choice between loving God or loving people, between seeking heaven and building the earth. No longer would we have to rely on some sweet morsel of satisfaction from the year-end *Time* magazine to tell us that our faith is still alive, quivering and groping around for cultural legitimation. In the solitude of prayer's self-presence and the movement of God's Spirit in our hearts, in our standing ontologically naked before our gospel and Lord, in our mutual sharing of faith and aspiration, we will have discovered not only our God, but our very selves, and other persons as well. And it will be the discovery of the foundations of the only true and permanent revolution.

A revolutionary in the fullest sense of the word—a man or woman who lets the imperative to be human take its deepest hold on his or her being, who becomes wholeheartedly committed to the service of people and a world of justice, who lives as he or she would call others to live—is nothing other than a saint. Francis of Assisi, Loyola, Gandhi, Dorothy Day, Barbara Ward, and E.F. Schumacher are the real revolutionaries. They move people's lives as Christ himself did; they have no time to shift musty furniture. They alone challenge and change the structures of oppression—because they call forth change in the human heart.

A qualitative revolution takes place in the monk who feels with his whole being the total claim that dying to oneself makes upon one's life; it drives him to deeper identification with all humanity, to the service of prayer and simplicity, to the purification of the intolerances within his heart.

Revolution is not in the swinging couple that is "into" liberated sexuality; but it can be found in the man and woman who live a life of sustained committed intimacy and fidelity to each other and their children. Their love and constancy will not only purify themselves and sustain others in their struggles; it will continually lead them outside of themselves into service of community, the transformation of their own style of living, and an abiding confrontation with all the social forms of human impoverishment.

True change is not brought about by the week-end radical or the seasonal rebel or the five-year planner; but it is brought about by the activist whose long-haul commitment radiates with a respect and love for persons. True revolution occurs only when one aspires with the full reach of one's hope to be disengaged from the deadly wheel of the idolized Thing and the violent injustice it necessitates.

It is only the saint who is the true revolutionary. For sanctity is not the quietism of formal rigidity or passionless interiority. Holiness will never occur where there is no passion or zeal for justice. It will never be found where there is no sense of one's own personal poverty nor a correlative love of the poor.

Sanctity is the acceptance of one's humanity, the acknowledgment that one is a loved sinner, and the overflowing of that experience of being unconditionally loved into compassion and honest labor. The saint is not one who displaces old regimes with the latest tyrant or idol. No, the saint does the only utterly new and sacred thing on the face of the earth. The saint has learned to give all—even his or her very self— freely away in a true revolution of life and love.

Saints are all around. One is a pastor to the handicapped who refuses to leave his "little ones" or the poor of his now no-longer-fashionable neighborhood. One is a judge who has long advocated the rights of the poor and adopted a homeless child as her own. Two of them are a suburban couple who hound supermarkets for unsold food to bring to guests at a Catholic Worker house.

One is a sister without religious garb, working through medical school, praying daily, living in the inner city among the disenfranchised; another is a sister in habit, a hospital administrator, who works for justice at the highest levels of medical leadership while quietly ministering to the poor at each sudden opportunity.

Some revolutionary saints, like Archbishop Romero, Rutilio Grande, and the four U.S. missionaries killed in El Salvador, boldly place their lives in the service of the poor—even at the risk of expulsion, imprisonment, or death. Others, family people, are voluntarily choosing to live poorly so that they may both offer their services to the needy and not be forced to contribute taxation monies for war making or any other form of human destruction. Other families, while middle-class economically, are quietly setting limits to their incomes so that their labors and professions are determined by human need and the fruit of their work may be shared with those who have nothing.

A community organizer, living in utter simplicity, developing a spirituality of human failure while he fights to restructure a city's zoning laws, is a holy revolutionary. Others are single people living in community, teaching, healing, serving people in their neighborhood, growing in the sacramental life. Still others are retired persons, who yet serve, who contribute silently and anonymously to the building of the earth. Some, finally, have even gone to jail in the name of justice, life, and peace. In each of these concrete human lives there is an interpenetration of faith and history, of God and time, of spirit and society. Each of these lives is revolutionary. Each is holy.

Only when faith and justice are seen as being mutually constitutive, only then is the social and cultural content of spirituality acknowledged and acted upon, and only then does the sanctification of human life take place and the saint emerge. Christ only was, only is, when God enters and embraces history. Authentic sanctity, like authentic revolution, is discovered, finally, when human life is seen as so splendid and irreplaceable that our very God might become one with it.

Men and women are of inestimable worth, not because they might serve as instruments in generating a gross national product, or even in building the earth, and not because they are capable of production or power and domination, but because in the compassionate embrace of their own truth, in the poverty of their being frighteningly incomplete, they find themselves—vulnerable, yes, but radically opened in freedom to the Fullness of personal knowing and loving. They make incarnate their very God.

Here alone will we find people of holiness and grace. Here alone will we find brothers and sisters fully empowered and willing to change the face of the earth.

READING ABOUT CULTURE AND FAITH

FORMATION AND INFORMATION

One of the more common difficulties we face in the Consumer Society as a totalized system is information. In many ways, whoever provides us with information forms us; and if the information system is largely controlled by forces that legitimize the consumer way of life, we will rarely encounter perspectives that question the received "wisdom" of the culture.

All information comes to us from a perspective; thus, it makes strategic sense to examine multiple perspectives. In the case of the broadcast and electronic media, except from the Internet, we will not often find a view of life that rises in contrast to consumer ideology. This is true even of the Public Broadcasting television programs, whose news programs are largely composed of data provided by our own government and corporate world, although there are some courageous exceptions. Invariably, commentators and discussants are restricted to academic and state department officials from the East coast and especially the Washington area. A presentation of "diverse" opinions is usually interpreted to mean a range of positions from highly conservative to moderate and liberal; all of these adjectives, however, fall within the confines of a presumed nationalism and consumerism. Rarely is the media system itself questioned; rarely are our economic dogmas subjected to critique; rarely is a perspective presented which challenges the "givens" of national interest.

In the instance of the two wars with Iraq, for example, the preponderance of information presumed unquestioningly the "justness" of our cause. The Arab side was rarely heard, the history of the region hardly considered, the plight of Jordan's King Hussein or of the Palestinians almost never entertained. Instead we got an endless array of ex-generals and Pentagon correspondents commenting on news reports which had already been censored by our army and state department. It is difficult, to this day, to get any accurate account of Iraqi lives lost during "Desert Storm," the years of sanctions, the final assault against Saddam Hussein, or the consequent years of occupation with the acts of Islamist terrorism it precipitated.

The situation on television was mirrored in news publications, especially the weekly news magazines. Even the *New York Times,* so often termed "liberal" by ordinary Americans, served as a reflection of governmental and corporate policy. A case could be made that a number of its columnists were actually instrumental in drumming up the war mentality and demonizing Saddam Hussein.

The "marketing" of news, moreover, has been segmented for target audiences. Some people will read only the *Washington Times* and view only Fox News, seeking confirmation of truths they are willing to "buy" into. Others will gravitate to certain PBS programs critical of government policy and read only columnists who offer a liberal perspective confirming their own.

With this problem of "perspective" in mind, the following annotated bibliography is presented. It is, to be sure, not exhaustive. Rather it is suggestive, a recommendation of places to begin. It should also be complemented by an investigation of magazines and journals which supply alternative readings of contemporary events. In this case, I recommend as a matter of fairness, at least two opposite sources that one might consider consulting. A trip to the public library every other week will make possible a more rounded and critical information base for our understanding of contemporary issues.

In the area of general political and economic opinion, a magazine such as *The Nation* should be read and balanced by *The National Review.* The first is as critical of American life as the second is accepting of it. Both are highly tendentious and feisty but challenging. It is in *The Nation,* however, where one will find a rare alternative to the consumer ideology. After all, the founder of *The National Review* (William F. Buckley) hosted his own influential PBS program, "Firing Line." And a former speech writer for Nixon mounted two weekly programs: "The McLaughlin Group," a still-airing discussion group engaged in ideological outbursts—with no true alternative represented—and McLaughlin's discontinued "One on One."

Among magazines of Catholic opinion, *America* offers a more centrist and liberal position, although it is not strongly critical of cultural ideology. *Commonweal* provides a probing analysis and questioning of nationalism and capitalism. In Catholic newspapers, one might balance *The National Catholic Reporter* with *The National Catholic Register.* They are both concerned with social and political matters, as well as the spiritual life and the life of the Catholic Church. The *Reporter* is more highly critical of American political, economic, and military policies—often with outstanding reporting and in-depth analysis; the *Register* is more accepting and uncritical. The *Reporter* seems, however, more acculturated to American liberal secular ideology in matters of the church, sacraments, and human sexuality, while the *Register* is more resistant to acculturated views of family, religion, covenant, and sexuality. More sustained argument can be found in *First Things*, in many ways a Neo-conservative Catholic publication (although it includes a range of other Christian and Jewish writers). While often thoughtful and probing, it manifests an almost uncritical support of capitalism and American military action. It can be balanced by reading the personalist-inspired *Houston Catholic Worker*, a newspaper that provides sustained and trenchant criticism of U.S. economic and international policies as well as abortion and capital punishment. *Sojourners*, an ecumenical radical evangelical magazine, is strongly grounded in gospel values and discipleship. Committed to justice, spirituality and community, as well as peace and life issues, *Sojourners* appreciated the integrated vision of John Paul II in a more whole-hearted way than some conservative Catholic publications that seemed to ignore the late pope's social, economic and international vision.

In Jewish publications, the more conservative *Commentary* contrasts with the liberal journal *Tikkun*. *UTNE Reader* is a *Reader's Digest* of the alternative press.

Two groups evaluate the media on a regular basis: AIM (Accuracy in Media), from what can be considered a conservative perspective, and FAIR (Fairness and Accuracy in Reporting), from a liberal perspective. Attention to both groups gives one an idea of just how "tendentious" our news media are. If a library has it available, it is worth reviewing the quarterly *Communication Research Trends*, which regularly features an annotated review of media and culture literature, often surrounding particular themes, such as ethics or religion.

The greatest explosion of information, including topics of Consumerism, Media, Christianity, and Capitalism, is surely on the Internet. In the case of publications mentioned above, one can simply type their names into Google, Ask, or Answers.com to access their websites. Almost each morning I access aldaily.com, an "Arts and Letters" site that provides links to major news groups, commentators, and journals. It also has the benefit of giving short introductions to new books, scholarly articles, and news stories. Then, there are the blogs, a mammoth network of individuals or groups that monitor and comment on contemporary events, link with favorite sources, advocate their particular perspectives, and often promote their work. I usually check in with Amy Welborn (Google "Open Book"), who reads like a Catholic super-mom, taking on *The Da Vinci Code*, commenting on Church and faith issues, linking you with her favorite blogs. "Godspy" and "Getreligion.org" have their own trove of links and issues. If you peruse the *Christianity Today* website thoroughly, you will find a treasure of information and links to blogs. The "ekklesia project," not quite a blog, but an information center for serious countercultural faith, is a jewel.

That is just a glimmer of the information available, for the most part focused on faith and culture. I have found in researching the material of the last fifteen years that there is more information available than one can process or even bear. Information, as a commodity to consume, can consume one's life—a dangerous tendency I have felt in my own life. Rather than read or surf the net, what I need more is solitude; relating with friends, community, and family; simplicity and service to the poor. Perhaps you may find the same in your own lives.

In the listing of books below, therefore, I have pared down recommendations from the previous editions. The influential abiding works will still be noted, but the majority of the recommendations will reference new research or penetrating analyses from the last fifteen years. There is no pretense that everything, even the best or most strategic, will be covered. If you detect serious omissions, you can inform me by email at kavanasj@slu.edu.

THE COMMODITY FORM

Consumerism in Media and Advertising

Robert McChesney has contributed two major studies of the media in the context of politics, capitalism, and advertising. *Rich Media, Poor Democracy* (University of Illinois Press, 1999) and *The Problem of the Media* (Monthly Review

Press, 2004) are serious critiques from the political left. Well researched and crammed with data, they stand out from the typical rants from the right wing (Bernard Goldberg's *Bias* and Ann Coulter's *Slander*) or the left (Al Franken's *Lies and the Lying Liars Who Tell Them* and Michael Moore's *Dude, Where's My Country?*). Ben Bagdikian's *The New Media Monopoly* (Beacon, 2004) is a long-standing, often revised, and newly edited analysis of the control over our information in the United States.

Thomas de Sengotita, in *Mediated: How the Media Shapes Your World and the Way You Live in It* (Bloomsbury, 2005), presents an imaginative and deceptively breezy account of how the media act as an all-encompassing "blob" that consumes and depersonalizes every area of our lived experience. Joseph Heath and Andrew Potter's *Nation of Rebels* (Harper, 2004) applies this phenomenon to every facet of the "counterculture" itself, always co-opted and domesticated by consumerism.

Ian Mitroff and Warren Bennis offer a startling and challenging critique of media and culture in *The Unreality Industry: The Deliberate Manufacturing of Falsehood and What It Is Doing to Our* Lives (Birch Lane Press, 1989). Their theme: "In Thoreau's phrase, *we have become the tools of our tools.* We invented a whole range of amazing machines, and now they are reinventing us. Ironically, the more sophisticated they have become, the more primitive we have become; the more active they are, the more passive we are, and the real world recedes more and more."

Jean Kilbourne, perhaps more than anyone else, has investigated the themes of addiction and objectification in the treatment of women. Her documentaries and lectures are well complemented by *Deadly Persuasion: Why Women and Girls Must Fight the Addictive Power of Advertising* (Free Press, 1999). Specifically targeted advertising is exemplified in D. Kirk Davidson's *Selling Sin: The Marketing of Socially Unacceptable Products* (Praeger, 2003 edition) and Tom Reichert's *The Erotic History of Advertising* (Prometheus, 2003). Eric

Clark's *The Want Makers* (Viking, 1989) is an outstanding place to begin if one wants to read about the world of advertising. It is filled with interesting facts, documented quotations, and strong critical analysis. It could be complemented with two less critical histories of advertising: *Advertising: The Uneasy Persuasion* (Basic Books, 1984) by Michael Schudson and *The Mirror Makers* by Stephen R. Fox (William Morrow, 1984). Carol Moog, an advertising insider and psychologist, has written a more personal, engaging, and analytic account in *Are They Selling Her Lips? Advertising and Identity* (William Morrow, 1990). She also suggests more psychologically positive ways of presenting advertisements. In 1995, Michael Jacobson and Laurie Ann Mazur sent out a clarion call titled *Marketing Madness: A Survival Guide for a Consumer Society* (Westview Press). Although the alarming statistics are now dated—but even more alarming—it is prophetic with its early indictment of advertising to toddlers and the co-opting of educational and civic institutions.

In recent years, the formation of teens and young children as consumers has been the focus of many studies. *Consuming Kids: The Hostile Takeover of Childhood* (New Press, 2004) is an indictment of the ways that childhood itself has been colonized by capitalism. Juliet Schor's *Born to Buy: The Commercialized Child and the Consumer Culture* (Scribner, 2004) is a more scholarly and fact-filled account. Alissa Quart's *Branded: The Buying and Selling of Teenagers* (Perseus, 2003) is more popular, particularly incisive on the exploitation of body-image in teens. *Freaks, Geeks, and Cool Kids* (Routledge, 2004) by Murray Milner is an extensively researched and theoretically nuanced treatment of identity segmentation even within the teenage years.

In 1977 Marie Winn wrote *The Plug-In Drug: Television, Children, and the* Family (Viking). It was such an important contribution to the study of television and its effect on childhood that Penguin published a completely updated edition in 2002. Like the earlier edition, the new book deals not merely with the content of television programs, but, more strategically, with the effects of watching television during the crucial stages of early childhood development. It contains much data and many practical suggestions as well as a penetrating discussion of the relationships between television and the development of the brain, the decline in reading ability and logic, the loss of creativity, the increasing occurrences of hyperactivity and violence, and the decline of the family, play, and commitment. To be sure, Winn has expanded her analysis to include VCR and DVD technology, computers and video games. More recently James Steyer has examined the extensive effects of the media on children and the erosion of family in *The Other Parent* (Atria Books, 2002). It is noteworthy for its helpful chapter on "strategies for change."

Neil Postman, in *Amusing Ourselves to Death: Public Discourse in the Age of Show Business* (Viking, 1985), proposes that entertainment has become the primary category of reality. While his is an engaging and popular critique, on a more sophisticated level, Stuart Ewen's *All Consuming Images* (Basic Books, 1988) demonstrates how surface, style, and pretense dominate our media and cultural life. Ewen's more recent book *PR! A Social History of Spin* (Basic Books, 1996) is a magisterial account of "public relations" during the last century. Mark Crispin Miller's brilliant *Boxed In: The Culture of TV* (Northwestern University Press, 1988) combines the themes of amusement and surface reality in a devastating analysis of television's form and content. "We will squeeze you empty and fill you with ourselves." "Big Brother is you, watching." A more radical critique of television, incisive, but highly theoretical and influenced by the neo-Marxist "Critical Theory" school, is Douglas Kellner's *Television and the Crisis of Democracy* (Westview Press, 1990). A more conservative evaluation of the influence of television on culture and politics is William Rusher's *The Coming Battle for the Media* (William Morrow, 1988). For a fascinating, regular source concerning culture and media, one can look into the *Journal of Communication*, especially the writings by George

Gerbner, the journal-newsletter *Media and Values*, and the counter-cultural *AdBusters*.

James Twitchell's works provide a wholehearted (and often entertaining) rejection of the cultural critique offered in the present book. *Adcult USA: The Triumph of Advertising in American Culture* (Columbia University Press, 1996) is an illustrated celebration of consumerism, followed by an equally enthusiastic endorsement of materialism in *Lead Us Into Temptation* (Columbia University Press, 1999) and conspicuous consumption in *Living It Up: Our Love Affair With Luxury* (Columbia University Press, 2002). He roundly rejects the worries and themes of many books listed above. In a section titled "Academic Bandwagon," he chides: "Railing against the consumption habits of others does have a kind of self-satisfied allure."

Degradation of Personal Life

The core reality of depersonalization is the treatment of persons as objects, commodities, things. The prime instance of personal degradation, then, is to actually turn them into objects by killing them. Killing is facilitated by removing certain classes of people from the privileged category of "personhood"—construed not as something we *are*, but as something performed, achieved, or seen as worthwhile. There is no intrinsic personal dignity or value here. There is only a value "bestowed" on humans by cultural, scientific, religious, or nationalistic dogmas.

Edwin Black's *War Against The Weak* (Four Walls Eight Windows, 2003) is a riveting account of the Eugenics Movement in America. It examines the relentless logic of depersonalizing degradation that inspired Nazi Germany but also haunts much of our national consciousness. Black uncovers the hidden utilitarian agenda that renders people expendable, a characteristic not only of the Holocaust but also of any movement that characterizes "marginal" humans as non-persons and expendable.

William Brennan in *Dehumanizing the Vulnerable* (Loyola University Press, 1995) skillfully unmasks this tactic in the treatment of women, Native Americans, African Americans, ethnic groups, and especially the unborn. Wesley Smith in *Culture of Death* (Encounter, 2000) concentrates on the depersonalizing tactics often used in medical decisions at the margins of human life. Human persons, reduced to brain activities, are apt candidates for elimination if their brain is undeveloped or profoundly damaged.

Lt. Col. Dave Grossman, a former professor of psychology at West Point, has presented a chilling account of the psychological costs of killing people. *On Killing* (Little, Brown & Company, 1995) treats the spiritual repression required to kill someone and how it can kill something within the killer. What is more, the book investigates the ways that our culture and its media can make killing easier. Lee Griffith's *The War on Terrorism and the Terror of God* (Eerdmans, 2003) examines the horrific combination of religious zeal and the permission to kill. Although this book could be more even-handed, it suggests the ways that any religion can be manipulated to justify the wholesale destruction of human life. Lou Michel and Dan Herbeck see the lethal logic in Timothy McVeigh, the Oklahoma City bomber, with *American Terrorist* (Regan Books, 2001). Those people were "collateral damage." The descriptions of his first "kill" in Iraq and his discussion with Islamist terrorists are chilling.

For a theoretical and theological examination of the dynamics of violence and the counter-reality of Christ, I recommend the works of René Girard. You might begin with *The Girard Reader*, edited by James Williams (Crossroad, 1996), and *Violence Unveiled* (Crossroad Classic, 1996) by Gil Bailie. Both authors, I believe, offer a penetrating account of Christian faith as a response to human self-destructiveness.

Related to the issues of "degrading" persons and killing them is personhood itself. In the past two decades we have seen a mounting philosophical conflict over accounts of human personhood. My own *Who Count as Persons? Human*

Identity and the Ethics of Killing (Georgetown University Press, 2001) argues that to be a person is to be a certain kind of being, a kind of being that has endowments for self-consciousness and self-conscious relational activities of love, commitment, freedom. Thus, God, angels, disembodied spirits, possible extraterrestrial beings are persons if they have such endowments. Unique to human persons is the fact that we are animal-persons. Because we are bodies, we are persons whose endowments are revealed over time and may not even be expressed because of our bodied conditions: lack of organic development or education, trauma, senility. But we are human persons from the moment we begin existing as human beings till the moment we die. It argues, moreover, that personal endowments are not reducible to our materiality or our brains. (That is why some being like God, without an organic brain, could be a person.)

There is an array of thinkers opposed to this account of human personhood. They usually share the conviction that to be a person is to have certain mental states dependent upon a functioning brain. Thus, Peter Singer in *Rethinking Life and Death* (Saint Martin's Press, 1995) denies personhood to newborn humans or profoundly brain-damaged humans. That is why he thinks it is morally permissible to kill them. Other thinkers, like Evelyn Pluhar in *Beyond Prejudice* (Duke University Press, 1995), use this "marginal person" argument not to justify infanticide, but to affirm that more "person-like" animals should be given the same protection we give to humans who are not "full" persons. The most sustained presentation of this line of argument can be found in Jeff McMahan's scholarly but deeply troubling *The Ethics of Killing: Problems at the Margins of Life* (Oxford University Press, 2002). He shares such a strong utilitarian ethic with Singer (who highly praises McMahan's book) that he can recommend harvesting the organs from a healthy but unwanted newborn baby to help out three "wanted" babies. A newborn has not passed the "threshold of respect." Since "we are not human organisms," similar applications can be made to "brain-dead humans." Such a line of reasoning has already entered into op-ed pieces and common discourse. Some implications of the notion that the body is some "thing" we emergent persons are attached to can be found in Andrew Kimbrell's *The Human Body Shop: The Engineering and Marketing of Life* (Harper, 1993)

In academic philosophical circles, Richard Rorty has become something of a reigning figure. If one has a speculative bent, it is interesting to see how the values of consumerism and capitalist "pluralism" dominate much of academia—both in the style in which academia is lived and in the content of theories. In *Consequences of Pragmatism* (University of Minnesota Press, 1982) Rorty compares philosophical conferences to "flea markets" and philosophical eminence to Andy Warhol's world where one might aspire to fame for fifteen minutes. He believes that philosophers should dedicate themselves to the task of helping students suppress any questions about the "meaning" or "ultimate value" of life. In content, he is part of a large movement in contemporary thought which sees itself as displacing or deconstructing the person. The more technical writings of Derek Parfit (who holds that there *is* no self and persons make no difference) and Patricia Churchland (who avoids addressing the meaning of human personhood in five hundred pages of "*neurophilosophy*") exemplify the trend. While some American philosophers seem to make room for personhood, such as Richard Bernstein, Calvin Schrag, Robert Nozick, John Rawls, and Alasdair MacIntyre, perhaps the most brilliant (and recondite) pen taken up on behalf of the person is that of Charles Taylor in his magisterial historical-literary-philosophical *Sources of the Self* (Harvard University Press, 1989).

Capitalism and Persons

Since the 1980's a growing number of Catholic thinkers have risen to the defense of capitalism. Perhaps the seminal work here is Michael Novak's *The Spirit of Democratic Capitalism* (Simon and Schuster, 1982). A reading of this book and Novak's recent works, combined with a perusal of the Acton Institute's website (for which, Novak serves as a member of its Board of Advisors) will present the reader with the strongest challenge to the thesis and themes of this book. Novak sees capitalism as the system most appropriate for the institutionalized values of freedom and Christian faith. Since the economic system, the political system, and the cultural system are all independent, they provide in their interaction, a flexibility, freedom, and cross restraint which is unique to democratic capitalism. This book is well worth reading, although I believe it suffers from a failure to recognize how money, greed, and consumption have come to dominate our political life as well as our religious practice. *Is the Market Moral?* (Brookings, 2004) by Rebecca Blank and William McGurn is a recent balanced discussion (McGurn is sympathetic to the Novak approach) of the relationship of culture, faith, and economics. Pope John Paul II, in the 1991 encyclical *Centesimus Annus,* has been taken as endorsing a "new democratic capitalism" by Novak as well as writers like George Weigel and the Reverend Richard John Neuhaus — an assumption hotly contested by Michael Baxter. See his essay "Blowing the Dynamite of the Church" in the excellent collection *The Church as Counterculture* edited by Michael Budde and Robert Brimlow (SUNY Press, 2000). *Centesimus Annus* also serves as starting point in the collection *The Consuming Passion* edited by Rodney Clapp (InterVarsity Press, 1999). From a more secular point of view, Thomas Friedman's *The Lexus and the Olive Tree* (Farrar, Straus, Giroux, 1999), an enthusiastic endorsement of free-market capitalism on a global scale, has won considerable acclaim from many who see the American model as the most freeing and enhancing for people.

This view, of course, has been long contested. Over the last fifty years, warnings about the bad effects of Capitalism have been issued by the likes of John Kenneth Galbraith in *The Affluent Society* (Mariner Books, Fortieth Anniversary Edition, 1998); C. Wright Mills in *The Power Elite* (Oxford,

1962, New Edition, 2000), one of the earlier books dealing with the inequities of wealth and the lopsided lines of political power distributed according to economic power; Robert Heilbroner in *An Inquiry into the Human Prospect* (R. S. Means, Revised Edition, 1991), a terribly pessimistic (but somewhat prescient) picture of the future in terms of excessive consumption by the wealthy and unending expenditures on armaments; and Daniel Bell in *The Cultural Contradictions of Capitalism* (HarperCollins, 20th Anniversary Edition, 1996). Bell, like the others mentioned, offers analyses of the crisis in values in North American society. These analyses, while in many ways radical, are remarkably conservative in their underlying affirmation of traditional values.

Kevin Phillips's *The Politics of the Rich and Poor* (Random House, 1990) is a withering critique of the Reagan years by a conservative populist. He amasses statistics to show how American wealth was systematically redistributed from the poor to the rich in the 1980's. His *Wealth and Democracy* (Broadway, 2002) is a warning that the unjust distribution of wealth is itself a threat to true democracy. Amitai Etzioni's *The Moral Dimension* (Free Press, 1990) remains an important critical contribution from the academic world of economics. Since its publication, the absence of the "moral dimension" has become even more troubling in the world of Corporate Greed. Just as the early nineties saw a spate of books on the Savings and Loan debacle, so also at the turn of the new century similar treatments would be offered concerning the corporate scandals involving Enron, WorldCom, Arthur Anderson, and others.

Paul Krugman, a professor of Economics at Princeton and an op-ed columnist for the *New York Times* (two criteria that will likely disqualify him for economic conservatives) has written *The Great Unraveling: Losing Our Way in the New Century* (Norton, 2005). No matter what your political leanings, you should examine this collection, unfortunately undocumented, of his articles on what could be the revolutionary dismantling of our economic system. This critical evaluation of the American system can be complemented by a group of books that have raised the question whether more production and consumption actually yield a more rich personal life. Robert Frank's *The Winner-Take-All Society: Why the Few at the Top Get So Much More than the Rest of Us* (Penguin, 1996) looks into the tremendous gap between stars or executives and ordinary Americans. Marjorie Kelly's *The Divine Right of Capital: Dethroning the Corporate Aristocracy* (Berrett-Koehler, 2003) is a business ethicist's indictment of shareholder supremacy in the free market.

In the last few years a new literature has emerged to question whether the expansion of consumer fulfillments actually yields fulfillment in personal life. David Myers, a psychologist, proposes in *The American Paradox: Spiritual Hunger in an Age of Plenty* (Yale University Press, 2000) that the economic advantages of contemporary capitalism have actually eroded personal satisfaction, parenting, and personal identity. Tim Kasser's *The High Price of Materialism* (MIT Bradford, 2002) reveals that the world of working, spending, and consuming leaves little time for solitude, faith, community and care of the earth—all requirements for personal well-being. Barry Schwartz, in *The Paradox of Choice: Why More Is Less* (HarperCollins, 2004), presents a practical guide for navigating the almost infinite options for distraction in the consumer world. The psychiatrist Peter Whybrow offers evidence that "the pursuit of happiness through the accumulation of material wealth is proving to be a blind alley" in *American Mania: When More Is Not Enough* (Norton, 2005).

Jules Henry, in *Culture Against Man* (Vintage, 1965), raised the issue of the cultural and personal costs of capitalism. His critique of American values from the viewpoint of a social-psychologist is still enlightening and challenging, often prophetic in retrospect. Christopher Lasch's *The True and Only Heaven: Progress and Its Critics* (Norton, 1991), quite possibly the most valuable of his studies, offers a profound historical and psychological challenge to the myth of progress and the devastating costs it has exacted from men and women. His approach is neither liberal nor conservative in his critique of the ethic of consumption and his call for a return of family values, hard work, commitment, and consistent respect for human life. He confounds both right and left, and the reactions to his book by reviewers invariably serve as litmus tests to their own ideologies. Henry and Lasch saw the power of capitalism to devour personal, moral, and cultural life, a connection missed by other critics.

Allan Bloom, in his *Closing of the American Mind* (Simon and Schuster, 1987), offered a critique of academic life that caused a flurry of comment and countercomment. It is a strong book marked by a quarrel with the rampant moral relativism of our culture and our loss of continuity with classic civilization. A somewhat complementary book is *Straight Shooting* (Harper and Row, 1989) by John Silber, a philosopher turned university president turned political figure. "Our society is in trouble and we all know it. We know that something is terribly wrong—the way we might know it in our own bodies that we are seriously ill." Silber, like Bloom, however, seems unaware of the dominant influence of capitalism on relativism and education. Thus, what they propose as possible solutions do not reach down to the radical causes; and they uncritically cling to the nationalism, militarism, and unrelenting competitiveness which are intrinsic to the problem.

The Culture of Cynicism: American Morality in Decline by Richard Stivers (Blackwell, 1994) successfully reveals the connection between moral decline and the forces of media, advertising, technology, and uncontrolled economic freedom. Much of the power of Eric Schlosser's *Fast Food Nation* (Perennial, 2002) is found in the network of ways our economy damages not only health, but also personal, familial, and international relations. Alan During's *How Much Is Enough?* (Norton, 1992) investigates the damage suffered by the ecosystem under the sway of untrammeled consumerism, even as it fails to satisfy desire. David Callahan, in *The Cheating Culture* (Harcourt, 2004), draws the disturbing connections between the boardroom and the schoolroom in a culture of avarice and "getting ahead." And underlying the warnings of Francis Fukuyama's *The Posthuman Future* (Profile, 2002) is the subtle undertow of a market-driven commercialism that pulls biotechnology's assault on human dignity.

It would be a mistake, of course, to think that the problem of persons in relationship to consumerism, capitalism, and commerce is something new. For those who are interested in an historical survey of the ways philosophers and other writers have addressed the problem, Patrick Murray's scholarly collection, *Reflections on Commercial Life: An Anthology of Classic Texts from Plato to the Present* (Routledge, 1977), is essential. The selection from Aquinas may shock capitalist Christians.

THE PERSONAL FORM

For Catholics and an increasing number of other Christian communities, the papal social teachings (on the dignity of labor, on armaments, peace, and the poor of the world) continue to be important reflections on our tradition and its relation to the Commodity Form. See also the documents of Vatican II, the American Catholic Bishops' statements, documents from Latin American Bishops, and the writings of Pope Paul VI and Pope John Paul II. It is true that the late pope is not easy to read: part of this is due to his style, to be sure. But another source of difficulty for the reader is that John Paul II was truly a dialectical thinker, always systematic and integrative. On the same page, one might be confronted with economic theory, sexual ideals, sacramental life, militarism, and the life of prayer. This is not because he is disorganized. Rather it is due to the fact that he sees all of these different areas of our life as interconnective and mutually supportive. *Redeemer of Humankind, On Human Labor, On Social Concerns, Centesimus Annus, Rich in Mercy,* and *The Gospel of Life* all exhibit a powerful integration of faith and our sociopolitical worlds. If you have not read any of his encyclicals, a good place to start is *John Paul II: The Encyclicals in Every-*

day Language: Definitive Edition of All Fourteen Encyclicals (Orbis, 2005) edited in attractive sense-line format by Joseph Donders.

The ultimate foundation of a Christian's understanding of personal dignity, of course, is in the Scripture—not only in the prophets, but most especially in the Gospels. Reading of the early "Church Fathers" also provides some of the most radical commentary on faith and culture that can be found. Similarly, the lives of the saints invariably provide contrasts between Christian faith and acculturated practice.

The list below is only a sampling of the variety of approaches to the Personal Form—exemplified in the lives of individuals, in the relationship between faith and justice, and in a Christian personalist's approach to economics, war, consumption, and technology. It is a bibliography weighted toward the Catholic tradition—passing over valuable work by Robert McAfee Brown and other prominent Protestant social theologians—although recent work of countercultural Evangelical writers will be noted. In the Jewish tradition, one book I cannot fail to mention as having enriched my own life is Martin Buber's *I and Thou*.

The Witness of Persons

Mark and Louise Zwick, founders of the *Houston Catholic Worker* (Casa Juan Diego) have done a great service by writing *The Catholic Worker Movement: Intellectual and Spiritual Origins* (Paulist, 2005). Profoundly Evangelical and Roman Catholic, they integrate the themes of justice, service to poor, pacifism, and prayer that marked the lives of Peter Maurin and Dorothy Day. Joining the influences of monasticism and saints like Francis of Assisi, Teresa of Avila, and Therese of Lisieux with thinkers such as Nicholas Berdyaev, Emmanuel Mounier and Dostoevsky, the Zwicks present Christian life as a challenge to depersonalization in all its forms. Dorothy Day's *Loaves and Fishes* (Orbis, 1997), *On Pilgrimage* (Eerdmans, 1999), and *The Long Loneliness* (HarperCollins, 1997)—diaries, autobiographies, collections of short writings marked by a passion for justice and the Gospel of Jesus—are well worth reading. She is a stunning witness. An anthology of her writings is available in *Dorothy Day: Selected Writings,* edited by Robert Ellsberg (Orbis, Twenty-fifth Anniversary Edition, 2005). William D. Miller's history of the Catholic Worker, *A Harsh and Dreadful Love,* written over thirty years ago and newly available from Marquette University Press (2006), is well complemented by Rosalie Riegle's *Dorothy Day: Portraits by Those Who Knew Her* (Orbis, 2003).

In my own formation, I have found various lives of the saints and spiritual testaments to be always challenging and inspiring. Actually, there are too many from the history of Christian writers to enumerate here, although I must say that the *Confessions* of Saint Augustine continues to stir faith and zeal in me. He stands not only as a great bridge between ancient and modern cultures, but also as a profound searcher into the interior life despite the turmoil of a collapsing society. Similarly, John W. O'Malley's *The First Jesuits* (Harvard University Press, 1995) reveals how personal holiness and communal solidarity can help transform the Church in the midst of a chaotic Europe. This book had the strange effect of explaining to me why I am a Jesuit. Thus, I suspect that readers know best for themselves what sources and people to return to for inspiration. You can see this, for example in Daniel Berrigan's *Testimony: The Word Made Fresh* (Orbis, 2004) where he gives witness not only to his own life of resistance to violence, but to those who have inspired and taught him.

The best collections of personal witness have been offered by Robert Ellsberg (whom I must recommend, despite the possible conflict of interest that he is editor of Orbis Books). *All Saints* (Crossroad, 1997) is a rich ecumenical treasure of daily encounters with great men and women of faith, both ancient and contemporary. *The Saints' Guide to Happiness* (North Point Press, 2003) is an engagement with a litany of saints from Julian of Norwich and Gerard Manley Hopkins to Martin Luther King and Father Walter Ciszek. Most recently,

Ellsberg has published *Blessed Among All Women* (Crossroad, 2005) which complements his earlier *All Saints* with new accounts of women, famous and hidden, all marked with courage and holiness.

Paul Elie's *The Life You Save May Be Your Own* (Farrar, Straus, Giroux, 2003) is a splendid narrative of the lives of Dorothy Day, Walker Percy, Thomas Merton, and Flannery O'Connor. Charles Marsh provides a similar service to the civil rights movement in his outstanding *The Beloved Community: How Faith Shapes Social Justice, from the Civil Rights Movement to Today* (Basic Books, 2005), a stirring labor of love and prophetic hope.

In addition to the specific life-witness of people, I have found and heard of many works that over the years have been personally transformative for people. The impact of C.S. Lewis continues to be startling, as his writings continue to be reprinted. His *Mere Christianity* (Harpers, 2001), simple and direct, is excellent for the moral foundations necessary to mount a cultural critique. Evil is a concrete reality for Lewis, as it is presented in *That Hideous Strength* (Scribners, 2003), a science-fiction fantasy novel; in the marvelous parable *The Great Divorce* (Harpers, 2001); in the philosophical polemic *The Abolition of Man* (Harpers, 2001). In *Mere Christianity* he writes: "I should not have been honest if I had not told you that three great civilizations had agreed (or so it seems at first sight) in condemning the very thing on which we have (as Christians) based our whole life." The writings of Dorothy Sayers, Charles Williams, and J.R.R. Tolkein—contemporaries of Lewis—have transformed lives.

On a less overtly spiritual plane, Gerald May's *Will and Spirit: A Contemplative Psychology* (Harper and Row, 1982) is an example of many subsequent works that integrate psychology, spirituality, and a strong sense of culture. More popularly, the sustained presence of M. Scott Peck's *The Road Less Traveled* (Touchstone, 25th Anniversary Edition, 2003) shows the extensive interest of Americans in the life of the spirit and its importance to commitment and health. From a more religious and psychoanalytic point of view (as well as being rather easy reading), Viktor Frankl's *Man's Search for Meaning* (Pocket Books updated edition, 1997) and *The Doctor and the Soul* (Vintage reissue, 1986) are as inspirational as they are profound. The integrated vision of Robert Coles can be found not only in his psychiatric studies of youth (for example, *The Spiritual Life of Children* [Houghton Mifflin, 1990]) but also in his compelling biographies, *Simone Weil: A Modern Pilgrimage* (Skylight Paths, 2001) and *Dorothy Day: A Radical Devotion* (Perseus, 1987).

Humanistic writers have also led their readers into lives of deeper personal commitment. Rollo May, in *Love and Will* (Norton, 1969) and *Man's Search for Himself* (Delta, 1973) as a psychotherapist, probes in a popular manner the meaning of value-loss: in the first instance, with respect to human affectivity, sexuality, and commitment; in the second, with respect to the more foundational purpose and meaning of human life. Other important critical work in this area has been done by Erich Fromm in *The Art of Loving* (Perennial, 2000), *Man for Himself* (Owl, 1990), and *The Revolution of Hope* (Harper and Row, 1968)—all written from a psychological, non-believing point of view. They have well stood the test of time. Even more enduring is the work of Abraham Maslow, whose *Toward a Psychology of Being* (Wiley, 3rd Edition, 1998) and later treatments of values, religion, and peak experiences, remain a sustaining vision of human dignity.

Personal Faith amid the Consumer Culture

In *Christian Critics: Religion and the Impasse in Modern American Social Thought* (Cornell University Press, 2000), Eugene McCarraher provides a rich, thick history of American Christians confronting capitalist culture. Although written a bit densely at times, McCarraher's book is a nuanced and rewarding experience. Ranging from the Niebuhrs and Paul Tillich to Thomas Merton, Martin Luther King, Dorothy Day, and Michael Novak (and many others), it reveals the tension between cultural accommodation and evangelical witness in the context of "commodified spirituality" and the enthronement of therapeutic "choice." A treasure.

For an extended, almost retreat-like experience, the thirty-year trilogy of zealous research by Walter Wink, *Naming the Powers, Unmasking the Powers,* and *Engaging the Powers* (Fortress Press, 1984, 1986, 1992), is an investigation of domination and true Christian liberty. His 1998 *The Powers That Be: Theology for a New Millennium* (Galilee, Doubleday) summarizes his project, including his work on the problem of violence and forgiveness in South Africa.

Among the countercultural Christian writers that Francis Schaeffer and his L'Abri Fellowship have influenced are Nancy Pearcey and Os Guinness. Pearcey's *Total Truth: Liberating Christianity From Its Cultural Captivity* (Crossway, 2004), while seemingly not aware of the ways capitalism dominates the modern worldview, is an extended critique of the relativisms and false dichotomies in contemporary life. (She includes an extended critique of Darwinism.) One may start with Os Guinness by reading either *Prophetic Untimeliness* (Baker Books, 2003) or *Unspeakable: Facing Up to Evil in an Age of Genocide and Terror* (Harper, 2005). Both books are lucid, meditative and challenging. "Of all the cultures the Church has lived in, the modern world is the most powerful, the most pervasive, and the most pressurizing."

Stanley Hauerwas's motto might be "not to change the world or even our nation, but to have ourselves reformed to the extent that we live what we say we believe" (my own formulation). A stellar Christian contrarian, he has challenged my own hopes to transform our society. In *A Better Hope: Resources for a Church Confronting Capitalism, Democracy and Post Modernism* (reprinted by the strategic Brazos Press in 2001), *Christian Existence Today* (Labyrinth Press, 1988), and the solid collection called *The Hauerwas Reader* (Duke, 2001), he combines ethics, spirituality, and discipleship into a stirring prophetic message.

Two recent books that address the specific relationship between religion and consumerism, while warning of the ways that faith itself can become commodified, provide concrete responses. Tom Beaudoin's *Consuming Faith* (Sheed and Ward, 2003) is particularly instructive for its recommendations concerning an "economic spirituality." Vincent Miller's *Consuming Religion* (Continuum, 2004), as its subtitle announces, offers a way of "Christian Faith and Practice in a Consumer Culture." Richly theoretical and researched, Miller's work is a valuable introduction to recent literature.

The growing individualism and diminishment of civil community—see, for example, Robert Putnam's *Bowling Alone* (Simon and Schuster, 2001)—that has marked American culture in the last twenty years was prefigured in Robert Bellah's *Habits of the Heart: Individualism and Commitment in American Life* (University of California Press, 1996). Through the use of in-depth interviews and follow through, Bellah and his co-workers presented a portrait of American culture in the midst of profound change and even a possible loss of moorings. The impact of consumer capitalism, while never explicitly treated, haunts the lives of many people interviewed.

A number of Christian writers have combined their critique of culture with a critique of acculturated faith. *Rich Christians in an Age of Hunger* by Ronald Sider (Paulist, 1977) has been sharpened and surpassed in his *Scandal of the Evangelical Conscience: Why Are Christians Living Just Like the Rest of the World* (Baker Books, 2005). More scriptural and scholarly, meditative and evangelical, is Ched Myers's *Binding the Strong Man* (Orbis, 1989) and *Who Will Roll Away the Stone?* (Orbis, 1993). One would hope that similar challenges could be made from the Catholic community of writers.

In *The Call to Discernment in Troubled Times* (Crossroad, 2004) Dean Brackley, an American Jesuit teaching at the University of Central America in El Salvador, presents an uncommonly valuable confluence of themes from Liberation

Theology, American culture, social justice, and personal discernment under the guidance of Ignatius Loyola's *Spiritual Exercises*. In addition to the fact that this work is a wonderful retreat companion, it is enhanced by a striking introduction written by the copy editor who was herself "converted" in working on this book. The writings of Gustavo Gutiérrez, Juan Luis Segundo, and Dom Helder Camara are still solid representatives of liberation theology. Most valuable, however, are the writings of Jon Sobrino, providing a vision of spirituality that is both Christological and sociological. His most recent offering, *Where Is God?* (Orbis, 2004), probes the meaning of human suffering in the light of El Salvador's deadly earthquake, the attacks of September 11, and the war in Iraq. The confrontation between Christian faith and economic life was addressed in *The Catholic Challenge to the American Economy*, edited by Thomas Gannon, S.J. (Macmillan, 1987), and merits a fuller contemporary application to the new century. Less favorable estimations are offered by George Weigel in *Tranquillitas Ordinis: The Present Failure and Future Promise of American Catholic Theology on War and Peace* (Oxford, 1987) and *The Catholic Moment* by Richard John Neuhaus (Harper and Row, 1987).

Any of Jim Wallis's books are worth considering. See also the journal which Wallis helped found and still writes for: *Sojourners*. The articles range from prayer and spirituality to racism, abortion, disarmament, the prison system, the Third World, multinationals, martyrdom. Jim Wallis and Joyce Hollyday have edited an inspiring collection of interviews and profiles of contemporary saints and prophets, *Cloud of Witnesses* (Orbis, revised edition, 2005). Wallis's latest book is *God's Politics: Why the Right Gets It Wrong and the Left Doesn't Get It* (HarperCollins, 2005), a "beltway" book that has troubled both right and left—as Wallis may have hoped. By and large, despite the constraints of format, he hits our problem in the bull's eye. A much more concise and quietly persuasive proposal for an integrated life of faith in America can be found in Mark Neilsen's *Reaffirming Life in a Culture of Death* (Liguori, 1996), a thoughtful union, in the spirit of John Paul II, of the realms of abortion and capital punishment, poverty and labor, war, equality, and stewardship. A concrete example of such integration is seen in Wendell Berry's *Citizenship Papers* (Shoemaker & Hoard, 2003). Although all of his many publications are worth reading, the essays of this book courageously explore the response of "a citizen" to militarism, the terror of 9/11, abortion, biotechnology, labor, simplicity living, agrarian reform, and the miracle of life itself.

Vulnerable Personhood

In Annie Dillard's disarming extended meditation *For the Time Being* (Knopf, 1999), she travels history and world with an eye both to our frail creatureliness and to faith in a provident God. With an obvious care for the least human person, she nonetheless writes a litany of the greatest injustices and the deepest wounds borne by humans at the margins of life. It is a book that draws you to open your heart and mind to the plight of the poor, whether economically disadvantaged or physically and mentally disabled.

The rise of the internet makes updated information on world hunger available daily. *World Hunger Facts, 2005, Bread for the World,* and *Hunger World* are sites you may want to visit regularly. Jeffrey Sachs, in *The End of Poverty: Economic Possibilities for Our Time* (Penguin, 2005), makes an urgent plea for world financial reform in an extensive, sometimes exhausting, exploration of "extreme poverty" among the nations. Paul Farmer's *Pathologies of Power: Health, Human Rights, and the New War on the Poor* (University of California Press, 2003) is a physician's prophetic challenge to the first-world nations. John Iceland examines the causes and structures of poverty in America in the fact-laden *Poverty in America: A Handbook* (California, 2003) while Barbara Ehrenreich's *Nickel and Dimed: On Not Getting By in America* (Owl Books, 2002) is a troubling (and sometimes too self-conscious) narrative about her year of working for and living on a minimum wage.

These new sources of information, however, do not negate the value of earlier publications. Twenty years ago Frances Moore Lappé and Joseph Collins wrote *World Hunger, Twelve Myths* (Grove Press, 1986). Easily readable, this little book provides ample data and insight into the problems of population, distribution of wealth, and the causes of poverty in the Third World. Originally published in 1975, Arthur Simon's *Bread for the World* (Eerdmans, revised and updated, 1985) is still a cherished classic, informed, easy to read, radiant with compassion. The Christian and American response has been addressed in Paul Vallely's *Bad Samaritans: First World Ethics and Third World Debt* (Orbis, 1990). Although out of print, it should be found in libraries as an extensive and highly informative treatment of the economic relations between the United States and the poor nations of the world. One leaves it with a greater understanding of why Pope John Paul II would say that "the poor nations of the world will rise in judgment against the rich nations of the North."

Accepting the poverty of our very humanness—something that has haunted every generation—has entered a new stage in the last two decades. A crucial subtext of Francis Fukuyama's *Our Posthuman Future* (Picador, 2003) is that, lurking under the drive of biotechnological enhancement (genetic alteration, nanotechnology, pharmacology) is a wish to eliminate all human vulnerabilities, requiring the ultimate elimination of our nature. A more personalist and spiritual critique of the same tendency is found in Bill McKibben's *Enough: Staying Human in an Engineered Age* (Holt, 2003). Like so much of his work, it is written with a respect and even love for "people whose bodies eventually start to sag, by people who love and who grieve and who celebrate, by people who mourn and who know that they will someday die."

In the last few pages of a book cited earlier, *Sources of the Self*, the philosopher Charles Taylor suggests that Mother Teresa and Jean Vanier, having worked with the irremediably

broken and mentally handicapped, have a greater understanding of our humanity than those who look only to our
health and strength. Alasdair MacIntyre in *Dependent Rational Animals* (Open Court, 1999) points in the same direction.
The concrete experience of personal beauty in the marginal
can be seen in Malcolm Muggeridge's *Something Beautiful for
God* (Harper, 1986). His account of the life and labor of
Mother Teresa of Calcutta inspired not only countless readers; the author as well was drawn to a life of faith. Jean
Vanier's *Community and Growth* (Paulist, 1979), like all of
his books and lectures, is inspiring as well as challenging.
Through his life's work with the handicapped in the L'Arche
communities, he has discovered and lived the indispensable
combination of prayer, interpersonal covenant, justice, simplicity, and compassion for the "marginal."

Spiritual writers or people of faith are not the only ones
to unveil a luminous dignity of the human person even at the
"margins" of life. Oliver Sacks, a physician-neurologist who
has found acclaim as one of the finest medical clinical writers
of our times, has written *The Man Who Mistook His Wife for
a Hat* (Perennial-Harper and Row, 1987) and *Awakenings*
(Perennial, 1990 edition), among many brilliant studies. The
books are case histories of his patients, each of whom is
treated with the utmost compassion and with what can only
be called love. Toward the end of *Awakenings* (which was
made into a stirring motion picture) Sacks writes: "One sees
that beautiful and ultimate Truth, which has been stated by
poets and physicians and metaphysicians in all ages—Leibniz
and Donne and Dante and Freud: that Eros is the strongest
and oldest of the gods; that love is the alpha and the omega of
being; and that the work of healing, of rendering whole, is,
first and last, the business of love." Speaking of his brain-
damaged patients, he writes: "After spending fifteen years of
my life working closely with these patients, I think them the
most afflicted and yet noblest persons I have ever known."
After reading him, you believe it. Two personal testimonies in
the face of enormous moral and social evil merit the long read

they will require. *Etty: The Letters and Diaries of Etty Hillesum* (Eerdmans, 2002) is the story of a soul's transformation, from an infatuation with a rather strange professor to the courageous, God-hungry servant of others as she faced her own murder at Auschwitz in 1943. A more extended and harrowing diary is Victor Klemperer's two-volume work, *I Will Bear Witness* (Modern Library, 2001). Spanning 1933 to 1945, it reads like a moral tsunami, as everything is stripped from this gentle German Jew and his Christian wife, except their abiding love and eventual return to normal life.

The voice of "the marginal human" suffering great physical evil (or disability) can actually be heard in Christopher Nolan's *Under the Eye of the Clock* (St. Martin's Press, 1988). This book, with his earlier *Damburst of Dreams*, is a handicapped man's profoundly moving testimony to the nobility of the human spirit. Both books are autobiographical, although the earlier work contains Nolan's poetry, which he composed after he started communicating with the world at the age of eleven.

Written from the perspective of someone in the prime of life but shattered by a profound stroke, *The Diving Bell and the Butterfly* (Knopf, 1997) is an unforgettable encounter. Jean Dominique Bauby, a father of two and chief editor of Paris *Elle*, dictated this book by blinking his one good eye to letters of the alphabet. His "locked in" diagnosis did not constrain his care for his often inadequate caregivers. "They carried out as best they could their delicate mission: to ease our burden a little when our crosses bruised our shoulders too painfully."

So may it be for us all.

INDEX

Made in the USA
Monee, IL
28 February 2020